THE HISTORY OF
MISSED OPPORTUNITIES

THE HISTORY OF
MISSED OPPORTUNITIES

British Romanticism

and the Emergence of the Everyday

WILLIAM H. GALPERIN

Stanford University Press · Stanford, California

Stanford University Press
Stanford, California

Printed in the United States of America on acid-free, archival-quality paper

Library of Congress Cataloging-in-Publication Data

Names: Galperin, William H., author.
Title: The history of missed opportunities : British romanticism and the emergence of the everyday / William H. Galperin.
Description: Stanford, California : Stanford University Press, 2017. |
  Includes bibliographical references and index.
Identifiers: LCCN 2016052469 (print) | LCCN 2016054147 (ebook) |
  ISBN 9781503600195 (cloth : alk. paper) | ISBN 9781503603103 (electronic)
Subjects: LCSH: English literature—18th century—History and criticism. |
  Romanticism—Great Britain.
Classification: LCC PR4470 .G35 2017 (print) | LCC PR4470 (ebook) |
  DDC 820.9/007—dc23
LC record available at https://lccn.loc.gov/2016052469

Typeset by Bruce Lundquist in 10/15 Minion

For Tina and in memory of Gabe

CONTENTS

ACKNOWLEDGMENTS

This study has been so long in the offing (not to mention a continuation of interests going back over thirty years) that the number of colleagues and friends who have touched it in some way and to whom I remain indebted is considerable. There are people, accordingly, whom I will fail to mention here to whom I apologize at the outset for their omission. The naming, however, begins with two truly indelible colleagues—Colin Jager and Susan Wolfson—who read the book in its entirety and whose suggestions and interlocution were invaluable for thickening and sophisticating the project and, just as crucially, for saving me from all sorts of embarrassment. Other colleagues in the field who've been important to the study's (and my) development during the decade or so that I've been writing it, and in the decades during which it was germinating in some form, include Ian Balfour, Marshall Brown, Julie Carlson, James Chandler, David Clark, David Collings, Jeffrey Cox, Neil Fraistat, Michael Gamer, Sara Guyer, Keith Hanley, Geoffrey Hartman, Jennifer Jones, William Keach, Theresa Kelley, Jacques Khalip, Yoon Sun Lee, Marjorie Levinson, Peter Manning, Anne Mellor, Anahid Nersessian, Susan Oliver, Adam Potkay, Forrest Pyle, Tilottama Rajan, Jacob Risinger, Michael Scrivener, Clifford Siskin, Garrett Stewart, Orrin Wang, Andrew Warren, and Deborah White. Extra special thanks go to Mary Favret, Frances Ferguson, Lynn Festa, Marilyn Gaull, Sonia Hofkosh, Deidre Lynch, Adela Pinch, and Nancy Yousef.

Equally important (because it happens all the time and almost always when one least expects it) has been the exchange with and feedback from Rutgers colleagues past and present: Harriet Davidson, Elin Diamond, Uri Eisenzweig, Kate Ellis, Kate Flint, Sandy Flitterman-Lewis, Martin Gliserman, Virginia Jackson, Jonathan Kramnick, John Kucich, David Kurnick, Ron Levao, George Levine, Meredith McGill, Michael McKeon, Jackie Miller, Richard Miller, Andrew Parker, Barry Qualls, Dianne Sadoff, Jonah Siegel, Michelle Stephens, Henry Turner, Rebecca Walkowitz, Michael Warner, Carolyn Williams, and Abigail Zitin.

My tenure at Rutgers University's Center for Cultural Analysis, as director and occasional seminar leader, has brought me in contact with colleagues, both intra- and extramurally, from whom I've benefitted in numerous ways. Of particular importance were the members and guests of the seminar on the Everyday and the Ordinary that I led in 2010–11: Derek Schilling, Ann Fabian, Louis Sass, Emily Van Buskirk, Seth Koven, Andrea Baldi, Loren Goldman, Laura Brown, Jonathan Farina, Chris D'Addario, Anna McCarthy, Michael Fried, Robert Pippin, Paul Steege, Thomas Dumm,Timothy Corrigan, Tom Conley, Kristin Ross, and Jane Bennett. I am grateful, too, to Rutgers faculty who've been involved in Center life as seminar participants—Frances Egan, Ken Safir, and Susan Sidlauskas—and to several postdoctoral fellows who've been attached to the Center over the years, including Elaine Auyong, Stephanie Hershinow, Rachel Feder, and Avi Alpert.

None of the books I have written would have been possible or have taken the form they did without the input, curiosity, enthusiasm, and plain rigor of the students in my graduate courses, where I not only have contrived to model what current research in romanticism might look like but also, and just as valuably, have served as a cautionary example. Special thanks, in any case, go to Sean Barry, Ignacio Infante, John Savarese, Greg Ellermann, Julie Camarda, Jesse Hoffman, Lizzie Oldfather, Melissa Parrish, and Nellickal Jacob, whose feedback—and pushback—was critical, along with that of many other students, including Nick Bujak, once an undergraduate and now a romanticist.

I am grateful as always to Rutgers University, where I've taught for over thirty years, especially to the English Department and the School of Arts and Sciences. I want to thank my department chairs, Cheryl Wall, Kate Flint, Richard Miller, and Carolyn Williams, for the kinds of assistance that only a chair can furnish, as well as Humanities deans Barry Qualls, Ann Fabian, and James Swenson, for providing me with a research stipend, leave time, and a general sense that what I was doing somehow mattered. Thanks are also due to the English department's superb staff: Courtney Borack and Cheryl Robinson in the graduate office; Leandra Cain and Carol Hartman in the undergraduate office; and Angela Piggee, Zelda Ralph, Derek Jablonski, and Carol Spry in the business office. They are a boon to me and my colleagues and to our academic lives, in and out of the classroom. I likewise want to acknowledge Curtis Dunn, the CCA's principal administrator during my tenure as director, whose talent and resourcefulness kept that institution running at peak capacity.

There are friends, in and out of the academy, to thank as well, both for conversation that is professionally focused and for exchanges that are always stimulating. They are Gideon Bosker, Karen Brooks, Tom Butkovich, Marcia Ferguson, Lisa Jane Graham, Charlie Gross, Eric Halpern, Tom Leclair, Fred Lind, Leslie Mechanic, Raji Mohan, Kate Nicholson, Joyce Carol Oates, Monica Potkay, Bill Ray, David Robinson, Ralph Rosen, Mort Schoolman, David Sedley, Gus Stadler, and Lisa Steinman. Susan Wolfson gets another shout-out here for reasons that are self-evident (certainly to anyone who knows our long relationship), as do Timothy Corrigan, Jonathan Kramnick, Michael McKeon, and Adam Potkay.

I also want to thank the various audiences who have heard versions of these chapters and for always helping to make them better. These include groups at the University of Colorado, CUNY Graduate Center, Harvard, Indiana University, Johns Hopkins, NYU, the University of Michigan, the New School, the University of Pennsylvania, Princeton, Rutgers, SUNY–Albany, and the Jane Austen Societies of New York and Southeast Pennsylvania. Versions of the chapters were also delivered as conference papers at several NASSR gatherings, the MLA Convention, the International Conference on Romanticism, ASECS, the Chawton Women Writers Conference, and two ACLA annual meetings.

I can't emphasize enough my gratitude to Stanford University Press, and to Emily-Jane Cohen especially, for taking this project on and for the reports she solicited from Deidre Lynch and Orrin Wang, which proved both indispensable and models of the genre. The editorial process, done right, is always daunting but a reminder too—as was the case here—that editors and peer reviewers are the custodians of a conversation on which knowledge ultimately depends. I also want to thank Marthine Satris, Gigi Mark, and those at Stanford who oversaw the book's production and Matthew John Phillips ("MJP") for all his help in getting my manuscript into final form.

One of the main arguments of this book is that the everyday came to consciousness in the romantic period as an opportunity that had not so much been lost as missed or overlooked. Scholarship is always autobiographical in some fashion. But in this case everyday life for me, specifically with my wife and partner, Tina Zwarg, is a plenitude that is always present and an endowment I happily cherish in real time. This book is dedicated to her and to my late father, with whom I spent some extraordinary days over the past eight years.

THE HISTORY OF
MISSED OPPORTUNITIES

PRELUDE

The Panorama and the Everyday

By midpoint in the romantic period, Barker's Panorama in London was in full swing, featuring images not only of battles and sieges throughout Europe where the large circular paintings performed as newsreels but also of various cities, beginning with a 1791 panorama of London and expanding outward to representations of Paris, Venice, Constantinople, and other places. Developed by Robert Barker, whose initial painting of Edinburgh in 1788 was promoted as an unprecedented innovation in prospect painting and patented as such, the Panorama quickly became a staple among the "shows of London": first, under Barker's supervision with the exhibition of a partial panorama of London, and later under the supervision of his son Henry Aston Barker who, like his father, was also the principal artist. The Panorama subsequently passed into the hands of John Burford and his son Robert and concluded its run in the 1860s.[1] The 1791 panorama, depicted as though viewed from the roof of the Albion Mills on the South Bank of the Thames (fig. 1), was relatively small, covering approximately 1,500 square feet. And it was smaller yet when Barker moved the painting to the upper rotunda of his new exhibition space in Leicester Square, where it was immediately dwarfed by a panorama of *The Grand Fleet off of Spithead*, which provided a 360° view over 10,000 square feet (fig. 2).

Very few images of the many panoramas that came and went over seventy years survive. Thus in reconstructing what they looked like and what the panoramic experience may have entailed we are limited by an archive that is slim and largely suggestive. In addition to the observations of famous viewers such as Sir Joshua Reynolds and William Wordsworth—visitors to the picture of London and, in Wordsworth's case, to the two-tiered exhibition—we have advertisements and reviews, as well as the explanatory keys or guides, including one of the London panorama that transforms the image into something remarkable in its own right (fig. 3). There was eventually, inevitably, a panorama of the battle of Waterloo, developed from sketches made on site (fig. 4), featuring a unique temporality that both distended and collapsed the battle in a never-ending simultaneity: an impossible union of timescape and landscape that Waterloo's duration of

FIGURE 1. (*top*) Henry Aston Barker and Frederick Birnie after Robert Barker, *Panorama of London from the Albion Mills*. Hand-colored aquatint. 1792–93. Courtesy of Yale Center for British Art, Paul Mellon Collection.

FIGURE 2. (*bottom*) Robert Mitchell, illustration from *Plans, and views in perspective, with descriptions, of buildings erected in England and Scotland: and also an essay, to elucidate the Grecian, Roman and Gothic architecture, accompanied with designs.* 1800. Courtesy of Yale Center for British Art, Paul Mellon Collection.

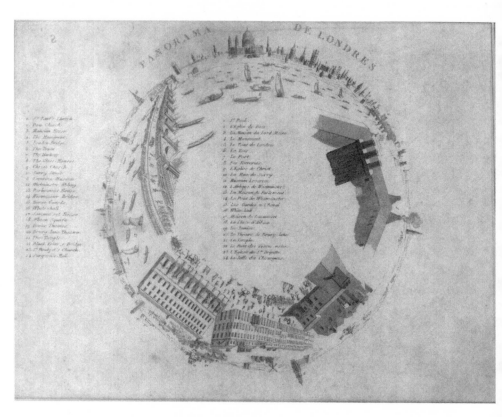

FIGURE 3. After Robert Barker, *Panorama de Londres*. Print. 1800. © The Trustees of the British Museum.

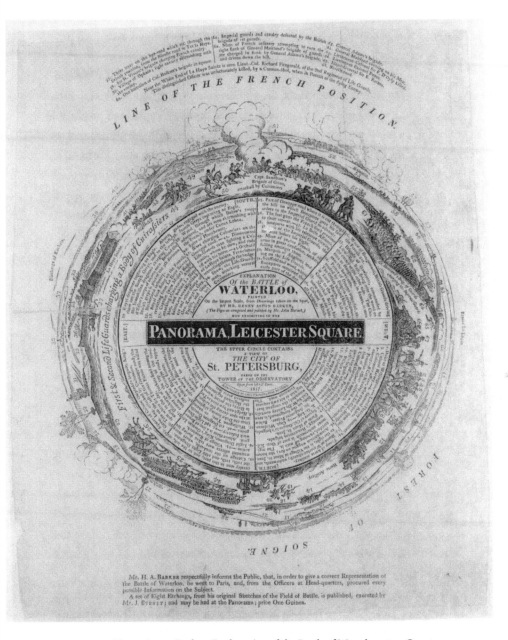

FIGURE 4. Henry Aston Barker, *Explanation of the Battle of Waterloo.* 1817. Courtesy of Yale Center for British Art, Paul Mellon Collection.

over just twelve hours undoubtedly inspired. What the mash-up reproduced was not a battle unfolding but something more like a participial present: time was *standing* and the glance, however extended or transformed, remained what Barker rightly termed "a coup d'oeil."

Barker actively solicited the opinion and interest of Reynolds. Initially skeptical about the painter's innovation, the academician reportedly changed his mind after seeing the London panorama, which he deemed "capable of producing effects, and representing nature in a manner far superior to the limited scale of pictures in general."[2] Among these "effects" was likely an uncanny illusionism, where viewing and reviewing combined to make visible and—for the purposes of my study—conceivable what "we never see a first time, but only see again." These are Maurice Blanchot's words regarding "the everyday," which for him "is in the street—if it is anywhere," rather than "at home" or "in offices" or "in . . . museums."[3] This was not so for Barker's near contemporary Jane Austen, for whom the everyday was substantially at home. But it bears on Barker's image, where the everyday that typically "escapes" on Blanchot's reckoning (Blanchot 1987, 18) is eventually captured in an endless loop where time and the image are versions of each other. This visual loop encompasses subject matter that is mobile and multiple, making city life both a panoramic mode and the result of a special, period-bound phenomenology. Every view of London ghosts a parallel or possible world that is "only seen again," at which point it becomes visible (a coup d'oeil) as well as thinkable for essentially the "first time."[4]

As the experience of re-seeing suggests, the emergence of the everyday as a distinct category at the moment of Barker's exhibition is linked in various ways to retrospection, in which a stratum that the "everyday" might serve to name comes to consciousness as a missed opportunity and, by extension, a history of missed opportunities. The sum of this re-view, and the consciousness it subtends, is a history distinct from "real" history: a counter-actual history that shades and provokes the emergence of a previously missing world, along with a conceptual framework for it.

Because these opportunities, as Blanchot elaborates them, abound in the street, I begin with Barker's London image and with Wordsworth's residence in that city as recounted in *Prelude* 7. Here he delivers both a description of city life at the very moment the panorama captures (further explored in chapter 2), and, for my purposes now, a conventionally "romantic" account of Barker's actual spectacle, where its "effects" are notably disquieting:

cf. The Simultaneity of Milton,
Mononoke

At leisure let us view, from day to day,
As they present themselves, the Spectacles
Within doors: troops of wild Beasts, birds and beasts
Of every nature, from all climes convened;
And, next to these, those mimic sights that ape
The absolute presence of reality,
Expressing as in mirror, sea and land,
And what earth is, and what she hath to shew;
I do not here allude to subtlest craft,
By means refined attaining purest ends,
But imitations fondly made in plain
Confession of man's weakness and his loves.
Whether the Painter—fashioning a work
To Nature's circumambient scenery,
And with his greedy pencil taking in
A whole horizon on all sides, with power,
Like that of Angels or commissioned Spirits,
Plant us upon some lofty Pinnacle,
Or in a Ship on Waters, with a world
Of life and life-like mockery to East,
To West, beneath, behind us, and before. (7.244–64)[5]

Despite its contempt for the panorama and the ersatz "world / Of life" apparently on view there, the critique is partly self-reflexive, particularly the greed with which the artist takes in the scene before him. Such animus is certainly consistent with what Wordsworth sometimes decries as the tyranny of the eye, where the more sublime and ennobling workings of the imagination are overwhelmed. But it does not prevent him from collating something similar in a scene just after London that is meant as an antithesis:

Immense
Is the Recess, the circumambient World
Magnificent, by which they are embraced.
They move about upon the soft green field;
How little They, they and their doings seem,
Their herds and flocks about them, they themselves,
And all which they can further or obstruct!

Through utter weakness pitiably dear,

As tender Infants are: and yet how great!

For all things serve them: them the Morning light

Loves as it glistens on the silent rocks,

And them the silent Rocks, which now from high

Look down upon them; the reposing Clouds,

The lurking Brooks from their invisible haunts,

And Old Helvellyn, conscious of the stir,

And the blue sky that roofs their calm abode. (8.46–61)

Like the aforementioned panoramas of London and Spithead, which are described only generally, this more elaborated rural scene (of which I've given only a part) also features a "circumambient world" that is "tak[en] in." And more greedily, arguably, than the view in the panorama. Leaving virtually no aspect of the scene unobserved, the poet's glances settle into a series of gazes or meditative embellishments, subordinating distraction to compositional and discursive authority.

The problem with the London panorama is not its opposition to the grand panorama of "Nature" (8.62) but, if anything, its similarity to "Nature's circumambient scenery" on the Wordsworthian model. Both invoke a characteristically romantic movement from the "earthly and material" to the "mental" and "celestial"[6] that is reversed indoors, rendering the seen and "seen again" continuous and collapsing the distance interposed elsewhere. By the "power" that fixes him in an environment where his only recourse is to continue to look about rather than to move along some narrative axis, Wordsworth is engaging a number of things. He is responding to an experience that, by comparison to the outdoor spectacle, is fundamentally involuntary; and he is referring to an order of experience that emerges on review—or what is mandated for review—in which the overlooked (or looked over in the second example) is uncannily visible and, he grudgingly acknowledges, lifelike.

One image of the London panorama that has survived—Frederick Birnie's aquatint of Barker's 1791 painting (fig. 1)—is composed, like the original, of separate panels. But more visibly than the original it is a series of discrete views that can be disarticulated from the whole in ways that bear on both the panoramic effect, where there is no vantage from which to view the whole apart from viewing it piecemeal, and the panoramic yield, which is nothing less than an aperture onto a present sufficiently, even oppressively, recurrent that what is missed is eventually encountered. Take, for example, the third panel featuring a street scene at one end of the bridge, which in context or as part of the illusionistic continuum may be easily ignored (fig. 5). Upon review, however, which is only a matter of time (viewing being circular and recurrent), this panel takes on a completely differ-ent character, precipitating a stratum or substratum that the image—lacking any compositional intention or integrity—flushes out of hiding. Displacing the pan-oramic sweep with a largely parallel world, the panel-image, along with the double take it figures, accomplishes two things. It focalizes what has been hiding in plain sight; and it creates what amounts to a conceptual void, which it provisionally fills.

To call this image photographic may be an indulgence in that photogra-phy—the technology for which was being developed at this very moment—would initially be put to more conventional uses, such as portraiture. And yet as Peter Galassi observes of oil sketches also made at this time, which hearken toward a mode of seeing that compact and reflex cameras would capture later, there is a sense in which the panel is not just on the threshold of photography or "before photography" (Galassi's term) as we know it in "street photographers" from Eugène Atget onward, but a meditation, in advance, on the way the pho-tograph shuttles between what Henri Cartier-Bresson has termed the "decisive

FIGURE 5. Henry Aston Barker and Frederick Birnie after Robert Barker, detail of Blackfriars Bridge from *Panorama of London from the Albion Mills.* Hand-colored aquatint. 1792–93. Courtesy of Yale Center for British Art, Paul Mellon Collection.

moment" and the continuum that that moment interrupts and, in fracturing, brings to view.[7] On one recent elaboration, the decisive moment is akin to what Wordsworth famously called "spots of time," chiefly in "the transcendent whole" into which "vision and composition" apparently "merge" in certain photographed images.[8] But it is just as much the case that these moments are fragments—to invoke another romantic topos—in which wholeness, whether compositionally or synecdochically, dissolves into what is ongoing (what Cartier-Bresson calls "movement") and where the photographed instant, far from being discontinuous, is the record of a present that is indecisive save for its recovery by photographic or (in the panorama) recursive means.

The capture of London life that the isolated panel performs, and that the panorama achieved in allowing viewers to look finally at the overlooked, seems eminently suited to a discussion of the everyday, which is often understood (*pace* Blanchot) in the light and context of urban experience. Yet the point to stress, which the panorama stages in a "history of the present" where discovery and recovery are forever linked, is the *emergence* of an experience—an order of experience—that is less a matter of consensus or understanding at this moment than one of surprise, even shock, over something that only history of a kind exposes. For Wordsworth this discovery is wrenching, since what is at stake, how-

FIGURE 6. John Linnell, *Study from Nature: At Twickenham*. Oil painting on board. 1806. Courtesy of Tate Gallery, Millbank, London.

ever inchoate, is a possible world—an environment to which he is "turned," as he will later describe it—that is also close at hand. Opposing the imagined worlds associated with romanticism as well as the probable worlds linked to empiricism that are notably devoid of surprise or wonder, the thickened or distended present that the panorama "effects" not only divests the poet of the multiple sanctions on which his project—and the romantic project generally—can be said to depend; it works in the manner of the disarticulated image as an interruption or pause to which perception modulates in becoming an intuition.

Wordsworth is not alone in this discovery. The work done in the panorama and the thinking it enables impinge on the romantic moment generally, where the procedure I've just traced is recapitulated in other writing and, as I've mentioned, versions of art like the oil sketch, where, as Galassi has written, "a new and fundamentally modern pictorial syntax of immediate, synoptic perceptions and discontinuous, unexpected forms" (Galassi 1981, 25), is suddenly in evidence (fig. 6). The operative word here is "discontinuous." For what the dis-continuity exposes in the striking form it takes is a "world" that is "too much with us" to be noticed except in aftermath—in an (after)image through which the everyday peers as a history of missed opportunities.

INTRODUCTION

"The everyday is what we never see a first time, but only see again."

Maurice Blanchot

I

Probability is central to the empirical project: the result both of an inductive method in which, as Hume noted, "what we have found to be most usual is always most probable" and of the growing stability of life in Britain and elsewhere, where predictions became increasingly measurable rather than mere guesswork.[1] Still, when Annabella Milbanke (the future Lady Byron) signed off on this development in describing *Pride and Prejudice* as "the most *probable* fiction I have ever read," her elaboration concerning Austen's rejection of the "common" and sensationalistic "resources of novel writers" missed the larger point of her hyperbole, which draws a bright line between probability and something else that the novel registers.[2] As early as the canonical first sentence of the novel,[3] both the marital imperative and its correlative, the marriage plot, are not just stipulations that are by definition limited; they form a bounding line where the pivot on "must" ("must be in want of a wife") marks a tension suddenly between the "usual" and its exasperating origins in female vulnerability and desire. Restricted to the probabilism that this "most probable novel" is already straining against, the imperative exacted through consensus (and vice versa) is "a truth" that needs buttressing, or "universal acknowledge[ment]," because it is no longer or shouldn't be the whole story.

Lady Byron may not have gotten at all of this precisely, but many of her contemporaries took their lead from the sentence as I've described it in regarding the marital trajectory, and the parallel narrative of error and correction, as more of an accompaniment than a defining feature. To these readers, as I've shown previously, the abundance of detail here and elsewhere in Austen took precedence over the novels' plots, prompting no less a reader than Maria Edgeworth to describe *Emma* as having "no story in it except that . . . *smooth, thin water-gruel* is according to Emma's father's opinion a very good thing & it is very difficult to make a cook understand what you mean by smooth thin water gruel."[4] A twentieth-century reader such as Roland Barthes finds a seamless and sinister continuity between a novel's ideological work (read plot) and the "reality effect" of such circumstantial information.[5] But when Austen's novels initially appeared their oft-noted verisimilitude was typically a synonym for something distracting and disarticulated rather than a naturalizing apparatus. One contemporary, Lady Vernon, tartly described *Mansfield Park* "as not much of a novel," but "more the history of a family party in the country,"[6] and another, Edgeworth's friend Anne Romilly, made a nearly identical claim in noting how "real natural every day life" in that novel took precedence over its "story vein of principle."[7]

These observations point to more than a blurring of diegesis and mimesis attributable to the novel's—and realism's—instability at the juncture when Austen was supposedly codifying the genre. They mark an abiding conflict between what Walter Scott termed the "narrative" of Austen's novels and what he called their "prosing," which, like Edgeworth, he listed "among the [author's] faults." In disrupting the progress of a heroine "turned wise by precept, example, and experience"[8] the "prosaic" was not simply a problem because it was a detour and a different turn. It was a problem for Scott because there is a necessary relationship, as he elaborates, between Austen's "narrative" and its ideological and pedagogical shape and the regress of probability, which counts similarly on "experience," or on precepts based on precedent, in prosecuting its claims and conclusions.

Two modes of history, Scott correctly inferred, were in play. One uses the past—the empiricism of an aggregated past—as a template for human life and nature including women desperate to marry. Another is a history in which the prior is sufficiently singular and prosaic (see Edgeworth) that its reproducibility in any form apart from what Romilly called "every day life" is largely undermined. The world and milieu that Austen engaged, reengaged and made the defining feature of her practice as a writer during the nearly two decades in which her first published novels underwent continued revision, becoming in the process "realistic,"[9] was far from static or immediately transhistorical. It was a particular world in the welter of time or what, in the advertisement to *Northanger Abbey*, she explicitly called "considerable changes." We generally restrict the changes mentioned in the advertisement to the world of "books," especially the gothic novel, which in the interval between composition and publication had ceased to be the vogue it was in the 1790s. But there were "considerable changes" in "manners" and "opinions" that Austen hints at as well—changes in the world of *her world*—that she was able to register and, in a style striking to her contemporaries, provisionally to reverse.

In this latter style—very different from the sublime detachment that D. A. Miller has recently termed "Austen Style"[10]—-details of a world seen as if for the first time prove more significant than either routine sensationalism or the probabilism in which unmarried gentrywomen are forever in search of single rich men. That's because the unprecedented representation of "every day life" that impressed Austen's contemporaries (for better or for worse), and that Scott was only partly right in calling prosaic, would have been unnecessary were it not also a history where the real and the possible were linked, a "retrospect," in the words of one character, "of what might have been."[11] The *Literary Gazette* was being nostalgic when in 1833 it singled out Austen's "absolute historical pictures" of "country dances" and the "delights of tea-table" for special praise.[12] But what it marked, however superficially, was the literary absolute (to expropriate a term) for which the "historical" was a placeholder. It marked a present, or "thickened present" (in Husserl's notion),[13] that was representable thanks to narratives that had *become* archives. In the archive of literary representation everything deducible from experience on Scott's empirical model is secondary to what was sufficiently unappreciated—or bothersome when reading for "story"—to count as both an alternative world and a missed opportunity.

This opportunity, this possibility, symptomatically involves heroines who for a good portion of their narratives resist their disposability to the formal or disciplinary imperatives outlined in *Pride and Prejudice*'s inaugural sentence. Their resistance is symptomatic because the counterplot that abides in the rich and static present of the novels—especially *Mansfield Park*—hearkens back to a moment when prospects for women were less restricted than they were by the time of the novels' publication and by the "considerable changes"—notably the entrenchment of domestic ideology and its doctrine of separate spheres—that had transpired since the mid-1790s. The historical status of an intransigent Elizabeth Bennet or an Emma Woodhouse or a Catherine Morland or even a Mary Crawford is more than a precondition for eventual compliance with the imperatives of plot or heteronormative desire. It is part of an abiding anteriority, whose afterlife or transposition to the present is additionally guaranteed by the temporal or linear progress in which something prior—a woman's life and world *before* marriage—is persistent and strikingly different.

Limning a world, where "the quiet power of the possible" (as Martin Heidegger later phrased it)[14] is tantalizingly close at hand, Austen's retrospect looks in two directions: to a past whose (re)discovery propels the everyday—or what was the everyday—into an appreciable state, and to a present whose peculiar and prosaic eventfulness is an "under-recognized mode of historical manifestation" and a transit back to the future.[15] Like trauma, also an "experience . . . not fully assimilated as it occurs,"[16] the history that impresses, yielding a stratum of life that the everyday might suffice to name or to describe, is analogous to the train wreck "from which a person walks away . . . only to suffer the symptoms of shock weeks later" (Caruth 1998, 6), but at a level that amalgamates concept and experience rather than being confounding. It bears affinities with trauma not as a wound whose registry is delayed, but as a "disquiet" (in Harry Haroo-tunian's term)[17] in which past "arise[s] where immediate understanding" of the everyday "may not" (Caruth 1998, 11).

II

Austen's writings seem tailor-made for a discussion of the everyday: both in their reluctant subscription to probability and in their striking embrace of the prosaic. But what they share with the writing of her more recognizably romantic contemporaries—specifically Wordsworth and Lord Byron—is a "retrospection" that transforms "what might have been" from an open possibility into one that counts on historical distance in becoming what Ernst Bloch terms "real possi-bility."[18] In Wordsworth's "Intimations Ode" there is not only an idealized past whose disappearance is famously mitigated through the joint agency of memory and imagination; there is also a more immediate history running sideways where an alternative world peers through in contrast to the palliatives of either vision or what increasingly seems like special pleading. Readers will remember very clearly the probabilistic course of human existence that the "Ode" outlines in place of what elsewhere in Wordsworth is a more clearly defined developmental trajectory involving a paradise regained through the interaction of mind and nature. The "Ode" is more qualified. After four stanzas in which the barely re-membered plenitude of childhood is juxtaposed to a present marked by disen-chantment, the poem proceeds haphazardly to answer the question on which its inaugural stanzas and, not coincidentally, its initial phase of composition came to an abrupt halt: "Whither is fled the visionary gleam? / Where is it now, the glory and the dream?" (56–57).

It is tempting to view the two years that it took to fashion an answer to these questions—or the answer produced during that vexed interval—as homolo-gous with Austen's revisions of her first novels and with the renewed sense of the world onto which they opened. But there is a critical difference even as the questions gesture toward something similar in suggesting that the glory and the dream are potentially close by ("Where is it now . . . ?"). The difference is that while Austen had an archive to revisit in her own cursive writing, the past in stanzas 1–4, what stands as history in the ode, is sharply dissociated not just from the present but from anything that might have been a present. If the two years it took to complete the ode involved some kind of retrospection, it was less "a retrospect of what might have been—but what never can be now" (to quote Austen's statement in full), than a retrospect of what might have been because "[it] is now" with the benefit of hindsight.

But how exactly does one fashion such a history? The answer is very quickly or as rapidly as it takes for there to be an interval to create historical distance. The central example of this process devolves on the ordinary or "meanest flower" in the ode's final lines, the one that famously gives "thoughts that do often lie too deep for tears" (204–5). This is the same flower glimpsed early on: first, as a personification and, in that very instant, something less mystified:

> —But there's a Tree, of many one,
> A single Field which I have looked upon,
> Both of them speak of something that is gone:
> > The Pansy at my feet
> > Doth the same tale repeat:
> Whither is fled the visionary gleam?
> Where is it now, the glory and the dream? (51–57)

Without belaboring the difference between a declarative statement of loss and a question that bears the promise, at least rhetorically, of some recovery in the present, it is clear that the pansy does not simply repeat the tale spoken by either the tree or the field. It alters that tale in quickly shifting from a debased or fallen present to something immediate, if indeterminate. Out of nowhere, or so it seems, the prosopopoeia is inverted in deference to the flower, whose pressure or thingness is reflected in an interrogative that turns on "it." And it happens with a suddenness best encapsulated by a phrase from Austen's *Emma,* and from the memorable character of Miss Bates, who in a rare moment of economy states flatly: "What is before me, I see."[19]

This maneuver—where the immediate is prior and the prior immediate—is far from self-evident, especially when memory is also being enlarged as a form of vision. For the duration of the ode, then, as in so much of Austen, the history of missed opportunities remains a counterpart, and a mostly silent one, to a probabilistic account involving an inevitable transit from the "simple creed / Of childhood" (139–40) to the "earthly freight" of "custom" or experience (129–30). In Austen this transit is from woman to "wife" and linked to truths that, by universal acknowledgment, are just as openly contestable. But in Wordsworth, or at least *this* Wordsworth, probability is a placeholder that, far from subscribing to an empirical worldview, is highly aestheticized and largely a performance. This is especially obvious at the poem's close, when the speaker turns from the human condition he had been elaborating to talk about himself and the separate peace or compensation he has secured. Many readings follow the mythologizing here, attributing this compensation to a heroic, highly individualized, act of recovery through imagination and memory. But this turn, and the seemingly subjective valuation of nature it subtends, proves a turning from that stance as well.

Coleridge would later reflect on Wordsworth's power of "giv[ing] the charm of novelty to things of every day . . . by awakening the mind's attention from the lethargy of custom, and directing it to the loveliness and the wonders of the world before us; an inexhaustible treasure, but for which in consequence of the film of familiarity and selfish solicitude we have eyes, yet see not, ears that hear not, and hearts that neither feel nor understand."[20] While there is no disputing these observations, or their appositeness at the time, what Coleridge describes was frequently exposed to a second look, in which the charm of novelty disappeared and "things of every day," or something like them, suddenly reemerged. In the "Ode," the "one delight" that the speaker claims to have relinquished—"[t]o live beneath [the] habitual sway" of the "Fountains, Meadows, Hills, and Groves" (194, 190)—moves processually from an immersion that is prehistoric and idealized to opportunities *in time* that have been missed and are only suddenly realized: in the "Brooks," in the "new-born Day," in "Clouds that gather round the setting sun" (195–99), and, last and most important, in "the meanest flower that blows," all of which are seen essentially for the first time.

The gyrations leading to the everyday's emergence as something missed, recovered, and writable are reparative in fostering a sense of enchantment, or hope, that is neither intentional nor teleological so much as a prevailing afterwardsness. Here the possibilities of the world and the world of possibility are timebound in two different, if interrelated, ways: in the "event" to which the world is tantamount by this development and in the peculiar plenitude to which this event—a history dissociated from memory—gives access. Although necessary to the emergence of things in ways that are surprising and seemingly unprecedented, the historical distance from which the "meanest flower" peers forth, and from which the vibrancy of domestic life becomes visible on reflection, is necessarily collapsible and the guarantor of "real possibility."

III

Byron is important here as well, thanks to a history that is speculative in advance of becoming fact and to the specific event that comes in either case to count as a missed opportunity. The event, suitably, is marriage, beginning with the "Eastern Tales," written during Byron's courtship of Milbanke, where marriage is consistently figured as what might have been, and culminating in *Don Juan*, which turns out to be both about marriage and a work whose shapeless intimacy amounts to a marriage between the poem's speaker and an interlocutor whom, only partly as a critical thought experiment, I'm calling Lady Byron. Byron's preoccupation with marriage is linked most immediately to the separation scandal and to the separation from England that the break with Lady Byron precipitated. Of interest to me, however, is the way marriage was connected *before and after* to a mode of relation, habitual and ongoing, where separation was also temporal and historical. We can thank Stanley Cavell for this general insight regarding what Eric Walker has more recently described as a "furtive, contingent model" of marriage that should be "called remarriage" or "remarriage . . . day after day."[21] But, regardless, the linkage of the everyday and (re)marriage, particularly as they may be dissociated from probability, domestic ideology, and the marriage plot in all senses, joins with other aspects of the everyday in romantic-period discourse in the way a retrospective procedure opens onto something past and passing that Byron, in a slight modification, eventually called the "feeling of a Former world and Future." This feeling or "sensation," which is also the essence of "Poetry," describes what Byron insistently calls "Hope" in this same journal entry (January 28, 1821). And not just any hope but one that, as he works through it, is located less in "memory," where it is forever "baffled," than in something "retrospective but also prospective" (in Svetlana Boym's phrase), which the "Present"—both obscure and self-evident—might very well describe.[22]

If it seems too much to claim that Byron could will himself to marry in the first place only by valuing his future union from the other side, when what Heidegger calls the "not yet" was already what might have been, it is the case that marriage routinely gains prestige as a missed opportunity and as an alternative to Byronic business as usual. The sense of a marriage missed is especially striking in the Eastern Tales, beginning with *The Giaour*, where a triangulated story of sex and violence ends with a surprising paean to monogamy, both as a counter to a "life of sensation" and a counterfactual history. It continues in *The Corsair* and *Lara*, where marriage is consigned variously to a former world whose defining counterpart is not just the future but a present that found additional form in the exchange that was the Byrons' courtship and subsequently in *Don Juan*, which revolves around a speaker and, by extension, an interlocutor rather than the story of its eponymous character.

Along with the repetition of days it comes to mime as an endless conversation, *Don Juan* is additionally representative in the way a missed opportunity (the Byron marriage) is recognized and honored by the poem's form. I have already noted a similar development in the way Austen's detailism amounts to a history that is properly the prose of history versus a more conventional history in narrative form.[23] The ever-unfolding disposition of *Don Juan* does something cognate in aspiring to historical status or eventfulness rather than in giving shape and meaning to what is either prior or invented. Like the history to which revision provides access in Austen, the history which substitutes for memory, *Don Juan* is also a retrospect of the possible: a history that takes the form, not of retrospection so much, with its implicit claim to loss or even comprehension, but of what might have been. Byron's poem registers the gain, the "willingness for the everyday," that marriage produces in practice, and in this case poetic practice, and "in the repetition of days" (Cavell 1988, 178) to which *Don Juan*, like the endlessly digressive world of *Emma*'s Miss Bates, palpably conforms.

A great deal has been written about the fragment's remarkable prevalence during this moment of literary production and what I am flagging may simply be an epiphenomenon. Still, to the degree that *Don Juan* is a relational do-over, whose ending, properly enough, is a parting until death, it bears connection to other contemporary fragments by both Coleridge and Shelley and, just as crucially, to the related tendency in Keats's Odes to foreground a present that typically goes undocumented. The dynamic is a little different in these instances. However, each reflects the "unrounded immanence," as Ernst Bloch describes it, that makes its "presence felt" when the "all too stilled work of art" is "broken" so as to "never clos[e]" (Bloch 1985, 219). Rather than tracking the particular historiography by which the everyday comes to view, these poems suggest an anteriority internal to form in which the text, quoting Bloch again, becomes a "hollow space of a factual, highly factual kind" (ibid.). Like still-life painting on

Norman Bryson's formulation ("looking at the overlooked"), these vessels of fact, these forms of historical content, engage an everyday that is both a "residual deposit" (in Henri Lefebvre's phrase) and one that, by performance, is "immanent," ongoing, and where the "closedness of . . . content," much less of "form" (Bloch 1985, 219), is essentially inconceivable.[24]

Without discounting the circumstances by which romantic fragments were produced or alleged to have happened, whether in a surprise visit by someone from Porlock or in the actual death of the author, the fragments of the period resemble Keats's Odes in recurring to the overlooked—both as a condition of becoming fragments and as a goad to fragmentation regardless of cause. Coleridge's "Kubla Khan" and *Christabel* and Shelley's *The Triumph of Life* do not on the face of it seem especially motivated by the indissolubility of form and content that makes the fragment the form par excellence for representing the everyday. Yet each opens onto a site of the ordinary that marks a departure from poetic business as usual. The sublime of "Kubla Khan" quickly dissipates in a daydream and the Manichean allegory of *Christabel* trails off into a scene of present-day domesticity. Even *The Triumph of Life*, whose fragmentary status was, like *Don Juan*'s, sealed by the death of the author, finds its gravity (for want of a better term) in a "life"-style of self-perpetuating terza rima and enjambment that does not support the poem's infernal vision so much as vitiate it.

Then there are the Odes. Adhering to the fragment's formal logic in their representations of everyday phenomenology or musing, these real-time lyrics preserve something unremarkable, even banal, that closure simply breaks with. This is especially true of "To Autumn," which closes on a lights-out moment that does not resolve matters but stops them arbitrarily, registering a willingness for the everyday, a sense of life interrupted, where a moment written out of history is written into history in honor of what is otherwise lost to time.

I V

The subtitle of my study—*British Romanticism and the Emergence of the Everyday*—could easily be reversed, since this book tracks a development that came to light during the romantic moment as a missed opportunity and an opportunity, accordingly, for historical accounting, where what "happened," to borrow from Walter Benjamin, was "lost" but with the potential now of being recovered.[25] Anticipating the formulations of Heidegger and Lefebvre, for whom the everyday, as I discuss in chapter 1, is environmental, broadly integrative and, along with much recent thinking about the everyday, object- rather than subject-oriented, what was "missed" in the period—thanks partly to the romantic ideology itself—proved to be an order of experience that, with no tautology in mind, was finally "missable" and a "retrospect" of something possible and ongoing.[26] The everyday world that history came to focalize, and the conceptual void it exposed in so doing, remained a recovery on several levels: it involved not only "what might have been" but a "sense" as well "of something ever more about to be" (Wordsworth). It registered the "shock of *recognition*" that took place when, as Raymond Williams outlines, "an area of experience" that "lies beyond" was finally "articulat[ed]," or historicized in this instance, and a sense of potentiality, or hope, where something past but presumably present was grasped in advance of being understood and categorized.[27]

As a largely literary or aesthetic phenomenon, this emergence would appear to comport with a philosophic dimension to romantic discourse, explored under rubrics such as the "literary absolute" or "metaromanticism," in that the everyday is later mobilized in dismantling a phenomenology that had reached a high-water mark in romantic aesthetic practice.[28] But as a retrospective procedure, art's convergence with the critical is forestalled in the romantic moment by thinking that is inconclusive and beclouded, frankly, by what has been recovered. The retrospects I follow tell us something about the period, then, that neither the standard account, where romanticism names an interval of succession and opposition, nor the more reflexive or historicist accounts fully grasp. Subtractable into a series of presents—or "sideways" as Boym calls them (2001, 13)—the anteriority that doubles for the everyday at the time of its emergence is "historic" in the spirit of Benjamin's "now-time" and its disavowal of progress. It is historic in making the "past" a site of "hope" and, more important, in the way the conditions for possibility are historically repeatable.[29]

In regarding this development as a question of period, I am making a claim that is straightforward to the point of seeming naïve (especially as a defining feature of romanticism in Britain) and sufficiently distended or oblique to have no immediate bearing on the period and on the ways we construe it, save that it is of the literature and the moment. Even as we can map the everyday onto familiar cartographies and taxonomies, beginning with empirical thought and its investment in the probable from which the everyday—as a precedented and also possible world—is a departure, its emergence, beyond the still-critical matter of its contemporaneity, is random and surprisingly freestanding. None of the contexts we typically apply to British romanticism—from the philosophic one where phenomena do an end-run around things in themselves (and around the skepticism posed by noumena)[30] to the various historicisms that have transformed romanticism into what looks more and more like a burnt-over interval—is especially useful. Nor is the institution of "British romanticism" as a division of academic or critical knowledge. From its early function as a counter to hermetic formalism, to its more recent incorporation into the long centuries it straddles, "romanticism"—the *study* of romanticism—has been increasingly impatient with the aspects of period-based writing that I'm following, which are not only better appreciated up-close and with a much tighter focus, but re-minders as well—and here it gets tricky—of something specific to the period that its specificity by other lights has elided. Lodged in a seemingly contingent relationship of means and ends, or between certain retrospective procedures and their potential yield and bearing, the everyday's emergence underscores romantic literature's altogether unique role as both text and context, where the world onto which this writing opens is so veiled, so barely understood, that it is enough just to mark it.

A brief look at the *OED* indicates that the everyday (as opposed to the "ordinary" which was primarily a class designation) developed into a necessary descriptor sometime in the mid-eighteenth century, eventually achieving a conceptual apotheosis in the notion of "everydayness" in the 1840s. But what this means too is that the particulars of this development toward conceptualization, especially in the new century, require a special kind of attention. As a category in process, the everyday registers a series of distinctions that are easy to overlook but are crucial nonetheless. In Wordsworth, as I demonstrate in chapter 2, the everyday's emergence is enmeshed in practices of recollection that are seemingly instantaneous and distinct from both Wordsworthian memory in the usual sense and, just as important, the immersive immediacy of his sister Dorothy's journal, where the everyday (as Heidegger might put it) is everywhere and nowhere. In the writings by Austen explored in chapter 3, including her daily writing to her sibling, the everyday's proximity to probability, and to the routine and stability on which the probable depends, is interrupted by a distinctly possible world that is the hallmark of Austen's plotless and detail-laden style and sufficiently lost to time to be recoverable as a prelude to becoming present. In Byron, the subject of the final chapters, the anteriority to which the everyday—or, in Byron's case, everyday domesticity —is consigned before and after marriage makes loss the condition of what is suddenly possible save for the brief interval when, as something fully present, marriage "day after day" was just as suddenly unthinkable. Regardless of how it performs, then, as a pathway to discovery, "history" focalizes something missed that writing is then pressed to (re)encounter: whether as an "archive" including the one we know as *Don Juan* or, as I discuss in chapter 5, by process of interruption, in which the fragment—that quintessential romantic genre—forms a "constellation" (in Benjamin's famous description) "wherein what has been comes together in a flash with the now" as a condition of becoming representable.[31]

No study with the words "romanticism" and "history" in its title can proceed without some mention of romantic literature's "aware[ness]" of "its place in and as history" or, as James Chandler further frames the issue, with its "historical specificity understood as the product of political activity and with that activity of specifying as it takes place in literary representation itself."[32] Chandler has a very specific year and place in mind—"England in 1819"—and a quite specific politics and political climate through which these turns, leading to a distinctly "romantic historicism," are routed. Yet his general claim for literature "as history" in the "period we call Romanticism" (Chandler 1998, 5)—a two-pronged procedure encompassing the "place" of time in a historical field that is anything but empty or homogeneous, and the way that place is demarcated in literary representation—is especially relevant. Ranging in a direction that is conceptual rather than "case"-specific, the everyday's emergence is a "political activity" as well, if only in rejecting the conservatism in which everything is subsumed by precedent. But the more important point about this historicism, or historicity really, is that the reheated chronology to which literature bears witness as a history of missed opportunities—where Keats's Odes remain archives in real time, where *Don Juan* is history in the making—is a very specific conjunction where the past, in no longer dictating what is to occur, takes its lead paradoxically from a present that is suddenly fathomable thanks to its status "in and as history."

Something similar obtains for Mary Favret, whose conception of wartime (an explicitly romantic-period development in her view) also involves a thickened present—a "barely registered substance of our everyday"—suspended across geographies in this case rather than over time.[33] Time is far from incidental here. A zone or continuum inflected by messages from afar, by something missing that, like the missed opportunities, is uncannily *there*, "wartime" couldn't be more important. At the same time, what Favret ends up calling the everyday in this context—and in one special instance "everyday war"—remains an interval marked from without (a "sense of war") rather than by a sense of its own monadic plenitude: a zone colored and sufficiently "affected" to stand in relief but not the stand-alone entity, the emergent category, that history—and a very specific history again—brings to view.

It has long been a commonplace that the history of missed opportunities to which writing of the romantic period refers is the "Age of Revolution" and the renovated world that seemed imminent at one point. This study is concerned with another kind of history and another kind of possibility, where "what might have been" turns out to be less a matter of conjecture or fantasy than of historical distance that is collapsible and a resource accordingly for what Byron provocatively called "Hope."

1 THE EVERYDAY, HISTORY, AND POSSIBILITY

I

This study is about the emergence of the everyday as both a concept and a material event, and about the practices of retrospection where it came to consciousness during the romantic period in histories of the missed, the unappreciated, the overlooked. Much like the postmodern, then, which on Jean-François Lyotard's well-known argument finds an early counterpart in Kant's version of the sublime, the everyday in its "nascent state" (to borrow Lyotard's term)[1] stands not just in contrast to the anomie with which "everydayness" would become synonymous in the wake of modernization and urbanization; it represents a conceptual, or preconceptual, leap forward that it took a century and more to recognize and gradually to reformulate.

The aim of this chapter is twofold, therefore: first, to trace the "theory of the everyday" in the aftermath of "everydayness," where the everyday returns in various ways to the scene of its emergence as a parallel world and a site of possibility; and second, to review and assemble a constellation of thought emanating from that emergence. Here questions of history and potentiality remain paramount, both in the opportunity that the present harbors, on reflection or in retrospect, and as a reminder generally that, like many acts of recovery, this study is fundamentally a transit to the future, or a series of futures, in which the previously thinkable continues to be rethought.

The everyday and the ordinary have enjoyed a conceptual resurgence over the past half-century, both as a practical refuge from various systems of dominance and as an endgame in social and political theory. To political theorists especially, an appreciation of (and a submission to) ordinary actuality holds out what may well be the last promise for democracy and solidarity, not just between people but between humans and the environment.[2] For others, notably Michel de Certeau, everyday activity, however routinized, remains a productive site of resistance for all human agents.[3] The site of a politics at once progressive, ethical and local, the everyday is more than a hiatus in a world defined by various imperia; it is akin by theory's lights to a parallel or possible world on which these definitions and proscriptions, including the anomie typically associated with the quotidian, have surprisingly little bearing. The political theorist Thomas Dumm regards the ordinary as a "repository of freedom," in which the loss of what is familiar, meaningful, and eventful to most people is compensated by a new world and by a politics of "resignation," where "anonymity" and "commonality" join in an unprecedented sense of belonging (Dumm 1999, 33, 63, 70). Jane Bennett goes even further, viewing the ordinary as a site of enchantment, which she defines as "a state of openness" to the "disturbing-captivating elements in everyday experience" (Bennett 2001, 131). Such openness, she argues, bears ethical and political potential in making us responsive to persons and things, no matter how contingent, and "more willing," as a result, "to enter into productive assemblages with them" (Bennett 2001, 147, 131).

Political theory's romance with the everyday owes its origins broadly speaking to a Marxist tradition and to the nonalienated world it projects as an alternative to capitalistic modernity and individualism.[4] But in something of a curiosity, the most important effort to found a politics on the everyday—de Certeau's *The Practice of Everyday Life*—comes not from political theory or economy directly but indirectly from a theory of *history writing*, where, as de Certeau argues, the customary practice of narrating what happened invariably opens onto a less narratable, more heterogeneous past. On this counterintuitive claim, aspects of "the past" that are seemingly unintelligible and irrelevant to a "new understanding of [it]" are not simply banished or erased in historical accounting; they return at the "edges" of "[historical] discourse," in which the "resistances" endemic to such practice leave traces, "[remainders] created by the selection of materials," that complicate and "perturb the pretty order of a line of 'progress' or a system of interpretation."[5] By commitment to "intelligibility," in other words, history makes forgetting a condition of remembering. For the "ruptures" this writing creates "between a past that is its object ... and a present that is the place of its practice" (de Certeau 1988, 36) are more than just breaks or divides; they are apertures through which a history in all its fullness (as Benjamin might call it) becomes palpable and comprehensible.

The leap that de Certeau negotiates between conventional historiography, whose limitations he strategically celebrates, and the practice of everyday life, turns out to be equally counterintuitive. None of the "shards" or forgotten remnants that history writing typically jettisons, whose traces amount to a debit against historical practice *tout court*, involve the everyday in a particular historical formation (as they do for a historian like Fernand Braudel or even a theorist like

Benjamin). If anything, the everyday practice that de Certeau promotes in what he terms its "oppositionality" is largely structural or transhistorical, from the religious practices of indigenous societies in South America, in which to believe in miracles is to believe in an eventual, and miraculous, escape from domination, to the surreptitious practices of some French factory workers, who have traditionally made things for themselves when supposedly producing items for their employers (de Certeau 1984, 15–28). In something of a fractured homology the unnoticed and surprising heterogeneity of certain routinized or ritualized activities by ordinary people finds its counterpart *not* in what history writing leaves out, or in what is generally unassimilable to either Whiggish narratives of progress or conjectural histories based on principles of probability and intelligibility. It finds a counterpart in historical practice itself, in which the repressed or the "forgotten" returns, compromising the reach of historiographic protocol. The duality of historical representation is not a template for the everyday by reason of something fundamentally historical, however ordinary or unaccounted for; it proves a template because, like the coherence that history writing seeks to impose, social or cultural discipline on the Foucauldian model especially is fundamentally unequal to what *it* regulates:[6] specifically the practices, the everyday practices, where people "escape," but do not by the same token leave.[7]

This slippage between one theory and another may seem unduly fine, discounting the heterological disorder of things that characterizes de Certeau's worldview generally.[8] But the absence of a genuinely historical or historicized everyday in his analysis of history writing, along with a sense of when something that could be named the everyday emerged as an idea, is a lacuna worth pressing on, especially in conjunction with other theories (not to mention histories like Braudel's), where anteriority and the everyday are explicitly linked. While it is possible to conceptualize everyday practice as occurring at all times and in all places, there is, on other accounts, something fundamentally, even theoretically, anachronistic about the everyday that runs athwart de Certeau's projection, whether as a concept retrofitted to a range of practices in an agrarian, pre-capitalist past (Lefebvre), or as an aspect of the here and now that derives its sanction from a past that is alternately made and repeated in "the innumerable common occurrences of daily life."[9] Like those remnants that conventional historiography apparently leaves behind, the version of the local or the seemingly uneventful for which the everyday is a shorthand ranges in theory from something that might have happened but was overlooked or unappreciated to what

Lefebvre terms a "residual deposit" (Lefebvre 2008, 2: 64), where the everyday returns, as both an engine of critique and a prospect in which history and the end of history are projectively one and the same.[10]

The discovery of the everyday in history (and vice versa), whether through de Certeau's homology regarding the history that history writing represses, or in the late eighteenth century, in which the everyday, as this study argues, emerges as something missed or overlooked, is more than just a tic or a coincidence; it is the linchpin in the most sustained and conclusive engagements with the everyday where the past, to borrow Reinhart Koselleck's phrase, is typically a "future past"—a site of possibility, even hope—as opposed to a history from which inferences about the probable and its corollary, the marvelous, may be drawn. In the conceptual moves undertaken by Heidegger in *Being and Time* and by Lefebvre in his three-volume *Critique of Everyday Life*, the everyday turns out to be more than just a category of being from which we've been somehow separated by modernity or, in Heidegger's case, by a wayward subscription to subjectivity going all the way back to Descartes; it is dependent, practically as well as dialectically, on an entrenched orientation typically associated with idealism, or with romanticism in its "standard" formation, that being-in-the-world (as Heidegger describes it) at once predates and supersedes.

Thus even as they seek to reorient us to something beyond selfhood that is abiding and potentially liberating, Heidegger and Lefebvre are grappling, no less than their romantic-period forbears did, with a stance that can only be grasped *in relation* to the developmental narrative (and, on a personal level, the *Bildung*) on which the "modern," certainly the romantic modern, is routinely leveraged. In the romantic-period texts, where time slows sufficiently for the overlooked to become visible, this position and the continuum to which it extends oppose newer temporalities that, as Koselleck observes, are hurtling toward futurity on an otherwise progressive axis.[11] But what is interesting is that more than a century later this dynamic, involving possibilities forgotten or foreclosed on, remains relatively intact in the way "history," as Harootunian notes (with reference to Japan), is continually "concealed under the smooth surface of routine and sameness" (Harootunian 2000, 72). On one level, then, the richly conceptual life that the everyday has enjoyed as a subset of what Harootunian calls "history's disquiet" elaborates, in this case by reversing, the conditions of its emergence as a retrospect of what might have been, in which, routinized or not, the everyday is concealed *in* history. On another level, this elaboration finds its strongest justification in a potentiality that is primarily historical, where the everyday's emergence is largely restaged. Although removed from the condensation that I've been calling "a history of missed opportunities," such theories, among them Benjamin's famous theses on history, verge on something "below the threshold of representation" (Dumm) that the everyday might very well describe. And why? Because the sense of history linked to potentiality (and vice versa) in what Jane Austen again termed a "retrospect of what *might* have been" (emphasis added), in what Benjamin later calls a "weak messianism" (to distinguish it from something progressive and teleological) and in what Svetlana Boym describes paradoxically as "nostalgia" with a "future," is not only a constitutive feature of the everyday in its "power to imagine and recall" (Harootunian 2000, 154–55). It is also the very mechanism by which the everyday becomes readable and, by turns, writable as a condition of its emergence in the first place.

II

Heidegger (for all his antipathy to routine and alienation) is the critical figure here, writing at the end of a phenomenological tradition that reached its high-water mark in, among other places, the British versions of romanticism operating within and beyond the paradigms of "English" idealism. He takes aim at the subject/object dyad as a basis not just for skepticism in the empirical tradition, in which we are immured in a world of impressions, but for idealism in the romantic/phenomenological tradition, where Wordsworth, for example, regards perception as creation, while believing at the same time that there is something out there to be worked on and with. Mapping an alternative subjectivity that he famously calls Dasein or being-in-the-world,[12] Heidegger invokes "everydayness" as the "mode" in which being "operates . . . pre-eminently" where a "submission" to the "world" (Heidegger 1962, 86, 121) marks a shift from subject to object. This shift is especially evident regarding things present or "ready-to-hand" (98–99), such as tools or faucets or writing implements, whose constant and inconspicuous application (and generally unchanging status) entails an "uproot[ing]" or "abandon[ment]" (214, 216) of a self that is otherwise worldless. It is evident, too, in the peculiar temporality or "historicality" "constitutive for Dasein's 'historicizing' as such" (41) by which "*my* world" (or what is erroneously that) is a world that, as Hubert Dreyfus describes it, is "always prior."[13] Thus in the very way that being-in-the world amounts to "being with" the environment rather than an "isolable self-sufficient mind" opposed to the others and objects that typically "involve[e]" it (Dreyfus 1991, 76), it is the case too that being or Dasein "is as it already was," making the everyday " 'what' it already was" (Heidegger 1962, 41) and a dialectical image similar to Benjamin's "wherein what has been comes together . . .with the now to form a constellation."

There would appear to be a link between the "historicizing" of everydayness, or of being's operation "in the mode of everydayness" (as Heidegger describes it [1962, 86]), and the historicizing that, as I'm arguing, undergirds the everyday's emergence a century earlier as something at once prior and potentially present. But there is also a real difference. Where being and time are condensed or "constellated" in the "mode" of everydayness that Heidegger outlines, which remains, as Harootunian notes, "the least differentiated and determinate expression of Being's existence" (2000, 113), the everyday's emergence as a missed or unappreciated stratum of experience is ambiguously suspended between anticipating Heidegger's schema and very nearly deconstructing what both Heidegger and Benjamin deem a "history of the Present" (Heidegger 1962, 445). This difference persists because the link between what is missed in either Wordsworth or Austen and what abides amid the publicness that limits being, rendering it inauthentic for Heidegger (1962, 219–22), is a world of possibility that proves a pathway "from inauthentic back to authentic existence" (Harootunian 2000, 113): a world that Heidegger describes as both "ahead-of-itself" and "not-yet" (1962, 288) and that romantic-period writers regard variously as a missed opportunity. The notion of what might have been carries some promise of recurrence in the here and now if only on the evidence, or the intuition, of its having already occurred. But this potentiality, although structurally analogous, is a far cry from the anticipatory repetition on which being and the "possibility" (1962, 309) it harbors for Heidegger are based. For it is by retrospection—rather than the repetition endemic to being where "historicism" is "reconceptualize[d] . . . to rescue from surface routine the possibility offered by a buried past" (Harootunian 2000, 99)—that the everyday emerges in the first place: both as the site of possibility and as a "possible world" that, following what philosophers call "modal realism,"[14] is provisionally disarticulated from the one we inhabit, which is the very world of *Being and Time*.

It may be safer to say that the retrospection necessary to discovering the everyday in the late eighteenth and early nineteenth centuries—where it returns or emerges as something missed and apart from memory—anticipates the role that history plays, not only in de Certeau (his notions of the everyday notwithstanding), but also and more importantly in Heidegger and Lefebvre, who regard the everyday as either harboring or figuring a privileged, depersonalizing, anteriority. For Marxists like Lefebvre, the everyday marks a "moment" of integration prior to modernity and to alienation under capitalism. For Heidegger, by contrast, the historicality attached to being and to everydayness effectively temporalizes the same uprooting and relocation—and the potentialities therein—configured spatially in a shift from subject to object or to a state of being that is more properly being-there (Dasein). And yet, we must take seriously the everyday's constitution at the moment it first comes into view, along with the means by which it became conceivable as such. The everyday's emergence and early conceptualization as a history of what was missed, as something appreciable in retrospect but not in real time, is more than just analogous to what a Marxist like Lefebvre also finds missing and lacking; it is at cross-purposes—and significantly so—with the very developments of which romantic-period discourse, in its subscriptions to interiority and individualism, remains a signal manifestation.

One way to illustrate this manifestation, along with romanticism's perspicuity in discovering something beyond its ostensible operating procedures, would be to turn not necessarily to romantic-period writing directly but rather to a near-contemporary of Heidegger's—Henri Bergson—who, like Heidegger, was very much interested in the interrelation of mind, matter, and time. Bergson's classic treatise *Matter and Memory* could very well have been titled *Being and Time*, save for the distinct and depersonalized status that being, or being in the world, retains for Heidegger. Like Heidegger, Bergson is particularly struck by the way perception is inseparable in practice from memory, "import[ing] the past into the present" and "enriching it," in his phrase, "with experiences already acquired."[15] Even the most elementary sensations are activated from "two different sides" (Bergson 1988, 129): they are impressions sent by a *"real object"* through what Bergson refers to as actual or "pure perception" (129, 58) and from behind, or by memory's mediation, through what he terms "virtual" perception (129). Or put slightly differently, "perception is never a mere contact of the mind with the object present" or what Heidegger might call "ready-to-hand" but is always "impregnated with memory-images" in the same way that "pure memory" (the mnemonic equivalent of pure perception) is ultimately rendered impure "in the colored and living image which reveals it" (133).

Bergson has other things to say that anticipate Heidegger (which the latter properly acknowledges), notably the concept of *durée*, which follows on Bergson's general thesis in defining the present as we experience it as a "psychical state" allied alternately with the past and with "action or movement" as "determined" by an "immediate future" (Bergson 1988, 138). While all of this would appear to accord with Heidegger's notions of time and historicality in the way being, or being with matter, is both "ahead of itself" and "not yet" for Bergson as well, there is a notable discordance in their views. This difference involves Heidegger's rejection of memory as largely extraneous to his own sense of temporality and the "being" it subtends and a reluctance correspondingly on Bergson's part to consider the primacy of matter as an aspect of everydayness. These differences exist because, for all of his sophistication—especially regarding motor memory and the neurological aspects of recollection in general—Bergson remains wedded to a subjectivity, or to what Heidegger, in discussing him, terms a "personalis[m]," that the latter is only too willing to jettison.

Much the same can be said of the aspects of romantic-period discourse that I'm exploring here, which anticipate Heidegger and outstrip Bergson in postulating a history *without* memory. Such a history yields what is missed or indeed missing in the romantic stance to the world as typically understood in the way pure or actual perception returns in place of virtual perception. Bergson regards pure perception as "the lowest degree of mind" (1988, 222). However, for Heidegger and the writers who anticipate him in shifting the focus from the mind's grasp of things to the things (including people) that essentially grab it, such perception is actually a leap forward, particularly regarding "personalism" or what memory may be said to inflect and control. We see this movement in the double takes by which Wordsworth disencumbers history of memory in demonstrating what virtual perception forgets or misses. We see it also in Austen, whose practice of revision, especially of narratives that were drafted at least a decade earlier, enables a return to both a world and a milieu that time and "progress" have largely erased, and that reemerges, if only by previous documentation, as something different and valuable. And we witness it most palpably in Byron, thanks to the "history" to which marriage and everyday domesticity are consigned *before* the fact or by a nostalgia that, in lacking mnemonic support, is radically anonymous. Relegated rather to a "future past," the everyday is not valorized in Byron by being missed or unappreciated at the time; rather, it gains value, and the particular prestige that helps drive its emergence, because there was no such time—no memory but only a history of missed opportunities.

Byron is an extreme case. But his use of history, however hypothetical, in place of "memory," which he notably distances from "Hope," squares with the phenomenological gyrations in Wordsworth and even Austen, which effectively backtrack from the amalgam of matter and mind outlined by Bergson to a purer perception of things in themselves, or of a world in this case, that emerges independently of a practical or conceptual sanction. This disarticulation is especially evident in Austen. Here revision is both a historiographic procedure, involving an archive previously assembled, and a procedure accordingly whose primary yield is a "style" that finds its purest exponent in a character like *Emma*'s Miss Bates, whose transport "by the looks of the world" (in Heidegger's phrase [1962, 216]) or by what Miss Bates describes as what she sees "before" her, amounts to a collective uprooting involving both a character and a historian for whom no detail or aspect of everyday life is apparently too small or uninteresting. Miss Bates's remarkable proclivity to what Heidegger also calls "idle talk" or gossip—a disposition that locates her "everywhere and nowhere" (Heidegger 1962, 217)—is obviously instrumental in her remarkable ability to raise the everyday above what Dumm again terms the "threshold of representation." But even as it is a characterological matter, or the by-product of some imagined pathology, Miss Bates's reportage of minutiae is just as pointedly an act of recovery, registering the surprise and wonder at what is typically overlooked that the Austen archive, rather than a consciousness in this instance, provides. Eventually, the history with which the everyday is allied at the moment of its emergence will split into several distinct histories, at least in theory, from the material continuum that, as Braudel reminds us, has long linked everyday life and practice to a persistent and surprisingly unchanging past, to an anteriority prior to capitalism and alienation (Lefebvre), to a history that, on Heidegger's redaction, is more local and immediate yet related to the preceding two. However during the everyday's emergence as a category at the turn of the eighteenth century these conceptually disparate pasts are condensed on the model of Benjamin's "now time," where a possible present, which is to say the past, turns out to be what Stanley Cavell hyperbolically calls "all the Eden there can be."[16]

III

This movement back to the present, which is at the core of Benjamin's messianism, is especially characteristic of Lefebvre, whose agrarian paradigm, and the humility it mandates in (re)connecting individuals to the environment, offers an escape from alienation and a pathway to the restoration of total man. And it describes, too, the project of Cavell who regards romanticism, or the aspects of romanticism he derives from writers like Wordsworth, Coleridge and Thoreau, as a discourse of authentication where things of the world are redeemed willy-nilly from the division of subject and object, which is the basis not just of alienation but of "the way" more generally that "human beings have come to think" (Cavell 1988, 66). Far from a narrative of progress, what Harold Bloom once termed an "internalization of quest romance,"[17] the "romantic quest for the ordinary" (4) involves a different messianism for Cavell, culminating in a world or "heaven" that is close by in contrast to the typically romantic state where the "world" brought "back . . . to life" (52–53) disappears and "we . . . become," quoting Wordsworth, "a living soul." What Cavell does not stress—although he confirms it—is the necessary link between this weak messianism, where "heaven" is suddenly visible "in the light of common day" (in a phrase appropriated from the "Intimations" Ode [75]) and the everyday's emergence as an informing intuition in Wordsworth's writing and elsewhere at that very moment. Although untroubled by the glass-half-empty phenomenology on which skepticism stakes its claim, never doubting that there is a world out there for which the ordinary might just turn out be a placeholder, Wordsworth is generally unaware that it is the everyday, much less a world suddenly authenticated, that nature frequently figures in his writing. This would explain why, despite a stated interest in aspects of life that he deems ordinary or common, Wordsworth's grasp of the ordinary and ability to press it in the philosophic register that Cavell outlines is routinely misrecognized and pegged to acts of recovery, or history, in which the everyday or some irreducible thing-ness comes haltingly into view. The scaling down so critical for Cavell, where the "extraordinary" (9) finds its level and possibly its essence in something quite "ordinary" like the environment, is not a philosophic or phenomenological reversal for this poet. It is more a movement *in time*—a double take or slowing down—where what was missed or overlooked is suddenly, even shockingly, close at hand.

Disarticulated in this way from many of the procedures that continue to run on a parallel track in romantic-period writing, what counts as the everyday in writing of the period works cooperatively, even prosthetically, with these same discourses, despite lacking their narrative or conceptual scope. By condition of its emergence as something belated and overlooked, the everyday imbeds a potentiality that bypasses the usual guarantors of something potential in replacing the "open futures" prevalent at this moment with open pasts in which history—not memory—proves a pathway to both possibility and continuity.

This differs certainly from the way Lefebvre views romanticism or what he terms "nineteenth-century literature," whose obsession with the "marvellous in the familiar" or "the symbol hidden behind the thing" amounted to "a sustained attack on everyday life which has continued unabated up to the present day" (Lefebvre 2008, 1: 105–6). But strangely enough the "world" that "constitutes the irreducible core of appearances" for Lefebvre (168) is a world that, by amalgamation of past and present, remains distinctly, if unconventionally, romantic in the way "humble, familiar, everyday objects"—"the shape of fields [and] of ploughs," for example—may be "see[n]" and "seize[d]" as part of the "immense wealth that the humblest facts of everyday life contain" (132).

For all his longing for an agrarian perspective that has been under siege since the nineteenth century and before, Lefebvre manages to join with "nineteenth-century literature," then, in projecting a "real" into which "the possible" has been "reintegrate[d]" (Lefebvre 2008, 2: 195) in the way certain "residual deposit[s]" (64)—what Byron termed a former world and future—succeed "momentarily" (3: 58) in raising the everyday "to the level of the Possible" (1: 247) and vice versa. Although "torn . . . from us and dispersed by alienation" (1: 168) and stymied by "the pressure of the market and exchange," these "intense instants" (3: 57) manage—as the "implicit, unexplored content of everyday life" (15)—to chart a regress that can happen at any moment, reversing a trajectory where the real and the possible have been disaggregated and revealing something familiar and uncanny that has gone unrecognized.

Projective applications like Lefebvre's—involving things and practices that we take for granted and are thereby removed from—are important for a number of reasons. In addition to modeling, or recapitulating, the retrospection by which the everyday first emerges as a previously missing stratum, the transit of the residual deposit is aligned also with a "concept of history," where potentiality lingers independent of narrative and of the telos to which narratives like Lefebvre's are pitched. Effectively coordinating de Certeau's cordoned-off theories of history writing and everyday resistance—in this case by linking certain oppositional "moments" to a specific and quite different past—Lefebvre looks also to a history "citable in all its moments" (in Benjamin's famous phrase) in the service of what both he and Benjamin regard as a "redeemed mankind" (Benjamin 2003, 390). This redemption is necessarily an endgame, and a backdated one at that. However, it routinely morphs into something ongoing and, in the manner of either de Certeau's opposition or Benjamin's messianism, into what is with us already.

IV

A similar conception of the everyday obtains in the writings of Jane Bennett, whose sense of an enchanted materialism echoes Cavell and Lefebvre in stressing the "extraordinary that lives amid the familiar and the everyday" (2001, 4). Cavell's interests are philosophical, involving a world that, in the shadow of skepticism, has been probable at best and whose sheer ordinariness is, by that measure, extraordinary. Bennett's are political and environmental and concerned with the way a "subintentional disposition in favor of life" (158) dislodges the human subject from its privileged and deleterious centrality. The issue of subintentionality takes us back to Heidegger and even further back to romantic-period writing in its uncanny retrospection. But Bennett's goal is more a leveling or networking of the kind espoused by Gilles Deleuze or Bruno Latour than a full-blown reconfiguration of the subject/object division. In treating things "as independent of human subjectivity," she speaks of what she calls "thing-power," where things—in for example a collage of trash—are entities no longer "reducible to the contexts in which (human) subjects set them" (351). Honoring the "nonidentity" of thing and concept, and the identity by extension of person and thing, such repositioning involves a "slow[ing]," as she terms it, of the "crossing from thing to human culture" in something like Benjamin's "now time" and with materials, like Lefebvre's, that suddenly demand recognition (362). And like Lefebvre, who wants us to "see and seize" remainders that have been "have been torn from us by alienation" and by the current order of "human culture," the slowing that Bennett proposes as a "practical exercis[e]" (with an assist from Adorno [362]) is motivated as much by the various deposits that persist in slow time as by a political possibility to which we have been hurtling since the age of revolution.

That is, when we weren't also slowing down and looking backward. In a paradox endemic to the revolutionary moment such futures could—and did—close as suddenly as they had opened, making the discovery of the everyday less a feature of modernity in its usual or propulsive formation (Koselleck) than an aspect of what Boym calls the "off-modern" (2001, xvi): a regression where the past is paradoxically the only future (as Byron intuited) and in which the world "is," as Heidegger puts it, "as it was." The challenge that subjectivity poses to what Cavell calls the "world as world" (1988, 53) in reducing it to either an impression or a concept is not only something that romantic writing performs in its customary passage from the material to the symbolic; it is also a performance that romantic writing frequently overcomes by regressive actualization where "the particular" rather than the universal is what one "looks back and yearns for" (Boym 2001, 11). Regardless of "the charm of novelty" that Wordsworth often gives "to things of every day" (in Coleridge's assessment), the transit from the material to the mental is not just reversible by the refusal to take idealism to its skeptical limit; it is reversible in the way that objects revert to things on recollection in what amounts to "a willingness for the everyday" or, amending Coleridge now, a willing suspension of belief. This undoubtedly makes Wordsworth a less-than-rigorous respondent to the darker side of "English idealism" where images and ideas are all we have to go on. But it suggests at the same time—and Coleridge's comments about "things of every day" are somewhat revealing—that the intentional structures of romanticism are continually shadowed by a subintentionality in which things are events in and over time.[18]

As a result, the self-involved holding pattern that Cavell calls "privacy," which abides "until . . . publicness"—the "participation . . . with whatever is alive"—is "recognizably established" (1988, 61, 64), describes a development that is largely inadvertent in the way an event provides access to "things of everyday"—in, say, the Ancient Mariner's review of the water-snakes (Cavell's example) or in Bennett's collage of trash—that the idea of questing essentially gets backward. Not only does the retrospection or slowing-down on which this access depends put considerable pressure on the ordinary as a *goal* to which the aesthetic—much less the private—is presumably directed; it also has almost nothing in common with the skepticism or state of "emergency" (as Cavell construes it), which goes one vowel too far in demanding formal or intentional mitigation.

More recently Cavell has described the "ordinary" as a "proto-state": "something there" that, "despite being fully open to the senses," "has been missed" and whose discovery amounts to an "ecstatic attestation of existence" (2005, 23, 11, 26). Here he anticipates a lot of what I'm exploring, particularly in the way our "historical everydays" (his suggestive term [130]) are not just recruitable to a "continuing effort to recognize the extraordinariness within the ordinariness of our lives" but concomitantly instrumental in forcing subjectivity and "original . . . narcissism" (202, 146) to part company. This "effort" is similar, of course, to his earlier sense of a romantic quest for the ordinary, where he may again be getting things backward. Even as history performs in the romantic period in the way Cavell suggests in discovering "something" missed on first pass, its relationship to the everyday as "there" and present is sufficiently provisional and referential that it is impossible for the two to coexist much less to join in a mass of "attestation."

It is more that the romantic substitution of anteriority for a dimension not yet formulated works, in the spirit of Byron's "Hope," to keep "memory" under wraps, so that the difference between one's world and the everyday world is roughly the same difference separating the probable and the possible. We typically regard probability, especially by the lights of skepticism, as a substitute for the certainty we lack as subjects and as a position, accordingly, that the romantics ultimately sidestep in making subjective life their ostensible focus. But what this means is that the subintentionality to which the everyday owes its emergence largely bypasses the idealism that the two-step of quest and discovery (or effort and attestation) recapitulates. Consigned to an anteriority accessible by practices that are fundamentally contingent or unanticipated, the everyday's emergence makes subintentionality the basis of a new, if necessarily weak, ontology that no amount of effort, memory, or even curiosity can possibly validate.

Thus it is important not just to establish what history is or performs as a pathway to the ordinary in the way I've been discussing, but to do so in conjunction with what history is thought to do, which Cavell in a related discussion attempts briefly to expand beyond parameters that are event-based.[19] In contrast to the three criteria that Paul Ricœur uses to define to an event—"something past, something done by or done to human beings" and "something unrepeatable"—Cavell offers a fourth: "something to which some fairly definite public already attaches some fairly definite importance" (1984, 190). The aim here is to consider a history that is "uneventful" and to consider in the process what it might mean for history to "escape from events" in dwelling on "what is not out of the ordinary" (193). For in so doing history may achieve a "closeness" (193) to the world that it typically lacks unless the historian is someone like Fernand Braudel, who tracks "man in his intimate relationship to the earth," thereby expressing what Cavell suggests is "the thought of an ambitious philosophy" (194).

The relationship to the earth and its vicissitudes that Braudel takes as his principal event might justify the attribution of an ambitious (and, for Cavell's part, anti-skeptical) philosophy to his method. But it points up a fundamental distinction between the ordinary as a philosophic phenomenon and its status as "something . . . missed" in the very writers and texts that Cavell explores elsewhere. Even as Braudel can be argued to escape from events in making the *longue durée* of life in early modern Europe the only event that literally matters, the more important point is that this "structure" (as he calls it) remains one where the "separat[ion]" of what [could] be done with little effort from what [could not] be done at all" was fundamentally unchanging, marking what he memorably terms "the limits of the possible."[20] In contrast to what the past—and as it happens that same past—harbors for Lefebvre, Benjamin or even de Certeau, or to a history that is as much about what *was* as about what might have been, the "material" or "everyday life" that concerns Braudel is a mostly abject condition where "the fragile lifetime of men" was "greedily and steadily swallow[ed] up" (1981, 28). "Ever-present, all-pervasive, repetitive" and "run according to routine," such life did more than discourage people from "explor[ing] the limits of what was possible" (28, 27); it was, as Cavell rightly intuits, a nonevent, where various "regimes" or "ceilings" (including those imposed by technology) consistently limited what was "doable" in contrast to what came later, where the previously impossible was increasingly possible.

But Braudel's is just one example where history and the everyday converge. The more that material and political existence proved a pathway to an open future, in which the doable knew fewer and fewer limits, the more it allowed for a concomitantly open past and for a present (by extension) that was reciprocally a site of discontinuity. "Missed" and separated by historical distance, thanks partly to an ever-accelerating sense of time, this past or present no longer belonged to a history that was unchanging. It was, in Cavell's phrase, a proto-state, where the possible and the historical were linked to completely different ends and in which an everyday—past but potentially passing—was suddenly fathomable in its historicity, immediacy and, yes, its eventfulness.

V

The claim to immediacy remains one of romanticism's most treasured assertions.[21] And it is a claim, accordingly, that has received its share of criticism, notably by Paul de Man, whose oft-cited essay "The Rhetoric of Temporality" tracks the impediments to the romantic "fus[ion of] inner states of the soul and the outward aspect of nature" in a "diction" that is presumably "of the moment."[22] According to de Man, the immediacy that romantic writing sustains in a "language that evokes the material shape of the landscape as well as the mind of its inhabitants" (1983, 199) is neither ordinary language nor a language fashioned out of whole cloth; it is, de Man insists, a language that is "inherited" and that, far from being "based on perception" or on a "dialectic between nature and consciousness" (203), is primarily allegorical. Referring less to something present, then, than to "another sign" or trope "that precedes it" (207), romantic language all but guarantees that any monument to immediacy in the form of, say, a poem will be built "in the void of temporal difference " (207), reflecting only loss or what de Man memorably calls an "authentically temporal destiny" (206).

Still, in making this a predicament to which language is fitted in reference to the "outside world" (1983, 200), de Man takes what turns out to be a circuitous route. For the loss he intuits at the site of immediacy and to which the "world" attests in what amounts to a reversal of sorts is already baked in. It issues less from claims that founder on the instability of the sign, or from the temporal shadow that the figuration either casts or occludes (depending on one's perspective), than from an original narcissism—what de Man describes as a "relationship that, in the last analysis, is the relationship of the subject to itself" (196)—which effectively dictates that the "outside world" is routinely overlooked and very quickly a matter of history. Thus far from misrecognizing absence as presence, the immediacy or eventfulness onto which certain romantic texts open is in the most basic sense a detour. "Something there," something "missed despite being open to the senses," is no longer an illusion in these instances but a recovery that neither language in its less-than-ordinary operations nor the "pure anteriority" into which reported experience is subsumed can fully obscure.

We see this discovery with particular clarity in a Wordsworth poem that de Man fortuitously analyzes at the conclusion of his essay in discussing the temporality that makes irony and its particular play with meaning possible:

> A slumber did my spirit seal;
>   I had no human fears:
> She seem'd a thing that could not feel
>   The touch of earthly years.
>
> No motion has she now, no force;
>   She neither hears nor sees,
> Roll'd round in earth's diurnal course
>   With rocks and stones and trees!

Noting, as have many critics, that the poem's temporal structure describes two states of consciousness, de Man focuses on the irony of "thing" in line 3, which in the shadow of death that elliptically divides then and "now" (and, not coincidentally, the two stanzas) proceeds from a word "used quite innocently . . . in a playfully amorous way" to what is "literally true in the retrospective perspective . . . of the second part," where "she has become a *thing* in the full sense of the word" (1983, 224). Of primary interest to de Man is the "temporal sequence" necessary to this disenchantment, where "first there was error, then the death . . . and now an eternal light into the rocky barrenness of the human predicament." While the speaker, he argues, seems capable of "resolv[ing] the tragic irony of lines 3 and 4 in the wisdom of the concluding lines," the particular difference that the poem introduces over time is unmoored from this ironic understanding "in the tendency of the language toward narrative," which follows "the fundamental structure of allegory" in "spreading out along the axis of an imaginary time in order to give duration to what is, in fact, simultaneous within the subject" (225).

The critical question for me, therefore, is the one that de Man asks somewhat inadvertently but in many ways unpacks: "what *is*, in fact, simultaneous within subject"? Is it the passage from innocence to experience crystallized in the understanding that "I," no less than "she," has been born for death? Or is it an altogether different "retrospective perspective" in which the beloved's materiality (versus her ethereality), and the visceral, haptic environment enveloping her, is seen and prosthetically *felt*, not just for the first time (or so it seems), but as the counterpart to a persistent slumber where "she" remains "a thing" in some purely figural register? I am not diminishing by any means the irony or the potential irony imbedded in "thing" especially in such a speaker as de Man describes. Nor am I discounting its persistence in the famous puns on "die" and "urn," which lend a distinctly figural dimension to a naturalism that bears the trappings of immediacy. But equally striking in the poem is the implication—however counterintuitive, since eros was presumably at work at some point—regarding the "slumber" by which the object (or in this case "thing") was somehow overlooked. Not only is this blindness continuous with the poem's irony and its culminating wisdom; it is just as continuous with a newfound awareness, where death is a kind of everyday unlife ("No motion has she now / She neither hears nor sees") and where the material environment is retrospectively a continuum, an accompaniment in and over time, that is fathomable, even shocking, rather than "a succession of isolated moments lived by a divided self" (de Man 1983, 226).

For all its focalization of a subjectivity in the throes of loss and sufficiently consolidated by passage from innocence to experience to enable a very grim irony, there is in the temporalization that de Man flags, which moves in two directions now, a "sensation of meaning," apart from "the despotism of the subject" (as Orrin Wang puts it),[23] in which the present (exclamation point and all) is fitted to the past in *its immediacy* rather than the other way around. The girl's or woman's thingness is more than just a prolepsis "in the tendency of language toward narrative" and the ironic wisdom it subtends; it is also a retrospect of what might have been: an aperture onto a history whose very possibility is recapitulated in the "rocks and stones and trees," which are also discovered and effectively found—hence the exclamation point—in the wake of being missed on first pass. Marjorie Levinson tracks a similar continuity between the poem's stanzas based on what she describes (following Spinoza) as "motion's inherence in matter": the way "rocks and stones," "like trees and persons," are "what they are through the conatus"—the drive to continue—"that sustains their relational physics."[24] This is clearly a more vitalist take than mine. However, it accords with the poem's retrospective procedures, as I construe them, and the life they both recognize and reconstitute, in transforming a woman presumed lost into one who has gone missing, which is also the state of the world, particularly as a prelude to discovery.

This finding or revelation looks a lot therefore like the triumph over skepticism that Cavell calls an "ecstatic attestation," where what is beyond reach or walled off by a very different revelation comes to life, finally, in rocky and vegetal concretion. But what this kind of worlding occludes is the process by which "what is, in fact, simultaneous within the subject" has transformed a narrative of wisdom and maturation (with a beginning, middle and end) into something distinctly fragmentary and continuous, where anteriority, far from "pure anteriority" or some infinite regress, is the condition of immediacy and of an everyday world—past and present—in which proximity and possibility are at a stalemate.

As a result, the "material event" that forces the poem beyond its temporally succinct parameters is virtually akin to what Derrida, in discussing de Man's late work on Kant and aesthetic ideology, describes as a "materiality without matter."[25] However waggish or perplexing this notion might appear at first glance, it speaks perfectly (and in the spirit of Kant's formal materialism as de Man redacts it) to the particular potentiality vested in everyday things, whose immediacy on review amounts to a distinctly impure anteriority, where rocks and trees are no longer in recession but, as poetry routinely demonstrates, present and eventful.[26] As the astonishment regarding these elements suggests, such presence by poem's end, or at the moment it breaks off, is at the same time thingness at a distance, beginning with the woman's everyday life as an embodied creature (versus an imago) and proceeding to the environment (however proximate or anterior) where any materiality linked to either irony or figuration is, for the exclamatory moment, in a losing battle with what might have been.

Such a history, where the "event" is mutable or "incalculable," in Alain Badiou's term,[27] and in which a potential past rises up against a probable much less personal one, gains particular traction in de Certeau: both as a riposte to history writing so-called, where many events are routinely banished as unintelligible excess, and with respect as well to everyday life, whose events are typically missing in action. Thus the particular possibility that history vouchsafes through an event that is on the move is secured by the impossibility of what Badiou calls its "situation" (2005, 207) along with the particular knowledge or calculability that situatedness either presupposes or permits. "Discover[able]" precisely by not "belong[ing]" (ibid.), the event or continuum that Wordsworth's poem registers, thanks to a subjectivity that inclines toward what Badiou (after Heidegger) calls being, remains a "history" that—to follow the figure in the Prospectus to *The Recluse*—is always "wait[ing] upon" the poet's "steps . . . pitch[ing its] tents before" him as he "move[s]." Wordsworth's complex referent—a "Beauty" that he terms a "living Presence of the earth" and a "Paradise" composed largely of "departed *things*" (41–50; emphasis added)—is clearly a possibility and an opportunity of some kind. However like the rocks and stones and trees of the Lucy poem, its immediacy as something irreducibly "before" the perceiver is both thickened and tried by its anteriority or departure as something equally "before" or prior, forming a continuum or *durée*, where movement—including the poet's in time and in-the-world—literally makes all things possible.

All of which brings me to my final point regarding possibility or the possible worlds now of which the everyday—as a retrospect of what might have been—is clearly one.[28] In discussing the everyday's emergence and its initial misrecognition in historical form, we are not only discussing a potentiality in advance of the everyday's conceptualization; we are talking about a possible or alternative world akin to what analytic metaphysicians have been exploring under the rubric of modal realism. Philosophy's engagement with the "the plurality of worlds" undoubtedly runs athwart the phenomenological framework that has governed my discussion here. However, the debates internal to philosophy's speculations regarding the "spatiotemporal" separation of potentially discrete worlds are relevant, especially on the question of time or on a world now to which anteriority holds the key. The philosopher David Lewis's position is especially rigorous as to "whether two worlds ever have a common part" or "whether any part of one world is part of another as well."[29] For a world to be possible within a temporal framework, according to Lewis, no single moment can overlap with another.

Such a world simply "perdure[s]" (1986, 204), in contrast to a world that we would deem probable, where there is temporal continuity and overlap from which inferences of all kinds may be drawn. Continuity of this kind is always something of a wish, whether in the penumbra of Lewis's thought experiment or even earlier for someone like Hume. But a probable world, however illusory, is necessary to understanding the particular possibility that characterizes the everyday, which—with Lewis's two questions in mind again—"whether two worlds ever have a common part" or "whether any part of one world is ever part of another as well" (193)—may be regarded as a contact zone, where an operator like Wordsworth perdures and endures in something of a dialectical dance. Although endurance presupposes a continuity that Wordsworth both disrupts and refashions, the subject that perdures is more austere: a being "made up of temporal parts" (204) with nothing in common, so that someone—say "David Hume" (210)—consists of different parts in time with no identity save for his body at a given moment.

That Lewis enlists Hume as his possible man is of course no accident. After all, there is probably no philosopher more committed to the idea of endurance, and to the continuities experience provides. Nor is there a philosopher more reliant on the epistemological yield of endurance and the inductions it permits than the eighteenth-century empiricist for whom probability is a compass—the only compass—in a world where nothing is knowable beyond a mere impression. But what Hume's philosophy also broaches, this time by counterexample, is a horizon of possibility—the possibility and plurality unleashed by perdurance—where neither personal experience nor collective or consensual wisdom are sufficient to dispel a world (or worlds) that are not just unknowable but, as Lewis doubtless appreciates, sufficiently separated from anything resembling our world to be remarkable as a condition of being discovered. Such worlds— which surely include the marvelous or miraculous worlds that Hume roundly disparages, but that analytic metaphysics happily entertains, in postulating places where donkeys, for example, can talk (Lewis 1986, 112)—are of great interest to both modal realists and certain versions of romanticism. What they both rule out of bounds, however, is the kind of possibility discussed here, specifically the "overlap" where perdurance and endurance, rather than exposing different and distinct worlds, bear mutually on a single, shared world.

The frameworks that favor continuity and may be deemed probabilistic are generally consolidated by experience of considerable duration or custom. But they also include frameworks based on experience of comparatively limited duration or on such personal experience as romantic poetry frequently relates. Correspondingly, the frameworks that allow for discontinuity and possibility replace those of either custom or memory with a historiography that, in practice at any rate, is more properly a do-over in contrast to both conjectural history and personal experience, in which things are seen from a single, sovereign vantage. Such frameworks allow, in other words, for the plurality of a previously familiar or singular world, where the opportunities raised by the everyday's emergence as what possibly happened are every bit as stunning, and a good deal more encouraging, than talking donkeys or dogs with two heads. These latter possibilities are no doubt interesting in philosophic inquiry. But the potentialities entertained by romantic-period writing, in its recovery and discovery of what is missed or obscured by the lights of either probability or narcissism (for which probability is in turn a compensation) seem a good deal more important. They are important as matters of literary and cultural history; and they are important as matters of *history*, where the possibility of a "greater world" mysteriously abides.

2 WORDSWORTH'S DOUBLE TAKE

I

At issue . . . is history as our own unassimilable alterity, our difference from the directions in which "history" is pushing us . . . a different conception of history—one where historical thinking is the dimension in which thought becomes responsible to what is other, lost, unconscious, or potential, yet to be.

Tilottama Rajan[1]

[T]he world is Eden enough, all the Eden there can be, and what is more, all the world there is. . . . Romanticism's work . . . [is] the task of bringing the world back, as to life.

Stanley Cavell[2]

"It was, in truth, / An ordinary sight, but. . . ." So writes Wordsworth in a memorable segue that I have truncated because my interest is not in the "ordinary" so much as in "ordinary . . . but": with something emergent and distinct in contrast to the sublime interiority to which Wordsworth immediately assigns the sight in a characteristic, but erroneous, move. My truncation might be viewed as a truncation of romanticism itself, which commentators from Coleridge to de Man have variously identified as incorporating a movement of mind from the particular to the universal or, in de Man's lexicon, from the "earthly and material" to the "mental and celestial." And, indeed, a seemingly "ordinary sight"—"A Girl who bore a Pitcher on her head / And seemed with difficult steps to force her way / Against the blowing wind" (*Prelude* 11. 306–8)—rises here to the level of vision. But equally important is the way the ordinary irrupts only to evanesce. For the ordinary's evanescence into something personal and aesthetic is not simply a foregone conclusion that the transitional conjunction ("but") anticipates and abets; it is an introjection where something ordinary and not ordinary is reconfigured, even counterfeited, as a romantic and mnemonic surplus. Although decades-old and necessarily a feature of memory, the passage of the ordinary into vision is as much an anterior negotiation as an abiding and still-pressing obligation:

> It was, in truth,
>
> An ordinary sight; but I should need
>
> Colours and words that are unknown to man
>
> To paint the visionary dreariness
>
> Which, while I looked all round for my lost guide,
>
> Did at that time invest the naked Pool,
>
> The Beacon on the lonely Eminence,
>
> The Woman, and her garments vexed and tossed
>
> By the strong wind. (11.308–16)

Wordsworth, by his own admission, is no painter. Were he one, he would have encountered considerable difficulty, since the scene is really a condensation of three discrete events that took place when Wordsworth was about five years old and that are presented in this "spot of time" as happening in sequence: his separation from his riding companion and guide; his coming upon a place "where in former times / A Murderer had been hung in iron chains" (11.288–89) and where someone had then "carved the Murderer's name" on the "turf" (11.294, 292); and lastly, his sighting of the woman with the pitcher upon "reascending the bare Common" (11.303). The traumatic conjunction of these events, involving an encounter with memorials of violence in proximity to what seemed like abandonment to a young boy, amply accounts for the additional freight that the "ordinary sight" is summoned to bear. But there is a sense, too, both in the image of the woman, and in the poet's backhanded and retrospective wish for painterly skills, that the peculiar excess of the only "ordinary" event of the three owes at least as much to a lived and residual actuality, to something palpable and material, that a painter might better capture. Wordsworth is no painter. Still, neither his incompetence as a visual artist, nor his implicit critique of painting as inadequate to the scene as he recalls it, work entirely to the benefit of his present business, poetry. If painting does not exactly serve the interests of interiority and memory, "words"— Wordsworth's words—are far from the vehicle par excellence for representing the ordinary or the "ordinary . . . but." By writing his-story rather than painting it, Wordsworth allows the "real"—the historical and material real—to "perish into art" (in Benjamin's strikingly apt description)[3] in the same way that the poet's *inability* to render the "ordinary sight" by visual means, even by a combination of words and colors, provides a momentary reprieve from death by representation.

By no means is this to argue that painting rather than poetry is the answerable medium for representing the ordinary, however charged. The point is that the force of the ordinary is such, even decades later, that its internalization is chalked up to a failure of representation even as that internalization remains, as the poet warrants and numerous commentators have shown, a triumph of mind. Thus while painting is deemed inadequate to the event, something akin to an impossible or "unknown" version of painting is simultaneously projected as the only the way to do justice to a sight whose transformation into vision is something of a missed opportunity, at least in representational terms. Although the problem confronting Wordsworth appears to be art's failure to capture a par-ticularly charged moment, the real failure lies in the misrecognition—admin-istered by "but"'s passage from qualifier to conjunction—where an "ordinary sight" is written out of history into Wordsworth's story.

If this contortion with Wordsworth reveals anything—beyond the custom-ary practice of turning his poetry to one exegetical purpose or another—it is the necessary connection between the misrecognition that defines and characterizes poetical representation in these lines and what is missed or transfigured in what de Certeau has termed "the writing of history." In verging on a history of what "was" before it wasn't, or in encountering the ordinary in a guise so arresting that it is immediately refigured as the work of imagination and interiority, Wordsworth makes art's failure to grasp what is close by, "pitch[ing] its tents before" him as he "move[s]," a confirmation of something lived and real. Far from a problem-atic tic, then, or a vitiation of the "romantic ideology,"[4] it is a characteristic, and representative, feature of Wordsworth's writing here that the material opportuni-ties it misses—or that variously evanesce—are recoverable and acutely palpable in consequence of being missed or misrepresented in what amounts to a history of missed opportunities. In such a history the claim to historicity is advanced in a way that the characteristic—indeed, temporalized—movement of something earthly into something refigured is very much a "history . . . of departed things" (in a phrase from the Prospectus again) where "things" appear to evanesce (or appear *only* to evanesce) in a romantic process that is intermittently an illusion.

This illusion is especially clear in the way the "meanest flower" in the "In-timations Ode" provides a running, if retroactive, commentary on both the probabilistic course of human existence that the poem narrates and, even more important, the exceptional compensation that the speaker claims to have derived from the exercise of memory and imagination in consort with the "philosophic mind" (189).[5] While the historical distance necessary to the flower's modification from thought to thing (or from pansy/*pensée* to meanest flower) in mapping an alternative to these trajectories is quite minimal, the perspective it provides in a look or double take that is at once awry and another of way seeing opens onto a "world" that has been unrealized and overlooked.

Grappling with the gratitude he feels as a result, the speaker finds himself repudiating the very argument or visionary time traveling that claims pride of place as the poem's later subtitle ("intimations of immortality from recollections of early childhood"):

> Not for these I raise
>   The song of thanks and praise;
>   But for those obstinate questionings
>   Of sense and outward things,
>   Fallings from us, vanishings;
>   Blank misgivings of a Creature
>   Moving about in worlds not realized,
>   High instincts, before which our mortal Nature
>   Did tremble like a guilty Thing surprized. (142–50)

Part of the difficulty of this notably cryptic passage involves the "force of things," which is being retrofitted to a past that is not just revised or reconfigured but simultaneously rejected as a "simple" or heavenly state beyond recall. That's because what the "Ode" and its speaker have been verging toward, and what has been trailing the speaker's arguments almost from the beginning, is precisely the condition described above, which is no longer a scene from childhood (all claim to the contrary), but a "noncontemporaneous contemporary,"[6] whose status as something seemingly unprecedented is highlighted in the staccato nature of the "realization" and in a clinching observation after which the pansy is suddenly a flower rather than a fallacy.

The "Thoughts that do often lie too deep for tears" (206) that the flower famously provokes at the ode's close would seem to presuppose a deep interiority consistent with our received sense of British romanticism. But this concluding move to depth and singularity—which is intermittent and disarticulated from the expressive functions typically associated with the romantic lyric—is preceded as well by a sudden, and decisive, turn to a condition and mode of sustenance that is unindividuated and presented as a human dispensation in general:

> Though nothing can bring back the hour
> Of splendour in the grass, of glory in the flower;

> We will grieve not, rather find
> Strength in what remains behind; (180–83)

"Behind" refers not just to the residue of the present, then. It also refers to something prior that precedes and supersedes the ostensibly romantic or idealistic resolution in the same way that the turn to the individuated speaker that follows ("To me the meanest flower that blows . . ." [205]) is fundamentally a turning away or, borrowing from *Prelude 7*, a "turn[ing] round." In gaining access to what has been previously overlooked, and in making that the signature of a subjectivity that is representative but by no means uniform, the single self that emerges in these lines is, like the world within its ken, a new and different formation: an operator sufficiently immured in nature that "alone" (22) is a matter of situatedness, embodiment even, rather than the qualifier of "To me."[7]

II

For all its success in establishing an alternative to both the probable and the purely phenomenological, the "Intimations Ode" is somewhat less clear in demarcating an alternative or possible world, where the ordinary takes precedence over both objects at a distance and the subject who typically gives thoughts in addition to receiving them. One reason is that, in addition to depending on individual witness, the ordinary, unlike the "ordinary sight" that we began with, is aligned exclusively with nature, which is easily fitted to the mind in contrast to the materiality that shadows the "Ode" and for which nature in the "meanest flower," or the "Clouds that gather round the setting sun" (199), or even the "brightness of the new-born Day" (197) may be reckoned a shorthand.

This materiality, a "thing"-ness at once surprising and shaming, is more prevalent when the encounter is *in* the field rather than with a landscape authorized to "speak." The "ordinary sight" of the girl with a pitcher is one example. A better one, perhaps, is the brief sketch from *Lyrical Ballads* (1798) "Old Man Travelling," later titled "Animal Tranquillity and Decay." Here the ordinary is linked to a double take and to a disclosure that, in estranging the speaker from his usual procedures, renders him a "guilty thing" disposed to listen:

> The little hedge-row birds,
> That peck along the road, regard him not.
> He travels on, and in his face, his step,
> His gait, is one expression; every limb,

His look and bending figure, all bespeak
A man who does not move with pain, but moves
With thought—He is insensibly subdued
To settled quiet: he is one by whom
All effort seems forgotten, one to whom
Long patience has such mild composure given,
That patience now doth seem a thing, of which
He hath no need. He is by nature led
To peace so perfect, that the young behold
With envy, what the old man hardly feels.
—I asked him whither he was bound, and what
The object of his journey; he replied
'Sir! I am going many miles to take
A last leave of my son, a mariner,
Who from a sea-fight has been brought to Falmouth,
And there is dying in an hospital.'

The corrective that the "old man" administers to the speaker's extravagant surmise would appear to mark a return to the ordinary—especially as a subset of what Wordsworth, in the Preface to *Lyrical Ballads* (and with the specter now of "distant war"), terms the "more than common."[8]

Yet if the ordinary is anywhere in this poem, it is located and characteristically missing somewhere between the initial phase, where a man is moved and animated "with thought," and the social reality that ensues, where the poem is compelled to a sociability and, with it, to a generalizing (read empirical) view of human nature in the way individual expression is normalized to another mode of communication. Marked only by a space, and by the dash preceding "I asked," the speaker's speechless curiosity, of which his question is mostly a supplement, registers something—something new or different—that neither imaginative projection nor recuperated speech nor even the man's disclosure can justify, much less figure. It is not that the reply lacks interest or even a kind of sublimity. It is that the force of the reply (and the reality onto which it opens) is different again from whatever roused the speaker to question him in the first place, interrupting the work of poetry in two distinct ways.

A related—possibly definitive—example of this interruption, and the history it inscribes in something like invisible ink, may be found in "The Two April Mornings," which—coincidentally or not—features another encounter with a woman bearing an object. Like other Matthew poems, this one records a conversation between the older man and his Wordsworthian interlocutor that is quickly displaced by Matthew's recollection of "a day like this . . . Full thirty years behind" (23–24). On that day, he recalls, as "[t]he self-same crimson hue / Fell from the sky that April morn, / The same which now I view" (26–28), he came upon the grave of his daughter Emma, who had died at the age of nine, and whom he remembers loving "more" at that moment "than . . . [he] e'er had loved before" (38–40):

> And, turning from her grave, I met
> Beside the church-yard Yew
> A blooming Girl, whose hair was wet
> With points of morning dew.
>
> A basket on her head she bare,
> Her brow was smooth and white,
> To see a Child so very fair,
> It was a pure delight! (41–48)

It may be fortuitous that it is a female carrying something on her head who is the placeholder again for the contingent and the more-than-common. But the transfiguration that follows, where she is likened to a "happy . . . wave . . . danc[ing] on the sea" (51–52), is hardly accidental and typical of the "intentional structures" to which the object often conforms in Wordsworth. In *Prelude* 11 this movement to "vision" is ultimately unidirectional. However, in "The Two April Mornings" it is limited and reversible thanks to a stubborn materiality that, to borrow from the first Matthew poem ("Expostulation and Reply") operates not "with" but "against" the subject's "will" (20):

> There came from me a sigh of pain
> Which I could ill confine;
> I looked at her and looked again
> —And did not wish her mine. (53–56)

Although Matthew's pain owes presumably to the recognition that the girl before him is *not* his daughter, it issues, at least by recollection, from a subject not exactly or continuously identical with the grieving father. This is even truer of the double take that follows, where Matthew is similarly divided: first, between looking and looking and then between wishing and not wishing. It would appear that it is the second look, rather than the first, that creates division leading to divestiture, in which the claim to ownership is relinquished and where the will is principally a negative way ("I did not wish").

But the real point of the anecdote, along with the doubling of the two mornings, devolves upon the double take, the look and the look. Like the pain within that comes seemingly from elsewhere, the looking and looking is not just an endless loop or circuit. It represents a new or different mode of seeing—a distension or splitting of the "look" over time (marked here, as in "Old Man Travelling," by a dash)—in which something lost or missed, the blooming girl, is recovered despite the loss that had threatened to subsume her. This recovery is painful since it involves, as the sigh alerts us, a letting go of the pain and love constitutive of the subject in mourning. Nevertheless what emerges is a dynamic, if evanescent, sense of the ordinary, where the movement or oscillation between one look and another leads nowhere but to the girl or, in the speaker's version of this same experience, to Matthew in a "now" different and defamiliarized formation:

> Matthew is in his grave, yet now
> Methinks I see him stand,
> As at that moment, with his bough
> Of wilding in his hand. (57–60).

The act of seeing Matthew so long after the fact is an act of both memory and imagination. But it is typical of the trajectory of this poem that, far from disappearing in a moment of vision, the ordinary emerges from the welter of interiority in the recollection of Matthew attached to a very particular *thing*. There may be some ambiguity over which moment is "that moment," and it is arguably the case that, like Matthew's double take, the moment of Matthew standing condenses the recollection of him at the "moment" of interlocution and the reported moment of encounter and letting go.

Still, it is the effect of the poem overall, along with the history it inscribes (however fleeting), to dispose of the titular pun through a mode of remembrance—or "now-time"—where "mourning" progresses to "morning." The concluding image of Matthew standing is a memory of course. However it is linked specifically to a thing (the wilding) and to a continuum—a noncontemporaneous contemporary—where feeling, meaning, and phenomenological dilation are secondary to a more basic, and persistent, locatedness. Like the letting-go administered by Matthew's double take, the emergence of the ordinary at the close, where something demonstrably overlooked irrupts to bear the freight of closure, is a telling divestiture: a submission to the world where, in a reversal of Benjamin's axiom, art and subjectivity disappear into the real.

III

When Wordsworth refers to the "din / Of towns and cities" (26–27) in "Tintern Abbey" and later in that same poem to the "dreary intercourse of daily life" (132), he is anticipating a strain of thought about the everyday as an urban or postindustrial phenomenon that theorists from to Benjamin to Blanchot have elaborated, if not always to the poet's point. In contrast to the environments that the everyday incorporates as an emergent concept—from natural particularity to the domestic sphere—Blanchot's everyday is site-specific, "belong[ing] first of all to the dense presence of great urban centers" or "in the street" (as he puts it) and not, he insists, to the "earth, the sea, the forest, light [and] night," which do not represent the everyday any more than do "our dwelling places," our "offices," our "churches," our "libraries" or our "museums" (Blanchot 1987, 17). Still, by insisting on what he describes as the everyday's "human"-ness, Blanchot hearkens to the way that encounters *in* the field extend in Wordsworth to the "earth" itself, where the environment typically performs multiple functions, including a reversion to something material (and overlooked) that "Nature"—as a broadly privileged category—intermittently includes.

The city is a different matter, though, chiefly because what "reigns there," in Blanchot's description, "is the refusal to be different, a yet undetermined stir: without responsibility and without authority, without direction and without decision, a storehouse of anarchy, . . . casting aside all beginning and dismissing all end" (1987, 17). This turns out, all differences aside, to be a fairly accurate gloss of *Prelude* 7 ("Residence in London"), where something cognate is present in the "blank confusion" (696) and "perpetual flow" (702) of the city, and where a seemingly dystopic London becomes on at least one memorable occasion the site of what Blanchot (in his rendering of the double take) terms the "inaccessible to which we have always already had access" (1987, 20). Just as the everyday has no real force beyond the conditions of its emergence, and no immediate effect for the poet beyond the toll it exacts on the subject/object dyad, so an encounter with a beggar "in the street" opens onto a continuum or "world" that, however present, is simultaneously below the threshold of either "knowledge" or understanding.

I have written previously how this encounter follows upon the poet's experience in London in struggling, with little success, to enlarge a sensory experience into a moment of vision akin to the poem's other "spots of time."[9] Here I want to change direction and focus on the way the encounter opens, like the "spot of time" in book 11, onto a category of experience defined mostly by subtraction. In book 11 this definition comes in the stutter or hesitation marked by "but," where memory leading to vision gives way briefly to something anterior and apart from the dreary condensation that words barely describe. In book 7 that process is reversed and distended as the people of London and, eventually, the beggar effectively wrest themselves—with the poet's cooperation—from the visionary formations to which *The Prelude* inclines and, just as important, from the dystopic uniformity into which London simultaneously dissolves.

Any reader of *The Prelude* remembers very well how the experience of the city or the mathematical sublime that *is* London thwarts all aspirations to a "romantic sublime" where the imagination might hold sway:[10] a blockage that comes to crisis and exegesis in the moment preceding the beggar when the Poet describes a recurrent experience:

> How often in the overflowing Streets,
> Have I gone forward with the Crowd, and said
> Unto myself, the face of every one
> That passes by me is a mystery.
> Thus have I looked, nor ceased to look, oppressed
> By thoughts of what, and whither, when and how,
> Until the shapes before my eyes became
> A second-sight procession, such as glides
> Over still mountains, or appears in dreams;
> And all the ballast of familiar life—
> The present, and the past; hope, fear; all stays,
> All laws of acting, thinking, speaking man
> Went from me, neither knowing me, nor known. (595–607)

The mystery that the faces of London evoke resembles the mystery onto which the speaker of "Old Man Travelling" earlier stumbles and that his eventual question is intended to clarify. Here, however, the "inaccessible" is protracted by a mode of perception that, in the description at least, resembles a double take ("Thus have I looked, nor ceased to look") splitting the subject into two: one who looks and looks, submitting to something there and incomprehensible, and another whose look dissolves into its near-cousin, second sight, where "familiar" or phenomenological "life" is bracketed from city life.

It is at this point—with the phenomenal and the everyday in juxtaposition—that the speaker shifts to the blind beggar:

> Amid the moving pageant, 'twas my chance
> Abruptly to be smitten with the view
> Of a blind Beggar, who, with upright face,
> Stood propped against a Wall, upon his Chest
> Wearing a written paper, to explain
> The story of the Man, and who he was.
> My mind did at this spectacle turn round
> As with the might of waters, and it seemed
> To me that in this Label was a type,
> Or emblem, of the utmost that we know
> Both of ourselves and of the universe;
> And, on the shape of this unmoving man,
> His fixed face and sightless eyes, I looked,
> As if admonished from another world. (610–23)

The final line in this passage makes more sense if we regard the analogy as bearing not just on the speaker's sense of being warned or cautioned or, better, "put . . . in mind of a thing forgotten, overlooked, or unknown" (*OED* definition 5), but on the "world" from which the reminder emanates. This latter sense—admonished "as if . . . from another world"—captures perfectly a feeling of something at hand and of *this world* whose remoteness or mystery, where it emerges to admonish, is a matter of perspective rather than imagination.

It is fitting that this culminating aperçu is preceded by "I looked," which in the description overall references a second look, juxtaposing materiality and deductive dilation in such a way that any synthesis or imposition that the "mind" might perform is forestalled. We see this in the speaker's struggle to move figuratively from the figure propped before him, where the effort to find the *mot* or *figure juste*, starting with the highly metaphorical description of the mind's movement, is impeded by something like "second sight." The difference is that where second sight is typically phantasmagoric on the order, say, of Poor Susan's pastoralization of London in the poem named for her, where "bright volumes of vapour through Lothbury glide, / And a river flows on through the vale of Cheapside" (7–8), it is an after-image here of something stationary, abiding and "unmoving." A "residual deposit" in which the "everyday" is "rais[ed] ... to the level of the Possible" (Lefebvre), the beggar introduces something here and there, beyond and close at hand, past and present, that Wordsworth, like Heidegger, calls the "world."[11] And not just any world, but "another world," whose alterity and proximity are acknowledged by "as if."

IV

Any discussion of the "world" in Wordsworth must reckon with the role(s) of nature and "Nature" in his writing. Criticism has long migrated—green readings aside—from the poet's status as a "nature poet" to the particular phenomenology to which his engagements with the world refer. But the persistence of the environment, even and especially in moments that are plainly imaginary, bears additional scrutiny: for what it says about nature and about a poetry in which the environment maintains special status. Wordsworth offers a brief on the "nature" traditionally associated with his writing in a well-known scene in *Prelude* 2, where, in observing a "Babe ... Nursed in his Mother's arms" (239–40), he draws a fairly common analogy between this maternal presence—"which irradiates and exalts / All objects through all intercourse of sense" (259–60)—and a broader, seemingly mythologized, nurturance where nature and mother are conjoined:

> Along his infant veins are interfused
> The gravitation and the filial bond
> Of nature, that connect him with the world. . . .
> From nature he largely receives, nor so
> Is satisfied, but largely gives again . . .
>   . . . his mind,
> Even as an agent of the one great mind,
> Creates, creator and receiver both,
> Working but in alliance with the works
> Which it beholds.—Such, verily, is the first
> Poetic spirit of our human life; (262–76)

There is much in this passage that is familiar: from the mind that half perceives and half creates to an equally familiar view of creativity as a distinctly privileged dispensation reserved primarily for "poets" in imitation of "the one great mind." But there is a tendency, too, both to generalize in an empirical vein (the first poetic spirit of our human life) and to conflate mother and "world" so that the anthropomorphism that comes to characterize nature (in the shift to mother nature) is just as much a naturalism, or environmentalism, in which creativity pertains mostly (as the passage hints) to the origin of "works" in an earthbound or geological sense. When some lines earlier Wordsworth speaks in an ostensibly mythopoeic vein about being "frame[d]" by Nature as "a favored Being" through various ministrations and visitations (1.363–64) and describes these as "Presences of Nature," "Visions of the hills," and "souls of lonely places" (all punctuated by exclamation points [1.490–93]), there remains, beyond the notion of some caring agency from without, a prevailing, even shocking, sense of things-in-themselves (presences, hills, places) in which the "surface of the universal earth" may be surface and nothing more (1.499).[12]

Wordsworth eventually describes these ministrations as "spots of time," where "the mind / Is lord and master, and that outward sense / Is but the obedient servant of her will" (11.271–73). While it is customary in most interpretations of *The Prelude* to retrofit this phenomenological supremacy to earlier moments in the poem—all the more in that "such moments" of mastery are apparently "scattered everywhere" (11.274–75)—there is a concomitant tendency to overlook their peripheral vision where the outward sense, or a version of it, is continually manifest. Virtually all the spots of time, including the three so named in books 11 and 12, take place "in" what is referred to as "Nature's presence," making them signs of election in which the poet has been "singled out" by Nature for "Holy services" (1.62–63). Still and all, the surround that "Nature's presence" invokes—as a necessary, if disarticulated, accompaniment to Vision—is just as much a material event to which the speaker is not only pointed in recalling these moments but also "turned" in what is both a re-view and a discovery.

We can take as an example the sight of "a heap of garments" (461) in *Prelude* 5 (the book on "Books") that belonged to someone who had gone swimming and drowned and whose corpse "bolt upright" (471) is eventually retrieved in particularly ghastly fashion. But this is not exactly what Wordsworth remembers or recalls experiencing. What he remembers is in many ways twofold: that, as a consumer of fairy tales, he had imagined such frightening experiences in advance, which protected him even as a boy from a "fear" that at that moment was merely sensational or "vulgar" (473); and secondly, the man's clothes, which are seen—or seen again—not as portents that have gone remarkably unclaimed but as common things that, for the moment, are part of the environment and eventful in an uneventful way.

> Twilight was coming on; yet through the gloom,
> I saw distinctly on the opposite Shore
> A heap of garments, left, as I supposed,
> By one who there was bathing; long I watched,
> But no one owned them; meanwhile the calm Lake
> Grew dark, with all the shadows on its breast,
> And, now and then, a fish up-leaping, snapped
> The breathless stillness. (459–66).

These various details would arguably have gone unnoticed—certainly un-remembered—were it not for what happened the "succeeding day," when a "Company . . . with grappling irons" finally retrieved the "dead Man" (466–70). But the point to stress, about the garments and the leaping fish and even the stillness here, is the way these sights and impressions, like that of the girl with the pitcher, are distinct and freestanding as much by proximity to what is memorable, or traumatic, as by the way this contiguity is broken to reveal something ordinary or "vulgar" on second or sustained "watching." It might be too much to argue that the very notion of a "spot of time" imbeds or honors this ancillary feature, where the environment or a sense of place impinges on memory and time. Still, there is little question that these moments in nature's presence involve competing histories and "meanwhiles": a personalized one where, as evidence of imagination, they foretell the development of a "creative soul" (11.257); and a history that this "meditative History" (13.418) only partly suppresses, in which circumstance—a leaping fish, a pile of clothes—becomes an event in its own right.

An especially striking instance of this historical materialism, and its retrieval of the world from a supporting—merely circumstantial—function, is the epi-sode in *Prelude* 6 describing Wordsworth's crossing of the Alps, which the poet struggles to convert into a privileged moment. The episode is built (in the re-counting fourteen years later) around an anti-climax, where upon learning that he had in fact "crossed the Alps" (524) Wordsworth shifts immediately to the "Imagination" (525) and to its glories as if to compensate for an environment that—with all the usual expectations surrounding an alpine crossing—had failed to deliver anything comparable save for what happened next:

           downwards we hurried fast,
And entered with the road which we had missed
Into a narrow chasm. The brook and the road
Were fellow-travellers in this gloomy Pass,
And with them did we journey several hours
At a slow step. The immeasurable height
Of woods decaying, never to be decayed,
The stationery blasts of water-falls,
And every where along the hollow rent
Winds thwarting winds, bewildered and forlorn,
The torrents shooting from the clear blue sky,
The rocks that muttered close upon our ears,
Black drizzling crags that spake by the way-side
As if a voice were in them, the sick sight
And giddy prospect of the raving stream,
The unfettered clouds and region of the heavens,
Tumult and peace, the darkness and the light
Were all like workings of one mind, the features
Of the same face, blossoms upon one tree,
Characters of the great Apocalypse,
The types and symbols of Eternity,
Of first and last, and midst, and without end. (551–72)

It is hard to regard this as anything other than a performance, and Wordsworth even excised it from the as-yet unpublished *Prelude* for inclusion in the 1845 edition of his poems. Contextually, however, the passage registers a strain between a teleological movement toward vision and a non-movement that, amid every effort to make much out of little, is constrained to the moment and to the environment, where just previously—in anticipation of something ready-made for sublime witness—things weren't.

    This is not to dispute the hallucinatory register of the recollection; it is only to suggest that the slow step of the passage, figuratively and literally, amounts to a series of double takes (however recollected) in which things are seen again and for the first time, and where the quick step to apocalyptic vision is consistently bedeviled by on-site retrospection (e.g., "woods decaying never to be decayed," "stationery . . . waterfalls," "winds . . . winds," etc.). This is so much case that even the grand gestures toward the "workings of one mind" and the arc of history from an all-seeing perspective, are immediately reversible in the way the workings, for example, pertain as much to the "face" or surface of things (and their origin, again, in a geological register) and in the way the narrative scope of the final line is alternately collapsible into a present, or sequence of middles, or a continuum "without end" of which the event—a series of "nows"—is both a fragment and a synecdoche.

It may seem a little strange that this continuum or stratum, with its hallucinatory aura, represents a state of being or being-in-the world on the order of the everyday. However in the very way that the everyday comes to preconceptual awareness as a missed *opportunity*, the descent is also a belated and backhanded reminder of what was missed or glossed over during the ascent, where the environment as such (a "rivulet," a "Mountain," a "beaten road" [502–6]) was noted only in passing and as the circumstantial accompaniment to an itinerary that, at the time and looking backward, was a prelude to disappointment. Yet immediately after, and with no promise at stake, the periphery missed on the ascent becomes the sum and substance of what matters stepping downward. The explanation is that "Imagination," or an imaginatively driven interchange with Nature, had eventually replaced the alpine surround as the source of interest and requital.[13] Still, as the strain of the passage suggests, never more than in its apocalyptic vision, the peculiar and quite different attention permissible with no horizon at issue and with no sublime to rush toward is mostly inadvertent: a feature of being in the moment and in the world—one seemingly "without end"—rather than pressing forward.

The tendency of the *Prelude*'s "spots" to focalize more than one event—one memorable and mental, the other peripheral and material—is no doubt a matter of time or *durée* (in Bergson's sense), in which all matter is infused with memory (traumatic and otherwise) and where no detail, however innocent or circumstantial, is ever actual and freestanding. But the double focus speaks just as much to a different *durée* or space/time continuum to which the poet is "turn[ed] round" in an "admonish[ment]" shorn of any moral or psychological dimension. In the second of the spots in *Prelude* 11, recounting a day when Wordsworth, who was then at school, "repaired to" a "Summit" (355–56) to catch sight of the horses that would be transporting him home for the holidays, the memorial shifts between a memory of place that is mostly circumstantial and a review of the same place that, however leveraged by what followed—his father's death and the shame and recrimination that the poet remembered feeling over his previously "trite" anticipation of Christmas at home (373)—is bound visibly, audibly and sensibly to a moment that was missed the first time around. Although memorable—owing to what transpired in little more than a week's time—the environment at the summit initially oscillates between a sense of a place and a prospect or teleology where the surround or spatial "meanwhile" vanishes:

> 'Twas a day
> Stormy, and rough, and wild, and on the grass
> I sate, half-sheltered by a naked wall;
> Upon my right hand was a single sheep,
> A whistling hawthorn on my left, and there,
> With those companions at my side, I watched,
> Straining my eyes intensely, as the mist
> Gave intermitting prospect of the wood
> And plain beneath. (356–64)

But when Wordsworth revisits the same scene just thirteen lines later, he sees, hears, and feels it very differently, transforming a mnemonic surplus in which he is palpably central (like the belated witness to visionary dreariness we began with) into a more material, more sensible event in which he is merely present.

> And afterwards, the wind and sleety rain,
> And all the business of the elements,
> The single sheep, and the one blasted tree,
> And the bleak music of that old stone wall,
> The noise of wood and water, and the mist
> Which on the line of each of those two Roads
> Advanced in such indisputable shapes,
> All these were spectacles and sounds to which
> I would often repair and thence would drink
> As at a fountain; and I do not doubt
> That in this later time, when storm and rain
> Beat on my roof at midnight, or by day
> When I am in the woods, unknown to me
> The workings of my spirit thence are brought. (376–89)

I will demonstrate in a moment what Wordsworth may mean by "spirit" here. But it is clear even in this passage that, however much the speaker wants to convert this double take or do-over into evidence of imagination, or into some internal capacity that defines him as both a person and a poet, there is something outward bound about the revised memory and, even more important, its separation from the traumatic events linked to it, on which the decentered, or depersonalized, idea of "spirit" bears. What the poet chooses to remember and to repair to is neither the death nor the self-recrimination nor his abjection before God ("who thus corrected my desires" [375]). What he repairs to, by claim and by demonstration, is an environment, an environmental continuum, where the personal and (in this case) the autobiographical are, for the moment at any rate, the background to something immediate and ongoing—then and in "later time"—that the poet registers rather than frames.

The choice of "spirit" in place of, say, imagination or even soul is an interesting one, implying a detour from what Derrida, in discussing Heidegger's similarly qualified deployment of the term, famously calls the "metaphysics of subjectivity." While Derrida has some devastating things to say about Heidegger's use of spirit (*Geist*) in his infamous address on the German university, where the term is nationalized and politicized, he recognizes as well that in earlier works concerned with being-in-the-world, "spirit" invariably "names [something]" in Heidegger that "allows [it] to be salvaged," that makes it "acceptable," that "frees it."[14] The same is true of Wordsworth, who in discussing the "first poetic spirit of ... life" describes an alliance or connection "with the world" that is at cross-purposes with the concentered work of imagination "where the mind is," by definition again, "lord and master." Recalling his early grapplings with such metaphysics in *Prelude* 4, he goes so far as to stage a conflict between the difference imposed by the metaphysics of subjectivity, in which the object is subordinate, and a leveling, where in repairing to the environment or to what is always "there" if overlooked, the workings of "something" different, "freer" and continually circumspect are in evidence.

The episode takes place during a summer vacation from Cambridge and describes the poet's meditative perambulations, where his thoughts at the time are idealistic in several registers:

> I had hopes and peace
> And swellings of the spirits, was rapt and soothed,
> Conversed with promises, had glimmering views
> How Life pervades the undecaying mind,
> How the immortal Soul with God-like power

Informs, creates, and thaws the deepest sleep
That time can lay upon her; how on earth,
Man, if he do but live within the light
Of high endeavours, daily spreads abroad
His being with a strength that cannot fail.
Nor was there want of milder thoughts, of love,
Of innocence, and holiday repose,
And more than pastoral quiet, in the heart
Of amplest projects, and a peaceful end
At last, or glorious, by endurance won.
Thus musing, in a wood I sate me down,
Alone, continuing there to muse. (4.152–68)

The use of litotes ("Nor was there want"), in changing direction from a recitation of great expectations, speaks nicely to the latency of a world where the subject is quiescent rather than a protagonist. This proves preliminary to what ensues, where the poet changes direction yet again, resituating himself ("I sate me down") in an environment that he has thus far ignored:

[M]eanwhile
The mountain heights were slowly overspread
With darkness, and before a rippling breeze
The long Lake lengthened out its hoary line;
And in the sheltered coppice where I sate,
Around me, from among the hazel leaves,
Now here, now there, stirred by straggling wind,
Came intermittingly a breath-like sound,
A respiration short and quick, which oft,
Yea, might I say, again and yet again,
Mistaking for the panting of my Dog,
The off-and-on Companion of my walk,
I turned my head, to look if he were there. (168–80)

The shift from the grand horizons of the previous (supposedly simultaneous) musing to what is immediately "around" the speaker ("Now here, now there . . .") recalls the similar shift in book 11, where both the prospect of the plain beneath and the narrative to which it is connected are displaced on re-view by a more heightened sense of place or of place in the first place. This is because the suddenly unswollen "spirit" that attaches itself to the surround and to its temporal analog (the "meanwhile") is not only looking "around" but also looking backward, both at what was missed and at what, by extension, has always been there. It doesn't matter whether the poet's dog was actually present; what matters and is sufficiently notable to be remembered is the motivation by which the speaker was again "turned round / As if admonished from another world." Here, as in the encounter with the beggar, the parallel world of which the speaker is put in mind as something overlooked is, all proximity or simultaneity aside, a matter of history: both as a prelude to recovery in which it irrupts as the meanest flower in the "Intimations Ode," and as something "now" whose absence contrasts hope (that generic progress of the soul in "high endeavor") to what, with reference to the dog in the "meanwhile," is in fact "real possibility."

V

If no discussion of the environment in Wordsworth's writing can proceed without some account of the role of nature, then no discussion of either the environment or the everyday world it figures as something missed, forgotten or uncounted, can be complete without consideration of his sister's *Grasmere Journal*,[15] where what the poet is often feeling his way toward is almost always front and center. In addition to featuring an "embodied," or non-"appropriating," consciousness "absorbed in the environment" and rarely at a distance,[16] Dorothy Wordsworth's journal is a record, as Anne Mellor notes, of "ongoing" domestic life, in which events typically written out of history—the "physical necessities" of baking, gardening, making beds, along with the comings and goings of various friends, neighbors and strangers—are documented in representing a world that, while the subject of seemingly simple record keeping, is various and significant (Mellor 1993, 162).

And yet, for all of its attention to the "meanwhile," be it spatially (in the field) or as the daily, domestic counterpoise to the privative and concentered disposition of her brother's literary labor,[17] the journal goes about reproducing the everyday without recognizing it as a world—a possible world—to which the writer's brother, who sees it in the wake of missing it, is perforce turned. If anything, Dorothy Wordsworth's practice of forgetting nothing marks what Braudel, in retrofitting the idea of everydayness to early modernity, mordantly calls the "limits of the possible" versus what, for her brother representatively, is a sense of "something evermore about to be" (*Prelude* 6.542).

It is not therefore that the world of the journal is boring or uneventful or shorn of surprise. It is that the stratum of experience to which it attends is one of unrelenting seriality, or sameness amid variety, making it impervious to the defamiliarizing practices of recovery and the conceptual work that that retrospection entails.

Here is a fairly representative entry from June 2, 1800:

A cold dry windy morning. I worked in the garden & planted flowers &c—Sate under the trees after dinner till tea time. John Fisher stuck the peas, Molly weeded & washed. I went to Ambleside after tea, crossed the stepping-stones at the foot of Grasmere & pursued my way on the other side of Rydale & by Clappersgate. I sate a long time to watch the hurrying waves & to hear the regularly irregular sound of the dashing waters. The waves round about the little [Island] seemed like a dance of spirits that rose out of the water, round its small circumference of shore. Inquired about lodgings for Coleridge, & was accompanied by Mrs Nicholson as far as Rydale. This was very kind, but God be thanked that I want not society by a moonlight lake—It was near 11 when I reached home. I wrote to Coleridge & went late to bed. (D. Wordsworth 1991, 7)

Dorothy, as often noted, is sparing in her use of the first person pronoun ("I") in accordance with a characteristic openness that, as her admirers are quick to observe, lyric or poetic epiphany occludes. Thus even as "I" makes more than a casual appearance here, there is no attempt to discriminate among its functions and activities. Weeding is no different a subject-position from heightened and (in the fortuitous absence of any meddling company) meditative engagement.

What this also means is that in contrast to the "environmental turn" in William's poetry, which can take on a revisionary cast, the world according to Dorothy has no antithetical or dialectical force. Like her many tasks and encounters, in fact, the natural environment is just one more thing that keeps her busy:

It is a nice cool shady spot. The small Birds are singing—Lambs bleating, Cuckow calling—The Thrush sings by Fits, Thomas Ashburner's axe is going quietly (without passion) in the orchard—Hens are cackling, Flies humming, the women talking together at their doors—Plumb & pear trees are in Blossom, apple trees greenish—the opposite woods green, the crows are cawing. We have heard Ravens. The Ash Trees are in blossom, Birds flying all about us. The stitchwort is coming out, there is one budding Lychnis. The primroses are passing their prime. Celandine violets & wood sorrel for ever more—little geranium & pansies on the wall. We walked in the evening to Tail End to enquire about hurdles for the orchard shed & about Mr Luff's flower—The flower dead—no hurdles. (1991, 96)

It scarcely requires saying that—by comparison to what we've been tracking in the poetry—this "writing to the moment" is striking, both in its capture of immediacy or procession through "now-time," and in the way the environment amounts to a seemingly endless simultaneity that the writer is simply encountering or passing through. There are cognate instances of this in William's poetry, too. But hemmed in, as they are, by what they are pushing back against, directly or subliminally, such moments or double takes never achieve anything close to the worlding that Dorothy performs here and to the world, by extension, into which, as Heidegger might have it, she is almost willfully "thrown."

Critics have done their part to provide a conceptual framework for this unmediated vision and, for what it's worth, nearly paradigmatic capture of the everyday (or a sense of it surely) that the description—like Austen's more knowing account of the world according to Miss Bates—apparently honors. Although the Grasmere journal functioned, and was viewed accordingly for years, as a sourcebook for William's poems, it is typically held up as an *écriture feminine*, featuring "a self built . . . on a model of affiliation rather than a model of individual achievement" (Mellor 1993, 166) and a "genius," in Susan Wolfson's description, "for writing against, and in alternatives to, the forms and forces of her brother's imagination."[18]

A lot of this can be traced to the event of William's marriage, which happens toward the end of the journal and features the wrenching account of the wedding ring that Dorothy gives him on his wedding day having "worn it the whole of the night before" (1991, 126). Writing exclusively for her brother in the shadow of this impending development, Dorothy is at pains, or so it seems, to make the present an experience that, by the journal's conditions, is not just shared or mutually occupied but a virtual stay against futurity. Unlike the world that emerges retrospectively in William's writing, even on short notice, the everyday world of the journal is not a missed opportunity; it is if anything an opportunity that is time stamped, or fated to be missed, and, for all its presence, almost stubbornly undifferentiated.

Another way to put this way put this, perhaps, which recognizes Dorothy's achievement in contrast to what we have seen thus far and will encounter going forward, involves the degree to which, as Heidegger might say, she is "struck by actuality." For in "being struck" or compelled in light of what I've just touched on, Dorothy is simultaneously "debarred," in Heidegger's view, from a world that might otherwise "concer[n]" or "touc[h]" her "in the surely mysterious way of escaping [her] by withdrawal."[19] Refusing or unable to be "draw[n]" into what is elusive or to "turn" (in language proximate to William's) toward what necessarily "turn[s] away," Dorothy is not just immersed in the present and in the things and people that go with it; she is also, at some level, not "thinking," which, on the model Heidegger proposes, requires that one "be far away from what withdraws" and that what withdraws "may remain as veiled as ever" (1977, 358).

The difference or distance necessary to the double take and to "another world" that remains "veiled" as a measure of the everyday's emergence is much closer to this model of being far away—a "thought . . . responsible to what is other, lost, . . . potential, yet to be," in Rajan's words—and to the particular possibility that thinking as an endless prelude ultimately fosters. Like the dog in the "meanwhile" in *Prelude* 4, which is absent but necessarily present, the potentiality that thinking on this model exposes, and that the "everyday" figures as a world thinkable at this moment, remains, in yet another of Heidegger's phrases, "as it already *was*" (emphasis added). None of this is to suggest that the *Grasmere Journal* is somehow shallow (there are, after all, other withdrawals at issue) but only that the world to which it gives immediate access is as it already *is*—in for example, the tendency to identify the same flower over and over again—and a world, accordingly, that approximates "everydayness" in the ceiling or limit that such record keeping imposes, even if the aim is to stop time.

The differences, accordingly, between the journal's vision of domestic life and, say, Jane Austen's are similar to those separating the journal's sense of a surround from William's. Although the Wordsworths are typically differentiated by Dorothy's attentiveness versus William's introversion (Dorothy takes the measure of the leech-gatherer whereas her brother takes possession of him), their difference lies in the corrective—and with it the opportunity—that the double take introduces: both as a riposte to a certain order of subjectivity and as the measure of a certain privilege by which such "turns" and the "thinking" they mark are, as Wordsworth says of the Wanderer's capacity to suffer with others in *The Excursion*, eminently affordable.

A similar privilege obtains in Austen, whose "real natural every day" world is tied to a time and just as importantly to a milieu where domestic life and the prospects for women of a certain class were isolable in retrospect from what could be called domesticity. However unlike the poet, for whom this "meanwhile" issues from a turn that happens (or happened) more or less on site, such a world is appreciable and thinkable not as an actuality that Austen was "struck by" even after the fact, but as the yield of an archive that the versions of her first published novels came to constitute. The history of missed opportunities that the novels inscribe, both in their unprecedented representation of everyday comings and goings and in the equally unprecedented ephemera that resist, or complicate, the unfolding of story along a linear axis culminating in marriage, is thinking on the Heideggerean model. It is thinking thanks to the "veiled" world, or stratum, that the novels identify without penetrating or naming or making into a limit. And it is thinking thanks to a world whose very possibility is guaranteed by the past to which it has withdrawn as an archival matter and by the protest to time and progress that the novels wage in "thinking *back* to what is to be thought" (Heidegger 1977, 352; emphasis added).

3 HISTORIES OF THE PRESENT AND THE HISTORICITY OF THE PRESENT
Mansfield Park, Emma, Jane Austen's Letters

I

"As I cautioned you against Madame d'Arblay's novel," Dowager Lady Vernon wrote Mary Frampton in 1814, "I recommend you 'Mansfield Park' if you meet with it. It is not much of a novel, more the history of a family party in the country, very natural, and the characters well drawn."[1] Lady Vernon may have meant nothing more by "history" than an imitation of life—versus the female picaresque of what was likely Frances Burney's (now Mme d'Arblay's) *The Wanderer*. However, she gets at something—her reservations aside—that a number of Austen's early readers understood to have been a mark of difference, even from so influential a writer as Burney.

This was, first and foremost, her "incomparable" achievement in providing "true pictures of real life" (Frampton 1885, 226), thanks to what Lady Byron had earlier noted was a conscientious rejection of "the common" and sensationalistic "resources of Novel writers."[2] But it embraces another level of difference to which the category of "history"—as something other than a placeholder for the real or the uncontrived—refers. In its review of *Emma* in 1816, *The Champion* introduced this very notion to distinguish Austen's achievement from other representations to which "history" normally applied:

In history, goodness frequently makes but a dull figure,—because in the wide survey of events, little attention can be allotted to any thing but *actions* which immediately operate upon these.—But novels are rather fictitious biography, as romances may be called fictitious history.—To the historian's generalizing eye, unobtrusive virtue presents few features of prominence or splendour;—but the novelist has the license of ranging into the recesses of domestic life, and of distinguishing the *actions* of the mind, the temper, and the feelings. Surveyed in this microscopic detail, characters which, to a more sweeping observer, furnish only the uniform outlines of virtue and worth, will always be found to exhibit sufficiently distinctive traits of mental and moral individuality, to answer all an author's objects of giving them a personal identity and relief. The same observations which apply to history, apply more strongly, though on the same principle, to poetry,—for history is poetical as it deals in the grand, the general, and the aggregate,—without alluding to their primitive connection, the earliest poems being historical, and the earliest histories poetical.[3]

The Champion raises a number of issues familiar to students of Austen and her milieu: the emphasis on ordinary virtue or goodness; the author as miniaturist; and finally, the necessary difference between Austen's version of history (what the review terms "fictitious biography") and the more traditional view in which only great actions and events stand in palpable relief. And there are few readers who would doubt these assertions given what Austen thought about such matters. There are the well-known comments on her "little bit of ivory, two inches wide" to which a microscope might be usefully applied. There is also the amusing exchange with J. S. Clarke, the Prince Regent's librarian, where in response to the latter's suggestion that she next write an "Historical Romance illustrative of the History of the august house of Cobourg,"[4] Austen wryly notes that she "could not sit seriously down to write a serious Romance under any other motive than to save [her] Life" and that, even in this circumstance, she would likely be "hung before [she] had finished the first Chapter" (Austen 1995, 312).

The other matter of domestic or unobtrusive virtue appears to echo a conduct writer such as Thomas Gisborne, whom Austen had read, and whose directives to women stressed the degree to which "human happiness" is "affected [much less] by great but infrequent events than by small but perpetually recurring incidents of good and evil."[5] But here—doubtless because Austen disliked conduct writing—the issue seems more a question of vocabulary, since the "action" extolled in the *Champion* scarcely describes how women function in her novels, especially those prior to *Persuasion*. If anything, the action praised by the journal is virtually nonexistent in the works that the reviewer would have known—in, for example, the character of Fanny Price whose primary action is *inaction* ("No, indeed, I cannot act")—and always adjunct to the actions of empowered men such as Darcy, Knightley, or even Colonel Brandon. While it was clearly onto something in stressing the significance of individual action and in using history, or "fictitious biography," as a way of focalizing that activity, the *Champion* missed the larger point that the "history" that ordinary women are capable of making was, with no tautology in mind now, a matter of history by Austen's lights rather than domestic life generally.

This brings me to the title and point of this chapter. The nearly oxymoronic notion of a history of the present that Lady Vernon describes to her niece turns out to be an unusually precise description, not just of Austen's view of history as something made everyday (as the *Champion* argues), but of the otherness, or distance, that came to mark the everyday as a distinct order of experience for her. In the approximately fifteen years, during which *Sense and Sensibility*, *Pride and Prejudice*, and *Northanger Abbey* were all revisited and revised, Austen achieved a perspective on her milieu and an appreciation of it that would have been impossible had that interval been less protracted and less consequential. Thus it is one of the ironies of Austen's achievement that the importance of everyday practice that characterizes her world was in many ways an *accident* of history and a bad one. For the world of the novels, particularly the first three, was not only viewed through the lens of retrospection and increasingly a matter of history; it was also a reality whose temporal destiny coincided with the fate of certain social and political possibilities that by the time of the novels' publication had been subsumed and mitigated by the ideals that the *Champion* both names and misrecognizes. A fuller account of these ideals or ones similar can be found in the writings of Lenore Davidoff, Catherine Hall and other feminist historians, who trace the stifling effects of domestic ideology and its doctrine of separate spheres in the nineteenth century.[6] What is interesting, though, is the way these developments, which help forge what Austen increasingly understood to be a history of missed opportunities, are equally instrumental in a conception of the everyday as an earlier or anterior present, for which that of the novels is mostly a stand-in. By process of revision and reflection, a world and milieu that had been written out of history—whether by convention (as the *Champion* argues) or by time itself in Austen's case—was provisionally restored in a practice inimitably Austenian.

This restoration is especially evident in the two novels composed just after the period of revision—*Mansfield Park* and *Emma*—whose worlds remained both an unprecedented representation of "real life" to contemporary readers and a repetition as such of a present lost to time of which the novels were largely a resuscitation. Thus when Edmund Bertram expresses worry late in *Mansfield Park* that a particular "retrospect of what might have been—but what never can be now" will likely cause Fanny Price "pain" rather than "pleasure,"[7] the novel rises in effect to meet and to conceptualize its procedures thus far. To be sure, the referent of Edmund's "what"—the missed opportunity of marriage to Henry Crawford—is not exactly a loss that either Fanny or most readers are immediately inclined to regret. However, it is probably no accident that it devolves on the most obtuse of Austen's heroes to lament something whose foreclosure the narrative is unambiguous in celebrating. The crowning irony of Edmund's mistake lies not in his misreading of the heroine; it is in the conceptual framework he provides in bracketing a story that has been misfiring throughout in seeking to sway readers to a position that the novel's "might-have-beens" actively mitigate. In addition to memorializing what Lady Vernon and others found themselves calling "every day life," such retrospection is a reminder that narratives like Fanny's are also histories, albeit ones written from the standpoint of the victorious. Regardless of how victory and loss are eventually distributed, then, there is no clear or necessary distinction between what has been consigned to history in *Mansfield Park*, of which Austen's practice is the answerable "style," and what cultural, historical, and now narrative progress are determined apparently to put behind them.

That *Mansfield Park* received *no* reviews despite its proximity to two works, *Sense and Sensibility* and *Pride and Prejudice*, that had been published recently and generally well received—and to which readers were alerted on the new novel's title page—is surely a missed opportunity for literary historians. But it speaks more immediately to a certain difficulty or opacity, which Austen's contemporaries, including those whose responses she actively solicited, variously acknowledge. Many of the responses by friends, acquaintances, and family members were opinions on specific characters, notably the kleptomaniacal Mrs. Norris. But the more developed observations, including those that compared the new novel to Austen's previous works, invariably came to an impasse for which the novel's striking verisimilitude or "natural[ness]" (as Austen's brother Frank put it) is more a euphemism than an achievement whose virtues are self-explanatory.[8] There were inevitably members of the Austen circle who preferred *Mansfield Park* for its moral theme. For those, however, who admired it for "scenes" that, as Lady Gordon described them, are "so exactly descriptive, so perfectly natural," the reality that the novel describes seems relatively uncontained and continuous with life, rather than a world circumscribed by narrative deliberation and closure. Or, quoting Lady Gordon, "there is scarcely an Incident or conversation, or a person that you are not inclined to imagine you have at one time or other in your Life been a witness, born a part in, & been acquainted with" (Southam [ed.] 1968, 1: 51).

If the mimetic power of Austen's writing was a tribute to her artistry in this instance, it was the world onto which the novel opened that took precedence for contemporary readers. There is Lady Vernon's "not much of a novel but more the history of a family party in the country." There was also Anne Romilly who, writing to Maria Edgeworth, compared the novel favorably to *Waverley*, which she disliked for being too much of a novel and too concerned with its hero rather than with "general manners." A good novel "must be true to life," she wrote, "which [*Mansfield Park*] is, with a good story vein of principle running thro' the whole"—though it was the last, curiously, leading to an "elevation of virtue" or "something beyond nature," that was also missing. What the novel gave Romilly—and this is critical—was "real natural every day life" so that "in spite of its faults," it could "amuse an idle hour very well" (*Romilly-Edgeworth Letters* [1936], 92).

It would not be very long of course before the "story vein of principle" that was lost amid the novel's surplus of "every day life" would come to characterize Austen's achievement here and in general. In his influential assessment of Austen's career, occasioned by the posthumous publication of *Northanger Abbey* and *Persuasion* in 1818, Richard Whately saw a greater cooperation between the verisimilitude of Austen's representations and their ability to impart "moral lessons." Acknowledging that Austen's "minuteness of detail ... produces ... a degree of tediousness" that "has also been found fault with" (notably by his *Quarterly Review* predecessor Walter Scott), Whately regarded "the vivid distinctness of description, the minute fidelity of detail, and air of unstudied ease" in Austen's representations as a device by which the illusion of reality, what he termed the "perfect appearance of reality," obscures and makes palatable a moral or religious message. In contrast to novels where the "purpose of inculcating a religious principle is made too palpably prominent," he wrote,

[t]he moral lessons of [Austen's] novels, though clearly and impressively conveyed, are not offensively put forward, but spring incidentally from the circumstances of the story; they are not forced upon the reader, but he is left to collect them (though without any difficulty) for himself: her's is that unpretending kind of instruction which is furnished by real life; and certainly no author has ever conformed more closely to real life, as well as in the incidents, as in the characters and descriptions. (Southam [ed.] 1968, 1: 98, 96, 95)

Whately may have been among the first to note how conformance to "life" serves—rather than beclouds—the novelist's commitment to moral principles. Still, his case overall was not very well served by *Mansfield Park*, where for other readers everyday life was a limit point rather than a naturalizing apparatus. It is true that Fanny begins as the frightened ward of the Bertram household and ends triumphantly as both Edmund's wife and the mainstay of the Bertram family. But it is the case too that, unlike Emma Woodhouse or Elizabeth Bennet, Fanny's progress is disjoined from her moral development, which largely precedes the narrative and from which "the circumstances of the story" are primarily a falling away. A good many of these "circumstances"—notably the private theatrical undertaken in Sir Thomas Bertram's absence—are certainly assimilable to a "moral lesson" that the narrator means to inculcate and where Fanny, whose perspective is frequently indistinguishable from the narrator's, abides as a paragon of virtue. The problem is that these circumstances are also the only examples—the only "real life"—that the novel truly engages.

Confronted with a novel suspended between "every day life" and a narrative or narrative perspective in which this same reality was found wanting, it is hardly any wonder that Austen's earliest readers routinely separated the world viewed in *Mansfield Park* from the world judged. Even as the novel was far from opaque in its distribution of praise and blame, its world was also one where "principle" is largely an imposition—or, like Sir Thomas's sudden return, an interruption—rather than an "unpretending" feature of the everyday. The invariable response of readers such as Mrs. Pole, who, like others, commended the novel's accuracy of representation,[9] is perhaps best seen as a subset of the silence with which the novel was met by professional readers upon publication. The missed opportunity of *Mansfield Park*—in this case as a considerable achievement by a living author—was strangely homologous with all that the narrative knows on earth, where virtually everything, from the theatrical at Mansfield to Mrs. Norris's parsimony to quotidian sociability, goes largely unappreciated.

II

In effectively siding with *Mansfield Park*'s imitation of life over its apparent judgment of the "every day," Austen's earliest readers were actually following the novel's lead in its necessary dependence on a society and a world in which there are precious few alternatives to those who, like the nominal villain Henry Crawford, are bent on "doing something." But these readers were also responding to something else that owes to the circumstances of the novel's composition, particularly in relation to the two works Austen had recently published, and to which she had returned in the years and months preceding. Although the extent and nature of the revisions to *Sense and Sensibility* and, more immediately, to *Pride and Prejudice* will always be a matter of speculation, the six years or so during which all of the novels were either written or revised for publication provided Austen with an aperture on her writing overall, and on the relationship of her achievement to the culture and milieu that she lived in, that is fairly unique. Her well-known observation in a letter to her sister, where *Mansfield Park* is described as representing a "complete change of subject—Ordination"—from the just revised *Pride and Prejudice* (Austen 1995, 202) is a comparative assessment that seems thematic in focus. However in light of the nearly two decades in which *Pride and Prejudice* was to one degree or other a work in progress, the comparison is temporal and historical as well.

Austen is much clearer on this point in the "Advertisement" to *Northanger Abbey*, where she explicitly notes the "considerable changes" in "places, manners, books, and opinions" in the years separating that novel's conception from what turned out to be its posthumous publication.[10] While these "changes" refer most immediately to *Northanger Abbey*'s treatment of the gothic novel, which was no longer an enthusiasm or an especially timely target by the second decade of the nineteenth century, they bear equally on certain prospects—or, quoting Edmund, certain "retrospects"—to which other aspects of that novel, as well as aspects of both *Sense and Sensibility* and *Pride and Prejudice*, refer. In the case of *Northanger Abbey*, as I have argued elsewhere, these "retrospects of . . . what never more can be" involve the practices and proclivities by which Catherine Morland resists her disposability to a narrative where growth and capitulation are synonymous.[11] This is similarly the case with the two other early novels, which bind content to form in making the eventual domestication of Marianne Dashwood and Elizabeth Bennet correlative to certain generic developments where the conflict of romance and realism remains, as it does in *Northanger Abbey*, a conflict of past and present. In all three early works the rise of the novel as a regulatory, realistic instrument, whose heroine, as Scott observed, is eventually "turned wise," is counterposed to a past in which the heroine's independence (or in Catherine's case strangeness) fashions a horizon of possibility that is foreclosed but scarcely forgotten. This memory persists not only thanks to the history in these novels, whose heroines are more expansive and more interesting early on; it persists

despite the literary history that *Sense and Sensibility*, for example, helped write
in its transformation from epistolary form—a form characterized by its constitutive indeterminacy—to the "[new] style of novel" that Scott, like Whately,
praised for being both probabilistic and didactic. (Southam [ed] 1968, 1: 63).

The most important formal feature of the "new" novel, whose subject matter, Scott noted, was "nearly allied with the experience of [one's] own social
habits" and unlikely to "tur[n]" the reader's "head . . . by the recollection of the
scene through which he has been wandering" (Southam [ed.] 1968, 1: 68) was
its mode of narration in free indirect discourse. There is no disputing Austen's
achievement here, or the pleasure she took in her particular exercise of narrative
authority. Nevertheless, her works generally, but particularly *Mansfield Park* and
Emma, are marked by an unwieldy fascination with "real life" so that, paradoxically, the more closely they conform to "life," the further they depart from the
realistic project that the "appearance of reality" supposedly underwrites.[12] The
"vividness of description" that *Mansfield Park*'s initial readers found so striking
was not just at variance with the moral lessons that the narrator and the narrative inculcate; it was redolent of a culture—an everyday domestic culture—that
was familiar, despite being under siege or, as the narrative urges, decadent and
increasingly moribund. That Mary Crawford's world or even that of the Bertram
sisters remains a "retrospect of . . . what never can be now" was no doubt news
to Austen's largely female and privileged readership; and it is news, too, to many
of the characters in *Mansfield Park*, whose actions, however derogated, stand in
problematic juxtaposition to the relative inaction of the heroine and to the more
modern—or, as a number of critics have described them, "Victorian"—standards
by which the heroine, the narrator, and the narrative collectively bring the mostly
female characters here to judgment.[13] Even as it works primarily to mark and to
justify the rise and fall of emergent and residual cultural practices, the division
of form and content in *Mansfield Park* is no less a division over time that, in the
spirit of Edmund's "retrospect" and its concern over "what might have been,"
looks backward simultaneously to a world where, among other things, women
do more than say "no."

Dubbed "Mansfield Park" in an ironic echo of Lord Chief Justice Mansfield's
recourse to Elizabethan precedent in describing England as having "air too pure
for slaves to breathe in," the world so vividly described in *Mansfield Park* is both
an *apostasis* from what the narrative doggedly insists is an improved mode of
social practice and a stay against this new and improved mode that the titular

irony quickly picks up on.[14] Although decadent and diminished on the arguments of both the narrator and readers like Whately, the primary content of
Mansfield Park remains equally opposed to what, in Hayden White's phrase, is
"the content of form" here: the Britain that is *becoming* "Mansfield Park," which
the narrative is at pains to defend. Mary Crawford's riposte supporting architectural changes wrought upon the chapel at Sotherton—"[e]very generation has
its improvements" (77)—is more than just an exercise in unprincipled relativism.
It attacks the developmental view of history to which the linear narrative plainly
subscribes. Mary's statement explains too, then, why *Mansfield Park*, whose title
is more importantly a referent, is a demonstrably poor vehicle of ideology. For
in its necessary situation along an axis of development over time, "Mansfield
Park"—the domesticated counterweight to an imperial Britain that cannot go
by any other name—also names a Britain in formation. It names a culture whose
values and whose instruments of value, including the institution of the novel
itself, are transparently self-serving, rather than a reliable measure of what the
narrative in this instance finds wanting or deficient.

But this is not all the novel does. For every prospect of improvement along
the lines I've described, there remain numerous "restrospects" that make reading
Austen an experience where the reader's head is in fact "turned" to "recollec[t]
... the scene through which he has been wandering," so that the "near alli[ance]"
with the experience of one's social habits, in which the "pleasure" of "reading"
Austen resides for Scott, was precisely as he describes: a *near*-alliance or differ-
ential now where historical distance prevailed. Marked by a necessary homology
between the superseded and the overlooked, the world to which the reader was
turned in *Mansfield Park* was a "retrospect" not only of a lost world but also of
a provisional *present* that could, by definition, only be seen again.

There is a difference, clearly, between *Mansfield Park*'s somewhat plotless and
episodic disposition and what Edmund, in reference to Henry again, describes
as a missed opportunity. But the standoff between the novel and its emplot-
ted content is pervasive, especially in the major set pieces, where "what never
happen[s]" (as Catherine Morland puts it)[15] or "can be" remains the persistent
other to what the narrative promotes in partnership with time. The result, in
each case, of Fanny's opportunistic reticence, the missed opportunity exposes
two things: the zero-sum logic that drives the narrative in the image of the im-
perium it serves; and the possibilities, cultural and aesthetic, that the narrative
and its heroine are impressed to expunge.

The first expungeable opportunity, presented during the visit to Sotherton, comes nicely in the form of a "prospec[t]" that Fanny and her walking companions, Maria Bertram and Henry Crawford, are prevented from entering by a locked "iron gate" and an adjacent "ha-ha," or sunk wall, that give Maria in particular "a feeling of restraint and hardship." Rather than waiting for their host, Mr. Rushworth, to unlock the gate with a key, Maria accepts Henry's assistance in "pass[ing] round the edge of the gate," leaving Fanny to remonstrate by warning Maria that she will hurt herself. But Maria does not hurt herself. She negotiates the prohibitions with Henry's assistance and the two are quickly out of view, leaving Fanny "with no increase of pleasant feelings" which soon descend to "disagreeable musings" (89–90). The cause of these "musings" turns out to be less clear than first seems. Although a feature of Fanny's prudence and seeming probity, her unhappiness is provoked as much by the bad behavior she has witnessed as by being left alone, both by her immediate companions and by Edmund and Mary Crawford as well. The "smiling scene" before her (as Henry describes it to Maria), and to which Maria assigns both a "figural" and "literal" meaning (89), stands in inverse proportion to a subjectivity troubled by more than it can comprehend.

Even as these companions are presented as cautionary examples, their irretrievability on moral grounds does not work to benefit the standards—and the standard-bearer—by which they are found wanting. If anything, the self-determination that Maria displays (both here and later on), and to which she is provoked by certain prohibitions, propel her to smiling prospects that belong "figuratively" at this point to a world—a woman's world—that is or *was* a good deal less miserable, even as it is getting harder to discover. Or to put it in terms distinctly (and historically) Austenian: were Fanny capable of entering the prospect—were she more like Elizabeth Bennet and less concerned with ruining her gown—we might well be contending with something other than her clear and present misery.

The two other prospects that Fanny eschews, leaving her similarly ensconced in states of misery, echo the first smiling prospect. Like so much else in a novel that moves in slow time, continually turning back on itself, they are an anterior lag on a future marked by a dogmatic investment in both Britain's and women's sanctity. This investment was especially evident in conduct manuals such as the one by Gisborne that Austen was reading as she was composing the novel, which make clear that activities, like the private theatrical mounted during Sir Thomas's absence, were unfashionable and already casualties of time. But in *Mansfield Park*, whose momentum forward is slowed by "retrospects" where "every day life" is front and center, things are not so simple. Even as she is on the winning side of history, Fanny's ostentatious refusal to participate in the theatrical ("No, indeed, I cannot act" [131]) is met by a concomitant misery that, while ostensibly a function of jealousy, simultaneously projects a smiling horizon of female agency and mobility: "Alas! it was all Miss Crawford's doing. She had seen her influence in every speech [of Edmund's] and was miserable" (141).

The third missed prospect is the "retrospect" that Edmund explicitly defines as such: the prospect of marriage to Henry. The least definitive of the various opportunities that both Fanny and the narrative reject, Henry's courtship of Fanny speaks as much to the possibility of marriage to a character—who (like Frank Churchill after him) is largely inaccessible to narrative intelligence—as it does to transformations in the novel generally in its shift from epistolary form to the more authoritative operation of free indirect discourse. There is no disputing Austen's investment in third-person omniscience or her understanding of her instrumentality in the development of what Scott, in discussing *Emma*, proclaimed the novel of the future. Nevertheless, it bears remembering (and repeating) that at least one, and possibly both, of the novels Austen had published thus far were initially in epistolary form and that this form was in many ways the antithesis of domestic fiction in its realistic and probabilistic formation. Or this, at least, is how Austen frames the situation in her only mature epistolary narrative, *Lady Susan*, written and transcribed over the same interval that generated the first two published novels. In ending as it does—with an abrupt and disingenuous turn to omniscience and moral authority—*Lady Susan* not only resembles *Mansfield Park* in looking forward to the new style of novel and the nation it serves. It also resembles the later work in looking backward to a pleasurable text that has been silenced along with its protagonist. Like Mary or Maria, the "retrospect" that the female libertine represents in *her* challenge to the future—and to domestic ideology—goes unmet in a narrative that, until its end, is marking rather than accelerating time.

What of *Mansfield Park* in this vein? Apart from the inculpatory force of narrative authority, the answer would seem to involve another remnant of the past or the literary past: Samuel Richardson's *Clarissa*. Austen's familiarity with Richardson's last novel, *Sir Charles Grandison*, is well documented. But it is *Clarissa* that resounds through concluding phase of *Mansfield Park*, dominated by Fanny's exile to Portsmouth as punishment for refusing Henry and by his attempt to win her affections in the interim.[16] In *Clarissa* it is the arranged marriage to Solmes that draws the heroine to the libertine Lovelace and renders Lovelace by turns an attractive alternative. In *Mansfield Park*, a mandatory exile to her parents' slovenly home—as punishment for resisting marriage to someone like Lovelace—softens Fanny in the face of Henry's entreaties. If it is not easy to know what to make of this intertext, in which the new style of novel and its epistolary antecedent are brought into strained compliance, one thing is clear: Henry's performance as Fanny's seemingly considerate and generous suitor is an echo of epistolary indeterminacy sufficient to drive the novel backward to a possibility that only another story, with its ham-handed disclosure of Henry and Maria's affair, miserably cancels.

III

The misery that impinges on both Fanny and the narrative perspective, where her view is often echoed or appropriated, demands some additional attention. The particular despair into which Fanny frequently shrinks, especially when compelled to say "no" to something, puts an all-too-human face on a narrative whose dogged commitment to rewarding virtue and punishing vice is manifest in a plot that must resort to clumsy inculpation—the elopements and dissipations that precipitate regime change at Mansfield—and in a sour perspective on those in whom value and virtue are vested. We sense this when the narrative, recounting the developments leading to Fanny's and Edmund's eventual marriage, shifts temporarily to the narrative first person and a positionality that free indirect discourse typically (or theoretically) should avoid:

I purposely abstain from dates on this occasion, that every one may be at liberty to fix their own, aware that the cure of unconquerable passions, and the transfer of unchanging attachments, must vary much as to time in different people.—I only intreat every body to believe that exactly at the time when it was quite natural that it should be so, and not a week earlier, Edmund did cease to care about Miss Crawford, and became as anxious to marry Fanny, as Fanny herself could desire. (429)

This is hardly the first time in Austen that marital closure poses a problem or that "natural" is explicitly ironized. There is the mortuary image of Marianne Dashwood, described as having been "taken from" her family by her marriage to Colonel Brandon, and on a lighter note, the "editor's" account of Frederica

Vernon's fate at the "conclusion" of *Lady Susan*, which could easily double as a gloss of the passage just cited:

Federica was therefore fixed in the family of her Uncle and Aunt, till such time as Reginald De Courcy could be talked, flattered and finessed into an affection for her—which, allowing leisure for the conquest of his attachment to her Mother, for his abjuring all future attachments and detesting the Sex, might be reasonably looked for in the course of a Twelvemonth. Three Months might have done it in general, but Reginald's feelings were no less lasting than lively. (272)

The structural similarities linking Reginald and Edmund are obvious enough. The same is true of the irony that migrates to Edmund's "unconquerable passions" and "unchanging sentiments." Yet irony aside, the description is marked by a nearly Aristotelian decorum, where the coming together of the hero and heroine is enough of a catastrophe now to be kept from view.

Binding narrative deliberation to an affect of aversion or misery, the union of Fanny and Edmund does more than simply undermine the comedic future to which the narrative has been proceeding; it remembers the pleasure and, just as important, the fate of pleasure in which a counterplot has been incubating throughout. To claim that only Fanny or Edmund or even Sir Thomas are the repositories of misery in the novel overlooks the fact that many, if not all, of the characters ultimately join with the heroes and supposed winners in projecting a horizon of unhappiness and discontent. There are no real victors in *Mansfield Park,* save in the most monolithic register. But there is a distinction in the novel that gains traction at the level of style between a prospect, aligned increasingly with things as they are becoming both at home and abroad, and a "retrospect" in which "real natural every day life" is infused with a sense of possibility.

Exactly "what might have been" is a little hard to calculate because almost everything in this—the first Austen novel to be published when written—appears to be a falling away, temporally and ideologically, from an impending future. But calculations can also work by subtraction, and they do here in the negative way with a set of people whose idleness and apparent decadence are a debit against the "duties" (as Gisborne described them) of men and women. It is frequently remarked that one of the primary features of Austen's first published novels is that nobody in them works for a living, in contrast to the later novels, where the rising professional orders (in, for example, Edmund's clerical and William Price's naval vocations) are held in general esteem. The subtraction of Henry and Mary

Crawford and of Julia, Maria and Tom Bertram from a projected sum of specifically defined duties, all pursuant to gender, runs in a different direction. It runs backward in time, or better still *in place*, to a sum or plenitude, where feminization is neither a pejorative nor a codification but bound up in an everyday world that is surprisingly dynamic, rather than rigidly circumscribed.

One aspect of this dynamism is the prerogative of saying "yes" as well as "no," which the leads the Bertram daughters, in particular, to actions that are also grist for the narrative's program. Another involves seemingly idle men, who have nothing better to do (in also saying "no") than to stage plays, converse, contemplate architectural or landscape improvements, or just be. This world is clearly on the wane, as evidenced by Sir Thomas and Lady Bertram, who are, if nothing else, man and woman respectively. Still, even as they give a sense, in their prototypically divided lives and separate spheres, of changes afoot, the Bertrams manage by comparison to make "doing something"—even if it's just a play or an outing or a conversation—more interesting than standing pat or, in Lady Bertram's case, not moving.

This latter stance typically involves demurring, whether to acting or to almost anything. But it also entails, in its avid subscription to tradition or received wisdom, a concomitant aversion to thinking. Here is Fanny rhapsodizing on family worship:

It is a pity . . . that the custom should have been discontinued. It was a valuable part of former times. There is something in a chapel and chaplain so much in character with a great house, with one's ideas of what such a household should be! A whole family assembling regularly for the purpose of prayer, is fine! (77)

And here she is on "Nature":

Here's harmony! . . . Here's repose! Here's what may leave all painting and all music behind, and what poetry only can attempt to describe. Here's what may tranquillize every care, and lift the heart to rapture! When I look out on such a night as this, I feel as there could be neither wickedness nor sorrow in the world; and there certainly would be less of both if the sublimity of Nature were more attended to, and people were carried more out of themselves by contemplating such a scene. (102)

And here, finally, on mutability and memory:

How wonderful, how very wonderful the operations of time, and the changes of the human mind! . . . If any faculty in our nature may be called *more* wonderful than the rest, I do think it is memory. There seems something more speakingly incomprehensible in the powers, the failures, the inequalities of memory, than in any other of our intelligences. The memory is sometimes so retentive, so serviceable, so obedient—at others, so bewildered and so weak—and at others again, so tyrannic, so beyond controul!—We are to be sure a miracle every way—but our powers of recollecting and of forgetting, do seem peculiarly past finding out. (188)

Mary Crawford, to whom two of these observations are addressed (and who is within earshot of the third), is described as "untouched and inattentive" in response to the last and as having "nothing to say" (188). While this silence is taken by the narrator to signify defeat and, worse, some moral or human deficiency, it is clear that, in contrast to Mary's terse but original "every generation has its improvements," it is Fanny who is saying "nothing," or nothing that isn't also a ventriloquization.

Mary by contrast is always thinking, and when she talks about improvements, she is saying something that accords with the counterplot in "thinking back," as Heidegger puts it, "to what is to be thought." For among the ways we might discuss the basic division of story and event in *Mansfield Park,* and the many retrospects that pile up as the narrative trundles on, is as a "turning" toward what "turns away" in Heidegger's description—where "improvements" are marked and countenanced, but only by dissociation from progress and by relocation to the "every day."

An example of this everyday, and the thinking it models, is the frequently cited moment of Sir Thomas's encounter with John Yates in what was the former's "closet" prior to becoming the temporary stage for the uncloseted performance of *Lovers' Vows:*

He stept to the door, rejoicing at that moment in having the means of immediate communication, and opening it, found himself on the stage of a theatre, and opposed to a ranting young man, who appeared likely to knock him down backwards. At the very moment of Yates perceiving Sir Thomas, and giving perhaps the very best start he had ever given in the whole course of his rehearsals, Tom Bertram entered at the other end of the room; and never had he found greater difficulty in keeping his countenance. His father's looks of solemnity and amazement on this his first appearance on any stage, and the gradual metamorphosis of the impassioned Baron Wildenhaim into the well-bred and easy Mr. Yates, making his bow and apology to Sir Thomas Bertram, was such an exhibition, such a piece of true acting as he would not have lost upon any account. It would be the last—in all probability the last on that stage; but he was sure there could not be a finer. The house would close with the greatest éclat. (164)

If there is a locus classicus of free indirect discourse, it is here, in this passage, which morphs effortlessly, like Yates, from Sir Thomas's point of view to the narrator's and finally to Tom's, where we are most palpably in thought. And like the pleasure it produces, such thinking—however "veiled"—is consolidated in the notion of "true acting," which speaks directly to a possibility that the narrative, by tracing the arc of "probability," works (like Sir Thomas) to devalue and to contain. This possibility does not just reside in Yates, who clearly embodies it; it is also evident among those who oppose it—notably Fanny—who is able to renounce acting in the interests of transparency or morality and capable of performance or duplicity whenever the occasion warrants, whether in appropriating sentiments and ideas or in the headaches and somatic complaints by which she gains attention and invariably gets her way.

The decision to make Fanny the novel's heroine may be reckoned an invitation to thinking. But it is just as characteristic of the novel, and of the missed opportunity that is *Mansfield Park*, that this invitation is simultaneously withdrawn, beginning with the many instances where Fanny's and the narrator's viewpoints are indistinguishable, and in the elements of plot that succeed in disposing of all challenges to the new, more codified, world that the narrative endorses in documenting the heroine's rise.

Austen's initial readers saw something very different, recognizing the novel's viewpoint as akin to Tom's in his father's closet. This is not because Tom is any way an implied or surrogate narrator that Fanny often models in her silent observation and pity. It is because the novel's remarkable way with the everyday proceeded in the same slow motion, and with the same invitation to "recollec[t] the scene through which [one] has been wandering," as the scene onto which Tom happens. This "retrospect" is closer obviously to Anne Romilly's sense of the novel's verisimilitude, which "will amuse an idle hour very well," than to the "humorous descriptions" that, in Whately's view, are inseparable from the novel's "moral lessons." But what is at stake finally with Tom as a guide is less bemusement than a recognition or appreciation that "every day life" in the novel enables. Such a stance exposes, in this case by exploiting, the representational opportunities that narratives, fictional or historical, discard in their subscriptions to probability and form.[17] And it recalls and commemorates—and here Edmund's "restrospect" is key—the opportunities, the missed opportunities, written out of "domestic life" by time and by what Austen later described as "the considerable changes in places, manners, books, and opinions."

I V

The discussion of *Emma* that follows will be brief, because its central point—that the novel is an exercise in rereading—varies only slightly from the thesis that anchors my discussion of the novel in *The Historical Austen*. But it is a point worth pressing on for the moment, because in disposing of story as a one-off event, rereading disposes of a rhetoric as well, in which story and detail, or progress and regress, are forced to operate at cross-purposes. That *Emma* went *Mansfield Park* one better in all but burying its narrative under an avalanche of detail was clear to readers from the beginning. In the most extensive critical treatment of Austen's writing in her lifetime, Scott praised the novel as a groundbreaking achievement but confessed to trouble with the way that "detail" in *Emma* mitigated "the force of narrative," in the way such "prosing" proved "as tiresome in fiction as in real society" (67–68). Maria Edgeworth had an even worse reaction and stopped reading after just one volume, complaining that "there was no story in it except that Miss Emma found that the man whom she designed for Harriets lover was an admirer of her own—& he was affronted at being refused by Emma & Harriet wore the willow—and smooth, thin water-gruel is according Emma's father's opinion a very good thing & it is very difficult to make a cook understand what you mean by thin water gruel."[18]

There are a number of things in Edgeworth's observation worth commenting on, beginning with the indirect claim that there is no story *save* for the one in *Emma*'s details. In volume 1, as perhaps nowhere else, readers are invited to join with the narrator in tracking and celebrating Emma's comeuppance in an extended episode in which the prosaic poses little complication, largely because Miss Bates—whom Edgeworth appears to be channeling—has not yet materialized, along with many other characters. Thus even as the impersonation may have been a coincidence, it points to a way of taking in the world in which the unforgettable spinster is in many ways symptomatic, even when the "moral lesson" springs relatively seamlessly, as it does in volume 1, from "the circumstances of the story."

More than a surfeit of circumstance, where no aspect of "every day life" appears to have gone unnoticed, *Emma*'s style is ultimately a condensation, where a world on which the future is encroaching is effectively put on life support, both in the imperative to reread, in which the everyday comes to view as something seen again, and by a mode of representation (also evident in *Mansfield Park*) where attention is exerted in such a way that reading and rereading are one and the same.[19] In the case of *Emma*, the imperative to reread is provoked initially by the suppressed narrative involving Frank Churchill and Jane Fairfax, to which a second reading provides amusing and illuminating access. Yet even allowing that the novel is a very different reading experience the second or third time around, there is more going on in the invitation to reread than the insider status that knowing the story confers. Rereading takes the reader in the opposite direction as well: to a limit point or ground-level claustrophobia that Edgeworth, in advance of the novel's more prosaic detours, experienced the first time.

Reginald Farrer noted something similar in 1917 when he observed that *Emma* is not in fact "an easy book to read" especially on first encounter. "Only when the story is thoroughly assimilated," he wrote,

can the infinite delights and subtleties of its workmanship begin to be appreciated, as you realise the manifold complexity of the book's web, and find that every sentence, almost every epithet, has its definite reference to equally unemphasised points before and after in the development of plot. Thus it is that, while twelve readings of 'Pride and Prejudice' give you twelve periods of pleasure repeated, as many readings of 'Emma' give you that pleasure, not repeated only, but squared and squared again with each perusal, till at every fresh reading you feel anew that you never understood anything like the widening sum of its delights. But, until you know the story, you are apt to find its movement dense and slow and obscure, difficult to follow, and not very obviously worth the following.[20]

The distinction here between the difficulty and the pleasure of the text is based on a particular knowledge that makes reading *Emma* a different activity than reading for plot. While this knowledge is not specified beyond a knowledge of the "story," it is pretty clear that, by Farrer's lights, there is no end to knowledge in *Emma*, and that what he alternately describes as the novel's density and its sublime pleasure are two ways of talking about the same thing. Any difference, then, between a novel that moves at a snail's pace on first encounter—thanks to a freewheeling attention unmoored from narrative—and one that, in its invitation to be reread, cultivates a similar attention ostensibly as a source of pleasure, turns out to be negligible. Not only does *Emma* foreground the overlooked *as the overlooked*, or as that which, as Edgeworth implies, we typically, indeed happily, ignore; it also transforms what we ignore into something—call it a missed opportunity—that we just as happily engage or appreciate for the same reason. We do this because the "infinite" or sublime that *Emma* performs in shifting from pain to pleasure is predicated in either case on a surplus independent of "story," and of the timeline necessary to story, in which history is both created and superseded.

Pointing to a lag or residue to which "story" is susceptible regardless of its movement forward, rereading reiterates the conditions under which *Emma*'s present emerged in the "dense and slow" form that Farrer and Edgeworth outline: namely, as a "retrospect" or "turning" in which "no story" is continually retrieved. Thus it also matters that the world to which *Emma* returns, whether on first reading or twelfth, is a world that has been superseded by time or, to quote Edmund one last time, "a retrospect of what might have been." For unlike the world of *Mansfield Park*, which remains, potentiality aside, a lost world ("but never can be now"), the world of *Emma*, and the density it opens onto, does two things: it maps a specific anteriority in Austen's life as a person and a writer; and it issues from what in rereading amounts to a *moving* anteriority in which historical distance (however foreshortened) provides a continuous accompaniment to a story where circumstance is irrepressible. The overwhelming assemblage to which *Emma* rises on multiple encounters is continuous with what is already readable or rereadable on first encounter: an everyday sublime from which there is finally no escape.

V

If Dorothy Wordsworth's daily writing in the Grasmere journal is linked to the shadow narrative of her brother's impending marriage and to a time line that her entries are motivated (however subliminally) to interrupt, the story imbedded in Austen's daily writing to *her* sibling is somewhat harder to discern, because she often seems, when writing to Cassandra, to have taken the day off. Lacking the density that she generously bestowed on similar materials as a novelist, the letters by Austen that have survived are largely gossip—the comings and goings of family and friends, births, deaths, illnesses, marriages, and meals, along with numerous social and domestic gatherings—almost all of which bears invidious comparison to the more crafted version of this discourse as practiced by Miss Bates.

Still, even as they are collectively a disappointment—particularly for readers expecting the attention and wit seemingly everywhere in the fictions—the letters track a narrative that, if nothing else, confirms that the "real natural every day" world so evident on Austen's printed page was of interest and thereby representable because, like the petticoat peering out at the close of her very last epistle, it is increasingly a prospect—a "good" as she calls it at one point—nested in a retrospect. Mary Favret speaks for many readers in noting the "unyielding" nature of Austen's correspondence as a personal record, even suggesting that—despite rumors regarding letters that were destroyed posthumously—"Austen may not have written the revealing letters we seek—at least not after the 1790s."[21] But in arguing, very plausibly, that the "familiar letter" in Austen's hands "functions" "as a mirror of the surrounding community" rather than "as a lens through which one scrutinize[s] the writer" (Favret 1993, 136), Favret inadvertently marks a connection that the letters underscore as a different kind of "personal revelation" (Favret 1993, 134), where the writer's diminishing prospects—in contrast to those of her brothers—compel her to look elsewhere for what she at one point calls "animation" (Austen 1995, 43).

The word appears in an early letter in an uncharacteristic moment of reflection. "Some wish," Austen writes, "some prevailing Wish is necessary to the animation of everybody's Mind, & in gratifying this, You leave them to form some other which will not probably be half so innocent." This potentially sober reflection is motivated by the incidental gift of the "pattern of our Caps" to "Martha [Lloyd] and Mrs Lefroy" whose gratification, Austen fears, will lead to more invasive requests. Still, lurking in the aperçu, and somewhat leveraged by what follows immediately in the letter—"I shall not forget to write to Frank.—Duty & Love &c" (Austen 1995, 43)—is a counternarrative of "prevailing . . . animation" that, absent a future like her brother's, cannot be served, or tainted for that matter, by desires that are requitable. It is more that what animates Austen's mind—as an opportunity more than a wish now—is almost always behind her or (to quote Miss Bates) "before" her, allowing what happened—or "what never happened" because it *always* happens—a capacity, an amplitude, an innocence even, in which gratification is beside the point and where the future, or what stands for it, is simply what comes next and by extension what came before.

We first encounter Jane Austen the letter writer as a still marriageable young woman with the apparent expectations of securing a single man and the less usual ones of becoming a great novelist. Early on these expectations intertwine, especially in the context of social gatherings where the novelist's eye finds objects of interest, while the letter writer is concerned equally with what she wears and her appearance generally. Austen may be exaggerating somewhat when she tells her sister that she "write[s] only for Fame, and without any view to pecuniary Emolument" ([1995, 3] a position she will later revise), but in her earlier letters especially she periodically enlarges or dilates on ordinary events, anticipating the techniques on which her "fame" would eventually be based. In the very first letter to Cassandra that we have, Austen enjoins her sister to "[i]magine" the "profligate and shocking . . . way of dancing and sitting down together" that she and Tom Lefroy displayed at an "exceeding good ball" (1995, 1). Several letters later she reports her "great Distress" in not knowing whether to give a servant "only five Shillings when I go away" (8). This is small-bore irony by way of hyperbole. However when such ephemera take center stage over events that are significant—for example, "the Beaches' loss of their little girl," which is mentioned in passing after a comparatively absorbed expatiation on Tom's Lefroy's "morning coat" as being "a great deal too light" (1995, 2)—certain signals, fueled by the writer's "wishes" and the style serving one of them, cross in ways that don't seem quite right.

The signals are more coordinated several years later (in 1799) when, alluding to the recently drafted "First Impressions" and to Martha Lloyd's propensity to take things (which have graduated, in the author's bemused fantasy, from cap patterns to what she is now convinced will be her intellectual property), Austen shifts to discussing male beauty and, eventually, to one Benjamin Portal:

She is very cunning, but I see through her design;—she means to publish it from Memory, & one more perusal must enable her to do it.—As for Fitzalbini, when I get home, she shall have it, as soon as ever she will own that Mr. Elliott is handsomer than Mr Lance—that fair Men are preferable to Black—for I mean to take every opportunity of rooting out her prejudices—Benjamin Portal is here. How charming that is! I do not exactly know why, but the phrase followed so naturally that I could not help putting it down.—My Mother saw him the other day, but without Making herself known to him.—I am very glad You liked my Lace, & so are You & so is Martha—& we are all glad together. (1995, 44–45)

The seemingly unconscious shift—as Austen herself admits—from "First Impressions" to dark men vs. fair men and, in the process, to age-appropriate males culminating in Mr. Portal, effectively comes full circle in what appears to be Mrs. Austen's ability to restrain herself in ways that Mrs. Bennet cannot. Nevertheless, the really interesting point here is that the writer's expectations, however consonant, are fundamentally competing ones, pitting a marriage plot (involving a fair man), in which she is potentially a lace-bedecked participant, against a courtship narrative over which, as author, she exerts—or should exert—absolute power and control. It will be some time before Austen fully recognizes that the only courtship leading to marriage that she will experience directly will be further testimony to her authority as a writer. Thus what the letters gradually reveal—increasingly by omission—is that the narrative of Austen as an author of narratives, in which she clearly took enormous gratification, stands in zero-sum relation to the life and world that the letters document and, with fewer and fewer exceptions, to the limited attention she brings to that world in treating it as news.[22]

Early on there is more equilibrium between these poles, and the reader is always the richer for it. Commenting, for example, on a ball populated by the "vulgar" and the "noisy" in which she "had a very pleasant evening . . . though . . . there was no particular reason for it," Austen adds—in a distillation of her position as it is apparently developing—that she does "not think it worth while to wait for enjoyment until there is some real opportunity for it" (1995, 38). There are a number of ways to interpret this. One is that opportunities for real enjoyment are few and far between. The other is that enjoyment, or such enjoyment as Austen is capable of deriving, is potentially everywhere—and that the opportunities for it are, in fact, missed opportunities, whose dividends come afterward. Being at the ball was probably insufferable. Yet in the shadow of just hours or a few days, it is a different experience entirely.

This dynamic is at work in the report of another ball that was not just "pleasant" but, as Austen qualifies it, "still more good than pleasant, for there were nearly 60 people, & sometimes we had 17 couple[s]." The attendees included the usual families of note and, in anticipation of the ball organized by Frank Churchill in *Emma*, a fair sampling of "the meaner & more usual &c. &c.'s." "There was a scarcity of Men in general, & a still greater scarcity of any that were good for much." The women were no better: "[t]here was commonly a couple of ladies standing up together, but not often any so amiable as ourselves" (1995, 53). So where lies the pleasantness, or, as Austen cryptically terms it, the " good"? Was it that she danced nine out of ten dances (as she reports), or that nobody "abused" her hairstyle, or that Lord Portsmouth was "attentive" in his "recollection" of the addressee? The answer, apparently, is that the "good" is good in retrospect and an enjoyment whose opportunities are not limited so much as archived, where they are retrievable and revisable.

Such a surfeit is available to more immediate (and memorable) effect in the novels, of course, and in *Emma* particularly, where the reports tendered by Miss Bates are arguably the best "letters" Austen ever wrote. Unlike her creator, though, Miss Bates is not just delivering the news, which the letters, to their detriment, do with ever less adornment and perspective; she is something more like Highbury's chief demographer and collector of information, without whom a lot would go unappreciated, and certain persons unnamed and unnoted. Emma finds herself in a similar position in the frequently cited view from Ford's store, which is notable as much for a scene that—with Miss-Bates-like acuity—the heroine takes in, as for the apparent "ease" by which a "lively" mind (like Miss Bates's) is tempered here to see things—and in so doing to compose them—in a state of what is best described as animation. The letters tell a different story, because they are seemingly the work of a mind "lively" and *not* "at ease," and because they reflect the disappointment and, stylistically, the agitation of someone for whom there is increasingly no future save for what replaces it in the twice-lived world that Austen has come to inhabit.

In the letters written as the family was relocating to Bath, the resignation is palpable, along with various retrospects by which the writer is propelled forward and backward at the same time. Allowing that she is more reconciled to the relocation with each day, Austen observes that there is also "something interesting in the bustle of going away," particularly from a place "where the Balls are certainly in decline" to a place "where summers by the Sea" will be "delightful" and where "we shall possess many of the advantages which I have often thought of with Envy in the wives of Sailors or Soldiers" (1995, 68). While this image does not exactly square with the close of Austen's last completed novel, where a "sailor's wife" seems hardly an enviable "profession," there is a sense, too, that Austen's fantasy wives are on existential as well as literal vacations, where neither children nor husbands figure and the marriage plot is plainly in arrears.

The relocation to Bath also features two extended vignettes that stand apart from Austen's usually minimal reportage. The first is of an adulteress who appears at a social gathering:

She is not so pretty as I expected; her face has the same defect of baldness as her sister's, & her features not so handsome;—she was highly rouged, & looked rather quietly & contentedly silly than anything else.—Mrs Badcock & two young Women were of the same party, except when Mrs Badcock thought herself obliged to leave them, to run round the room after her drunken Husband.—His avoidance, & her pursuit, with the probable intoxication of both, was an amusing scene. (1995, 85)

The second, in essentially two parts, describes a short-lived friendship with Mrs. Chamberlayne, a childless woman with whom Austen went walking:

It would have amused you to see our progress;—we went up by Sion Hill, & returned across the fields; in climbing a hill Mrs Chamberlayne is very capital; I could with difficulty keep pace with her—yet would not flinch for the World.—on plain ground I was quite her equal—and so we posted away under a fine hot sun, *She* without any parasol or any shade to her hat, stopping for nothing, & crossing the Church Yard with as much expedition as if we were afraid of being buried alive.—After seeing what she is equal to, I cannot help feeling a regard for her.—As to Agreeableness, she is much like other people. (1995, 87)

Five days later Austen walks again with Mrs. Chamberlayne in what proves to be their last encounter.

Mrs Chamberlayne's pace was not quite so magnificent on this second trial as in the first; it was nothing more than I could keep up with, without effort; & for many, many Yards together on a raised narrow footpath I led the way.—The Walk was very beautiful as my companion agreed, whenever I made the observation—And so ends our friendship, for the Chamberlaynes leave Bath in a day or two.—Prepare likewise for the loss of Lady Fust, as you will lose before you find her.—My evening visit was by no means disagreable. (1995, 89–90)

I cite these episodes, not only because they are sustained in contrast to the many Austen letters that are just congeries of details, but also because the presents that they briefly cling to are informed by loss. In the first account, which is one of the few occasions where the novelist's eye is visibly at work in the letters, the loss (which I take to be that of her previous life in Steventon) is reflected in a determination to make the most of what remains behind or "before" her now and to be amused rather than made "disagreable," which is often her default position. The second episode involving Mrs. Chamberlayne is framed explicitly by loss: both the implicit loss of old friends, whom new acquaintances can hopefully replace, and—just as suddenly—the loss of those who are becoming friends or, in the case of Lady Fust, disappear before they are even acquaintances. Here, as in the first description, Austen is at pains to remain in the moment, a participial present of sorts ("stopping . . . crossing . . . being"), quite possibly because she knows what she will be reporting in the second installment. This would explain her hesitancy regarding a new friend's "Agreeableness"—a stay, presumably, against further disappointment—and the litotes for that matter used to describe the "evening visit" in the second installment, where the verdict on the night's agreeableness is out just long enough for the event itself (as the letter subsequently shows) to be reanimated in the telling. At the conjuncture of relocation and maturation (the writer is now in her mid-twenties), the future is obviously fraught for Austen, making the present—or the erstwhile present—the only possibility, the only future in effect, currently before her.

The world of the letters, however, is generally not this present, much less the world of the novels, but a starkly probable world where sameness and a general flattening prevail. At one point Austen commends her sister for "such long Letters" and for the "little events" (131) they report and describes her own practice, several days later, as a round of "needful replys and communications" (133) on matters that, a week or so earlier, she memorably calls "important nothings" (125). The final term (beloved by Janeites) well describes the animation that the novels bring to ordinary life. But the use of "nothings" is in fact apposite. What the letters represent with numbing frequency—and in contrast to the moments I've already flagged—is a world made nugatory, or part of a continuum, where days and weeks repeat in "a constant succession of small events" (230). At one point Austen writes that she is "at leisure" and can "make the most of [her] subjects, as they are not numerous this week" and goes on to discuss the "right" of people (as she designates it) to "marry *once* in their Lives for Love, if they can" (159) in reference to Lady Sondes who has managed to do that. The "if they can" is a telling qualifier (Austen is now in her thirties) and while it merges unavoidably with the fictions she was writing and the wish-fulfillment they are arrayed upon plotwise, it is equally continuous with the loss and disappointment that her letters document—never more than when they are "full of Matter" (162) or of "many little matters" (179) or of the "nothings" whose importance remains dormant.

Sadly, there is no shortage of examples to illustrate this feature, but one that stands out, which is no small feat, does so in allowing something "important," specifically *Mansfield Park*, to be annexed to a world that barely rises from nothingness:

We did not begin reading till Bentley Green. Henry's approbation hitherto is even equal to my wishes; he says it is very different from the other two, but does not appear to think it at all inferior. He has only married Mrs R. I am afraid he has gone through the most entertaining part.—He took to Lady B. & Mrs N. most kindly, & gives great praise to the drawing of the Characters. He understands them all, likes Fanny & I think foresees how it will all be.—I finished the Heroine last night & was very much amused by it. I wonder James did not like it better. It diverted me exceedingly.—We went to bed at 10. I was very tired, but slept to a miracle & am lovely today; & at present Henry seems to have no complaint. We left Cobham at 1/2 past 8, stopt to bait & breakfast at Kingston & were in this House considerably before 2—quite in the stile of Mr Knight. Nice smiling Mr Barlowe met us at the door, & in reply to enquiries after News, said that Peace was generally expected.—I have taken possession of my Bedroom, unpacked my Bandbox, sent Miss P's two Letters by the twopenny post, been visited by Mde B.,—& am now writing by myself at the new Table in the front room. It is snowing. (1995, 255)

If Dorothy Wordsworth's journals are notable in recalling moments that are both immediate and immersive, what this letter captures, or boils down to really, is the scene of "writing by myself at the new Table" rather than the various referents, which typically fly by. Henry's response to the new novel is surely noteworthy in underscoring the moral equivalency of *Mansfield Park*'s characters as drawn and the "good," accordingly, of a narrative where goodness is, at the same time, relentless and problematic. But whether any of this is bound up in either his understanding or in Austen's at this moment is unclear. What *is* clear is the moment itself, which the letter reproduces almost viscerally, flitting doggedly from topic to topic. Unlike Dorothy Wordsworth, whose ceiling is a possible world that she is too absorbed in relaying to stand back from and truly see, the ceiling that descends on Austen's daily writing is palpably felt in the way "every day life" disappears and everydayness or routine—from reading practices that are superficial to writing practices that are, well, practices—takes hold.

    The limits that letter writing both represents and imposes are so great, in fact, that Austen virtually forgets both that she is "Jane Austen" and the "bit of ivory" that marks her as that author. After an extended account of a moment with "Lady B.," whom she liked "for being in a hurry to have the Concert over & get away, & for getting away at last with a great deal of decision & promtness [*sic*], not waiting to compliment & dawdle & fuss about seeing *dear Fanny*, who was half the eveng in another part of the room," she actually apologizes for "growing too minute" (1995, 251), even as the sequence, as she surely realized, plainly adds up to something. But Austen can be "Jane Austen," too. Thanking Frank for having kept her identity as the author of *Pride and Prejudice* a secret, which her brother Henry had recently failed to do, she recognizes that the unwanted attention she is currently receiving is really "a trifle in all its Bearings, to the really important points of one's existence even in this World!" (231). Austen might well have written "even and especially in this World," for despite the patina of religion at the edges of her *sententia*, the author is implicitly weighing the importance of celebrity on a grand scale (for her) against the greater importance of what, in the previous anecdote, is evidently "too minute," too pointillistic, *not* to warrant attention.

A brief critique of Mary Brunton's novel *Self Control* turns up something similar. Austen writes that it is "an excellently-meant, elegantly-written Work, without anything of Nature or Probability in it" and wonders drolly "whether Laura's passage down the American River is not the most natural, possible, everyday thing she ever does" (1995, 234). Such observations, framed by an apparent subscription to "Probability," may be taken as a defense of realism against the marvelous, the romantic, or the fantastic. However the ironic thought experiment on an "everyday" both "natural" and "possible" moves in a completely different direction, invoking a "possible" world that is not so much improbable or unnatural as overlooked.

We know from Harriet Smith, after all, that "the strangest things do take place." And the letters, for all their limitations and non sequiturs, do confirm this, never more than at the very end, when after complaining briefly about something that Cassandra thought later to excise, Austen determinedly changes direction, becoming the writer who in looking backward is always looking to something new and unappreciated:

You will find Captain . . . a very respectable, well-meaning man, without much manner, his wife and sister all good humour and obligingness, and I hope (since the fashion allows it) with rather longer petticoats than last year. (1995, 343)

It goes without saying that, stylistically, we are as close to the novels in this last letter as we are in any of the others, in part because the addressee—the daughter of one her brother's business partners—was someone whom Austen felt obliged (in a good way) to stand on form for. As a result we are treated—even amid illness—to an optimism in which growing minute turns out to be precisely that: an attention from which "hope" is extracted not by the prospect of future gratification, but now, more than ever, through a "retrospect" where amplitude is visible—literally fashionable—allowing a "natural, possible, every-day thing" finally to emerge.

4 LORD BYRON AND LADY BYRON

In chapter 15 of Henry James's *The Portrait of a Lady,* Mr. Bantling, the quintessential Englishman, reflects briefly on Americans and their proclivities.[1] Remarking to the writer Henrietta Stackpole, on "that extraordinary American way of yours" where husbands and wives "liv[e] away" from each other, Bantling quickly shifts to the topic of his sister whose acquaintance, he is certain, Miss Stackpole would enjoy making: "She writes herself, you know; but I haven't read everything she has written. It's usually poetry, and I don't go in much for poetry—unless it's Byron. I suppose you think a great deal of Byron in America."[2]

The indices of this innocuous bit of conversation are surprisingly clear in where they point. From the specter of marital separation, to the achievement and renown of Lord Byron, to the interlocutor, whose name temporarily belies her function as a portmanteau character representing American women writers, the not-so-hidden referent is the Byron controversy: the poet's brief marriage to Anne Isabella Milbanke and their ensuing separation, which an American writer with Stackpole's initials rekindled and stoked to a near-frenzy more than a half century after the event. The disrepute into which Harriet Beecher Stowe fell in her dogged advocacy of Lady Byron, whom she befriended in the 1850s, and rushed to defend following the publication of Teresa Guiccioli's well-received memoir of Byron (where Lady Byron figures poorly), is a well-known matter, since it effectively marked the end of Stowe's remarkable run as a writer of consequence. Indeed, what Bantling is all but declaring outright to Stackpole is that in the same way that you think a great deal of Byron in America, you must think comparatively little now of the woman writer who at one time had made as great a difference as any American writer, living or dead.

The zero-sum logic governing Stowe's relationship to Lord Byron points to the way Byron and his poetry had become dissociated. Bantling's calculus has less to do with his implicit claim that Byron is too great and important a writer to be reproached than with his more explicit sense of the ascendance of the "Byronic" on which the poet's posthumous ability to fend off Stowe's attack (specifically the charge of incest) depended. James returned to this very subject in "The Aspern Papers," the germ for which came from Byron, again, and more immediately from his surviving lover, Claire Clairmont, who lived to an old age in Florence, where James had unknowingly passed her door on numerous occasions.[3] Like that story's narrator, whose interest in the poet Jeffrey Aspern is lodged primarily in Aspern's aura rather than in what he wrote, Mr. Bantling's blanket admiration of a poet whose appeal to him is largely unpoetical speaks as much again to a Byronic hegemony as to the way Byron's art had been overtaken by mythology. If Stowe was the manifest loser in her engagement with a poet long-deceased, long-martyred, and long-mythologized, she shares that loss with Byron himself, whose vindication was predicated as much on the poetry he originally produced as on his mystification by popular sentiment.

In returning to the Byron controversy, and to the short, unhappy marriage that provoked it, I will be exploring several issues, the most important being the "singular," everyday world of relation that the marriage represented for Byron, both beforehand, where marriage was an abstraction performed in correspondence with Milbanke and viewed—proleptically and then retrospectively—through the lens of historical distance; and afterwards, when the Byron marriage and the world it figured was quite literally a history of missed opportunities that the poet contrived to recapture and to reinscribe in the endless conversation that is *Don Juan*. Consequently, the distinctly finite, largely epistolary, conversation that constituted the courtship was more than a trial run at marriage, particularly as the opposite of what Byron disparagingly called "love;" it proved a stay against a future that, on the relational front and in the contemporaneous Eastern Tales, was devoid of either hope or possibility. What is not in dispute, or of interest really—though it formed the core of the reaction against Stowe—are the material and recoverable facts of the Byrons' marriage. Stowe's principal claim, that Byron committed incest with his half-sister Augusta Leigh before and during his brief marriage, and that this activity, in conjunction with behavior that was erratic and intolerable, made the separation inevitable, was pretty much as she recounts (or as Lady Byron told her). There may well have been other factors at work, including certain sexual practices that the omnisexual Byron introduced and that Lady Byron may have found abhorrent.[4] But whatever the cause or complex of causes at work in the separation, two things are inescapably clear: the Byrons were dispositionally unsuited (or ill-adapted, as Lady Byron earlier put it); and the onus for the mismatch, independent of any intended malice or even greed, rested largely with Byron, and with his failure, finally, to be anything but Byronic.

The various attempts, then, by both Byron and his supporters to represent Lady Byron as an uncompromising prig—a representation that Stowe abets even as she contests it—reflect certain cultural imperatives to which Lady Byron may have conformed, but not without resisting. Similarly, the accompanying version of Byron as a genius at odds with the claims and restraints of domesticity—a position advanced by his friend Thomas Moore and assimilated by Mr. Bantling and by Stowe's opponents on both sides of the Atlantic—belies the poet's commitment, in theory, to certain possibilities and ways of being that the marriage of two people might conceivably foster.

That the Byrons proved unequal to such prospects, that their experiment quickly deteriorated to a degree that made them assimilable in kind to codes and commonplaces that the Byron controversy would draw upon even after both principals were dead, does not diminish either the prospect or its centrality to Byron's greatest achievement, which engages an auditor who—animus aside—had arguably worn the face and spoken the words of Annabella Milbanke. Nor does it validate Mr. Bantling's position and that of countless others for whom Byron is chiefly a discourse where there is simply no place for the domestic. What it does is shed light on what was always a fundamental distinction between the "Byronic," to which the poet gave sustenance in this and other occasions, and what is readable in Byron in the interval (1811–15) when he sought with considerable determination to marry. Here, in the sway of what may best be described as proleptic nostalgia, marriage would be suddenly fathomable and, like the monetary fortune of which Byron was in quest, valuable, but as a history of missed opportunities.

II

The details of Byron's courtship of and brief marriage to the wealthy and precocious heiress, whom he cheekily dubbed the "Princess of Parallelograms" in recognition of her mathematical abilities (more on this shortly), have been often told and require only the briefest summary. Involved in a destructive, if wildly exciting, affair with the married and obsessive Lady Caroline Lamb, Byron was instructed, cajoled and otherwise persuaded by Lady Caroline's mother-in-law, Lady Melbourne, to redirect his energies toward marriage and to one woman in particular. This was the highly intelligent, somewhat sheltered Miss Milbanke, the only child of Lady Melbourne's brother and an heiress to her father's legacy as well as to the considerable fortune of her childless uncle and aunt. Encumbered by debt—even at the height of his popularity, having recently published the first two cantos of the best-selling *Childe Harold's Pilgrimage*—Byron undoubtedly found the prospect of fiscal emancipation enticing. But he was consumed in his moment of fame with other "pursuits" to which marriage was anything but congenial. These included not only Lady Caroline but a variety of other, mostly older, women as well, from the Whig hostess Lady Oxford to Lady Frances Webster to (possibly) Lady Melbourne herself. Indeed, marriage of the companionate variety was probably as exotic to the twenty-five-year-old aristocrat as both Byron and his fictions (in Peter Manning's phrase)[5] were to his adoring, largely domesticated readership, which included not just Milbanke but the young Harriet Beecher.[6]

That Byron took Lady Melbourne's advice and allowed the relationship with Annabella to unfold would seem to support the argument that the marriage was a pecuniary matter for him, or, as Elizabeth Cady Stanton later observed, a crude exchange where "he married her for money, she him for a title."[7] And this interpretation, with certain modifications, remains posterity's verdict. My interests, then, are with what posterity has missed in uncanny similarity to Byron himself: specifically the parallel world that marriage came to represent as a missed opportunity and, for my purposes now, a missed opportunity in advance of eventually becoming one.

An examination of the letters that passed between Byron and Milbanke, between Byron and Lady Melbourne, and between Lady Caroline Lamb and all of the parties—not to mention the ways in which these letters were often available to readers to whom they were not addressed—makes this episode in Byron's life read like an epistolary novel, with the scheming Lady Melbourne in the role of Laclos's Madame de Merteuil (as Lady Byron would eventually note).[8] But the "theoretical" dimension of the exchange with Milbanke tilts elsewhere: toward a world and more immediately a "present" that Byron's writing and thinking, whether in the Eastern Tales or in "conversation" with Milbanke herself, inevitably turns.[9] Were Byron not a writer, or a relatively minor one, his life in letters, literally and figuratively, would be a somewhat puzzling sidebar to the "life of Sensation" for which he is almost as famous. But precisely because the relationship with Annabella marks a surprising convergence of the aspects of Byron's life that are generally opaque to both biographers and literary scholars, it bears directly on the scene of Byron thinking, where the courtship and whatever was projected through it actively contest the easy homology between "Byron" and his poetry that Bantling, Moore, and Stowe all espouse, and that the poet, for his part, was happy to let persist.

That Byron and his eventual fiancée spent virtually no time alone prior to her acceptance of his proposal and, even more, that their on-again off-again courtship over two years was almost exclusively epistolary, lends support to the argument that the relationship was circumscribed by Byron's financial worries and by Lady Byron's self-centered naïveté in advance of what Stanton later called her "cold indifference" (Ammons [ed.] 1980, 174). But what this underscores as well was the relationship's speculative dimension, both in opposition to the various physical encounters to which Byron was accustomed, where sex and some asymmetry were usually intertwined, and in conjunction with the retrospection, however contrived, where marriage—in both the letters and, more dramatically, the poems written during the courtship—remains an object of reflection and already a matter of history.

Abstraction was hardly sufficient in sustaining the brief marriage, which foundered on several shoals, most decisively the incest that Byron reverted to in typically regressive fashion.[10] Thus the separation that had earlier performed as a premonition and an aid to reflection not only came to agonistic fulfillment in the year or so during which the Byrons cohabited; it also consolidated the Byronic Byron to a degree that the tension, as Stowe representatively termed it, of "the pure and impure,"[11] was resolved in favor of the latter, and in a way that only death in a liberatory cause would eventually reverse. This is precisely where Bantling and readers like him enter the controversy, and where Stowe also enters, even as the incest had been a secret until she disclosed it. In making the Byronic a contested category according to its measures of purity and adulteration, what the long-standing controversy could not grasp, largely because Byron could not seize the opportunity himself, was the challenge that marriage—and the genuinely queer possibilities it limned—posed to the standard vocabularies of value and virtue. But this is just another way of saying that a surprising number of readers—on *both* sides of the question and the Atlantic—did not go in much for poetry, unless it was Byron.

III

Annabella Milbanke's "first impressions" of Byron clearly demonstrate the Byron effect in the wake of *Childe Harold*, where both the poem's "delineation of deep feeling" and certain mannerisms at cross-purposes are transferred to the poet himself, whom Milbanke encountered for the first time at Lady Caroline Lamb's in 1812:[12]

His mouth continually betrays the acrimony of his spirit. I should judge him sincere and independent—Sincere at least in society as far as he can be, whilst dissimulating the violence of his scorn. He very often hides his mouth with his hand when speaking. He professed himself very partial to Music, and said he could not understand how any one could be indifferent to it. It appeared to me that he tried to controul his natural sarcasm and vehemence as much as he could, in order not to offend, but at times his lips thickened with disdain, and his eyes rolled impatiently. Indeed the scene was calculated to show human absurdities. (Elwin 1962, 105)

In noting the slippage between Byron's sensibility—chiefly his love of music—and his demonstrable contempt, Milbanke joins with Stowe and others in underscoring the similarities between Byron and the persona of *Childe Harold,* who reflects the "general character of [Byron's] mind" in always "prov[ing]" that he *can* feel nobly but . . . has discouraged his own goodness" (Elwin 1962, 106). Accordingly—and in a spirit not unlike Byron's as she construes it—Milbanke "did not seek an introduction to him" on this occasion, "for all the women were absurdly courting him, and trying to *deserve* the lash of his satire." "Besides," she adds, "I cannot worship talents that are unconnected with the love of man, nor be captivated by that Genius which is barren in blessings." Subscribing to the notion of Byron as a tantalizing mixture of good and bad, Milbanke is equally careful to announce her independence in ways that resemble Byron, hinting at an equivalency, even a compatibility. Thus while she makes "no offering at the shrine of Childe Harold," she "will not," she adds, "refuse the acquaintance if it comes in my way" (Elwin 1962, 106).

The "acquaintance" came "in" her "way" some weeks later when, at supper at Lady Cowper's, Milbanke and Byron had "some very pleasing conversation" in which Byron "address[ed her] with great respect" on the cobbler-poet Joseph Blacket, whom Milbanke had patronized and Byron had recently mocked in *English Bards and Scotch Reviewers* and elsewhere. This leads to a somewhat different view of Byron, where he is suddenly "repentant for the evil he has done" (in criticizing writers like Blacket) but not so repentant as to be unByronic. Conceding that he is "without exception . . . more agreeable in conversation than any person I ever knew," Milbanke continues to view him in conventional terms: "I think of him that he is a very bad, very good man. Impulses of sublime goodness burst through his malevolent *habits*" (Elwin 1962, 109). No one would accuse the young Milbanke of being similarly malevolent. But her conventional view of Byron is curiously mimetic in adopting or in recapitulating a critical posture. Things take a turn in their next meeting amid a literary conversation that included Samuel Rogers, where Byron managed to dissociate himself from his fictions and hence from the Byronic. In response to an "interesting question . . . discussed in the course of conversation, 'Must a poet have felt, in order to make his readers feel,'" Byron, writes Milbanke, "asserted the negative" (110).

Milbanke's view of Byron was suddenly transformed, so much that she was, as Elwin speculates, cautioned by her mother against becoming too involved. "Conversation," however, was holding sway. "He is," she writes to her mother,

indeed persecuted to the greatest degree by those who know nothing of him except what they have learned from prejudice. On the other side he is as violently & unjustly exalted, but this affords him no gratification, for he has too much penetration not to perceive that his *talent* alone is considered, and that there is no *friendship* in all this *mouth-honour*. He has no comfort but in *confidence*, to soothe his deeply wounded mind. I consider it an act of humanity and a Christian duty not to deny him any *temporary* satisfaction he can derive from my acquaintance, though I shall not seek to encrease it. He is not a dangerous person to me. (Elwin 1962, 111)

If this "Byron" is the counter to Lady Caroline Lamb's "mad—bad—and dangerous to know," it is easy to see why this version of the poet, and the relationship or parity it projects, have also vanished from memory. In contrast to the Byron, who is both persecuted and exalted (often in the same "mouth-honour"), the Byron of Milbanke's free indirect discourse is a potentially domesticated figure with whom "friendship" is a possibility.

It's not clear that Byron was immediately aware of or affected by this revisioning or by Milbanke's sudden magnanimity. But his conversations with her clearly made an impression. Writing to none other than Caroline Lamb herself, he describes her as a "very extraordinary girl" with "much strength & variety of thought," and enjoins Lady Caroline to communicate "as much of this to Miss M[ilbanke] as you think proper." Equally telling are his concluding comments: "I have no desire to be better acquainted with Miss Milbank, she is too good for a fallen spirit to know or wish to know, & I should like her more if she were less perfect" (*Letters*, 2: 175–76).[13]

Regardless of whether we take Byron at his word regarding any future acquaintance, the more important feature is the prevailing sense that a relationship, now or in the future, is foredoomed, creating a pattern where union and separation are condensed or, as appears here, mutually dependent. If Byron cannot imagine a "better acquaintance," he cannot, in virtually the same stroke, imagine not pursuing one. The trajectories are linked not because Byron is somehow incapable of being anything but a roué (as he often calls himself). They are linked rather by logic of the "extraordinary," which turns out to be more like the "ordinary" squared, or, as Byron both intuits and gradually demonstrates, the opposite of everything familiar or customary. Moreover, when we consider the retrospection necessary to its focalization in the first place, this "opposite" is more than just the opposite of custom or probability for a fallen spirit. It amounts to a missed opportunity, in which the extraordinary that *is* the ordinary (as both Jane Bennett and Stanley Cavell describe it) comes to view as an order of "uncounted experience" and eventually a desideratum of which Byron is in "quest"—but always belatedly.

"Quest" may be a little strong. Still, there is little doubt that what counted as marriage for Byron, as he came increasingly to pursue it, was a "retrospect"—indeed a history of missed opportunities—that managed counterintuitively to leverage future prospects. In arguably his most unambiguous and unabashed expression of interest to Milbanke, where she is implicitly described as "the *only* woman to whom I ever seriously pretended as a wife," he immediately shifts from reflections on their "intercourse," which had grown "nearer" and more intimate in recent weeks, to noting the "value" of what he had obviously "lost—or rather never found" (*Letters*, 3: 178). This resignation was driven by worries that Milbanke had been entertaining other suitors and by the shadow of her rejection of his first proposal, awkwardly advanced through Lady Melbourne. But the dynamic of both a missed opportunity, and one sufficiently modeled by recent intercourse to count as retrospect of what might have been, is not just broadly characteristic of Byron's way with marriage generally, where he can "value" and therefore seek only what is already "lost." It is equally instrumental in what "marriage" or "intercourse" or "conversation" figured for him. "Separation," in other words, marks the distance, but also the proximity, of a parallel order that "intercourse" past, passing or to come brings to view.

Byron gets at this in his most famous and ultimately fatalistic description of his future wife. Writing to Lady Melbourne only days after his initial proposal was rejected, he thanks her for her "efforts with my Princess of Parallelograms," whose "proceedings," he adds, "are quite rectangular, or rather we are two parallel lines prolonged to infinity side by side but never to meet" (*Letters*, 2: 231). As in the later letter, where what "is lost" is never to be found (even as Byron may have believed otherwise), the description here of infinite or eternal separation is more than a grim premonition. It is preliminary to looking *back* to what, in the figure, is present and ongoing, suggesting a "willingness for the everyday" (in Cavell's term) where what is passing, elusive, and largely unappreciated is both notable and sustainable.

The prospect of never meeting speaks most directly, of course, to the impossibility of erotic closure in what Byron typically calls "love." But the fact that, in the figure, the "Princess" is forever present, and that "intercourse," all separation aside, is structurally alive, marks a paradox regarding the relationship itself, which comes to life as "separation" or in the version of marriage that Eric Walker, channeling Cavell, has described as "remarriage" or as "remarriage, day after day." Cavell is surprisingly dour on the point. "Marriage," he writes, is "an estate meant not as a distraction from the pain of constructing happiness from a helpless, absent world, but as the scene in which the chance for happiness is shown as the mutual acknowledgment of separateness, in which the prospect is not for the passing of years (until death parts us) but for the willing repetition of days, willingness for the everyday (until our true minds become unreadable to one another)" (Cavell 1988, 178).

An existential as well as a temporal distance, in which "days" or (or in Byron's case) "lines" are "historical everydays" (Cavell 205, 130), such "separateness" is just as instrumental in mapping a continuum where what is "passing" and immediate is also "lost" and the more valuable as a result. Thus as Byron continues to pursue Milbanke, he goes from generalizing about marriage as a convenience in which "all wives would be much the same" and, in the case of a "pretty wife," "something for the fastidious vanity of a roué to retire upon" to regarding marriage as a practice in which difference and some kind of distance abide. "What I want," he writes Lady Melbourne, "is a companion—a friend—rather than a sentimentalist" (*Letters*, 4: 34). Byron might have also said, "a friend rather than a moralist." Although morality is frequently at the center of his letters to Milbanke, generally at her instigation, their language of religion bespeaks what Bharat Tandon has dubbed the "morality of conversation" (rather than the converse),[14] which, with the eye of an historian who has "seen enough of love matches—& of all matches," Byron implicitly links to "the common lot of happy couples" (4: 34). When "intercourse" turns, as it does invariably, to Byron's "sentiments concerning Religion," "Christianity" is a topic of conversation with little relation to the Church as such. "Do not suppose I have a fancy to convert you," Milbanke writes, "first, I do not believe you need conversion—secondly, I do not believe it in my power to convert from infidelity . . . I am not a bigot to Church Establishments, which in my opinion deviate widely from the purity of the Christian dispensation—and I am disposed to spare those who doubt, because I *have* doubted" (Elwin 1962, 171).

And Byron reciprocates in a series of letters on religion and related matters that stand apart from his usual correspondence, constituting a rehearsal of sorts that marriage itself would fail to repeat. It was more that—shadowed by separation and by the abiding prospect of rejection on either side—the courtship achieved in advance what marriage or friendship or companionship continued to represent in theory, giving just enough sense of what marriage might be, or what it might have been, to make it a missed opportunity in advance of becoming one.

Letters to Milbanke written over three months in 1813 in response to her renewed interest bring this dynamic, and the friendship it postulates, into particular relief. The first of these, which is largely a rehash of the events and feelings leading to Byron's initial proposal to the only "woman with whom there appeared to [him] a prospect of rational happiness," is notable for its stutter in the name of "Friendship":

it is a feeling towards you with which I cannot trust myself—I doubt whether I could help loving you—but I may appeal to my conduct since our eclaircissement for the proof—that whatever my feelings may be—they will exempt you from persecution—but I cannot yet profess indifference—and I fear that must be the first step—at least in some points—from what I feel to that which you wish me to feel. (*Letters*, 3: 98–99)

If with Byron's metaphor in mind, this expatiation reads like "one step forward two steps back," it is largely because—in the related manner of Zeno's paradox—the number of steps between what Byron feels and what Milbanke wishes him to feel (or so he assumes) is infinite and of a piece with the parallelism that defines "friendship" as the opposite of sex. Part of the problem is that feeling and rationality are antipodes. But the real problem is that the problem itself is in many ways the solution, liberating Byron to a "cand[or]" (or an affect at any rate) and a distinctly measured, companionate eloquence that is unusual.

In a succeeding letter, written just six days later on August 31st, he returns to the scene of Milbanke's rejection, taking responsibility for the abruptness of his initial overture and, in an effort to revive things, expressing pride in the "regard" she had "bestowed on [him]" along with the resolve to avoid "the loss of it by vain attempts to engage your Affection." A pattern clearly is emerging where "correspondence & intercourse" are not just circumscribed by "limits," which Byron promises in closing not to infringe, but an outer limit as well. "I perceive," Byron continues, "that I *begin* my letter with saying 'I do not wish draw you into a correspondence' and *end* by almost soliciting it—admirably consistent—but it is human nature—& you will forgive it—if not you can punish. . . ."(*Letters*, 3: 103–4). The closing dash may not strictly signify the parallel line of Byron in "correspondence" versus the oblique line of Byron in love. Yet it works with characteristic circularity to keep things both consistent and in the moment rather than "progressing" to an interstices where "love" and "marriage," as Byron observes in *Don Juan*, are impossible to "combine."

Thus Byron opts in this moment of clarity and, in the succession of "presents" to which it amounts, to pursue "marriage": most immediately in correspondence where we discover him in remarkably companionable form and eventually as a goal in which marriage very quickly became the antithesis to what friendship— or what amounted in this interval to "marriage day after day"—had briefly retrieved from abstraction. Still, in the three-month-long exchange prompted by Milbanke's renewed interest, Byron remains, even in the face of queries over his apparent cynicism and lack of faith, open, undefended and genuinely relieved or so it seems to be in friendship rather than in love. In a long letter written on September 6th, which begins by discussing "friendship" (and implicitly their friendship) as something far rarer and more valuable than "love in this best of all possible worlds," the expatiation ranges from Byron's "despondency," which he counters by describing himself "as very facetious personage," to his ostensible "prejudice against" women, which he both rebuts by praising women and admits to being a problem that he (and others) must fix: "I think the worst woman that ever existed would have made a *man* of very passable reputation—they are all better than us—& their faults such as they are must originate with ourselves" (*Letters*, 3: 108). Finally, in discussing London "society" and its various "agremens," he makes a famously Byronic statement about life in the world that is typically taken as gospel even as he is contriving—in the present context—to move beyond it:

The great object of life is Sensation—to feel that we exist—even though in pain—it is this "craving void", which drives us to Gaming—to Battle—to Travel—to intemperate but keenly felt pursuits of every description whose principal attraction is the agitation inseparable from their accomplishment.—I am but an awkward dissembler—as my friend you will bear with my faults—I shall have the less constraint in what I say to you—firstly because I may derive some benefit from your observations—& next because I am very sure *you* can never be perverted by any paradoxes of mine. (*Letters*, 3: 108–9)

If this looks like a fairly conventional plea for a refuge from the seas of sensation and more broadly Byronism, it differs in one critical respect already evident in a style notable in its freedom from agitation. Framed by the capacity to describe it in just this way, the "Byronic everyday," involving pursuits of every kind, is not only constrained to this moment of articulation and to an interlocutionary continuum; it is also pitched in the process toward a very different "ordinary" that Byron is "in quest of" rather than in "pursuit."

Byron continues on the topic of his "restless doctrines" in a succeeding letter, contrasting the experience of being "on the ocean no matter how stormy" to the "insipid shores by which it is surrounded." Seeking to counter and to placate Milbanke, whose worry he appreciates and understands ("You don't like my 'restless doctrines'—I should be very sorry if *you* did"), the anchorage he implicitly postulates is arguably a third way, where sincerity and indecision (Byron's terms) are sufficient to ward off "stagnat[ion]," even when the topic turns to religion:

I was bred in Scotland among Calvinists in the first part of my life—which gave me a dislike to that persuasion. . . . My opinions are quite undecided. . . . I believe doubtless in God—& should happy to be convinced of much more—if I do not at present place implicit faith on tradition & revelation of any human creed I hope it is not from a want of reverence for the Creator but the created. . . . but the *moral* of Christianity is perfectly beautiful—& the very sublime of Virtue. (*Letters*, 3: 119–20)

If Byron is being unByronic, even apologizing for being "[un] amusing," it is because the exchange has effectively replaced one void, the craving that opposes and defines stagnation, with a void akin to what Thomas Dumm, in describing the "ordinary," has called the "unknown" to which "stagnation" and "boredom" remain something of a threshold experience.

Not surprisingly, the "unknown" or the unexperienced is where Byron turns next. Confessing his dislike of "society" or of "mixed company" as something he can bear for no more than "two hours," he projects a relational alternative that he initially extrapolates from friendships with "two or three men" before turning, in sympathy with Milbanke, whose friend had recently left England, to the "friendship of *good* women—more sincere than that of men—& certainly more tender." Unable to connect the two (this is, after all, the "unknown"), he digresses briefly to *The Bride of Abydos*, the "heroic" poem he is "scribbling," and to the preceding one, *The Giaour*, before broaching the possibility of meeting Milbanke when she is next in "town," adding that he is not in pursuit but confident that "we understand each other perfectly" and "may talk to each other occasionally without exciting speculation." "[T]he worst that can be said," he continues, "is—that I *would*—& you wont—and in this respect *you* can hardly be the sufferer—and I *shant*. . . . I shall keep out of the way" (*Letters*, 3: 159–60).

There is no question that much of this is complex diplomacy. However just as important is the relational horizon it projects, where mutual understanding and an otherwise unknown friendship suddenly coexist, making the brief digression to the Eastern Tales and to *The Giaour* in particular a good deal less puzzling. Although *The Bride of Abydos* (its title notwithstanding) is the only Eastern Tale that is *not* about relation on the everyday model that Byron is tentatively projecting, *The Giaour* is very much about the "unknown," which, there and in the two other Eastern Tales, is either missed or unrealized or unrepresentable. The letter to Milbanke that follows engages two related matters, then: the degree to which their "very intercourse" (or "nearer acquaintance)" has "convinc[ed]" Byron "of the value of what [he has] lost"; and the historical distance now through which the "singularity of [their] situation"—unprecedented because it is *already* a precedent—is recognizable and describable (*Letters*, 3: 178–79).

Consequently if it is "too late" for the situation to lead to marriage (which Byron claims to have given up on), there is time apparently for it to function in a cognate capacity and as an opportunity all the same.

The word *patience* reminds me of ye. book I am to send you—it shall be ordered to Seaham tomorrow.—I shall be most happy to see any thing of your writing—of what I have already seen you once heard my favourable & sincere opinion.—I by no means rank poetry or poets high on the scale of intellect—this may look like Affectation—but it is my real opinion . . . they say Poets never or rarely go *mad*—Cowper & Collins are instances to the contrary . . . it is however to be remarked that they rarely do—but are generally so near it—that I cannot help thinking rhyme is so far useful in anticipating & preventing the disorder. (*Letters*, 3: 179)

Byron goes on to praise the "action[s]" of soldiers and politicians in contrast to the "speculations of . . . mere dreamers of another existence" and to lament

his tendencies toward "speculation" and to being a "mere spectator." Nevertheless the commitment to exchange, in which he is suddenly a diminished figure
for whom writing is therapy and a stay against "disorder," involves speculation
of a different kind. It involves the parallelism that, in addition to marking a
continuum (and the letter is very clearly in medias res), is marked equally by
a sense of difference, or separation (in Cavell's sense) and by a "patience" with
the "unreadable" (Cavell)—or queer—that his "willingness" for the readable
underscores.

IV

The letters that Byron wrote to Milbanke between this series and their marriage
in January 1815 took on a different tone as marriage became a likelihood rather
than a missed opportunity. The "singularity" of the 1813 exchange as the marriage that wasn't thus not only proved instrumental in converting a lost cause,
however generative, into what was eventually a failed "estate"; it was also, in a
related register, the complement to the equally "theoretical" Eastern Tales, where
the world of relation that the correspondence with Milbanke limned as something lost or missed, is a central and animating concern. Composed six months
before the exchange of letters in the fall, *The Giaour* engages with the letters in
two related ways: in presenting marriage as a missed opportunity (the Giaour's
potential partner has been killed); and in making the paean to monogamy toward the poem's close a formal rejoinder to a work whose multiple perspectives
effect a "restlessness" in contrast to an "unknown" for which "stagnation" is no
longer the right word.

It is tempting to regard this multi-voiced narrative as an alternative and possibly a corrective to the monologic tendencies of romantic poetry generally. Yet
the more important point about *The Giaour*'s "disjointed fragments" (as Byron
called them) involves a certain stagnation or repetition, beginning with the
male principals who murder out of love, and extending to the narrative itself,
which is summarized in the opening advertisement, and *repeated*, then, from a
variety of mostly "Orientalized" perspectives. Set in the Levant when parts of
it belonged to Venice, the poem (as the advertisement recounts) centers on the
story of a female slave, Leila, who falls in love with a young Venetian infidel (the
"Giaour") and whose murder by her master and former lover in punishment
for infidelity is later avenged by the eponymous hero. The poem ultimately relocates to a monastery, where in the final phase the Giaour speaks to a confessor

not only about his love but also about his adversary Hassan, whose position he could easily have occupied:

> Still, ere thou dost condemn me—pause—
> Not mine the act, though I the cause;
> Yet did he but what I had done
> Had she been false to more than one;
> Faithless to him—he gave the blow,
> But true to me—I laid him low;
> Howe'er deserv'd her doom might be,
> Her treachery was truth to me;
> To me she gave her heart, that all
> Which tyranny can ne'er enthrall. (1060–69)[15]

In capturing the synonymity with his counterpart, the Giaour undermines any argument for repetition with a difference. Nevertheless his assertion throughout that Leila's love for him was a matter of choice or "affective individualism," makes the "Oriental tale" an allegory of contemporary conjugal relations in which a companionate, monogamous relationship emerges retrospectively.[16]

Especially noteworthy is the Giaour's imagery in reference to the marriage that wasn't. Here he is out in front of Byron in refusing to "alight on" what, about a year later, the latter had described as "the nearest *perch*" (*Letters*, 4: 111). Byron made this famous statement to Lady Melbourne at a moment when he was torn between "my A"—Augusta—-with whom he was incestuously involved and "your Niece," whom he would propose to a second time in September and, assuming "succe[ss] in that quarter," would "give up all other pursuits" in deference to. "[M]y wife if she had common sense," he wrote, "would have more power over me—than any other whatsoever—for my heart always alights on the nearest *perch*—if it is withdrawn—it goes God knows where" (*Letters*, 4: 111–12). At a moment when marriage had migrated from a "lost" horizon "never to be found"—save in the way it had been abstracted—into something imminent, Byron proved to be both a weak theorist and a bad ornithologist. Untrue to the species he claims metaphorically to be imitating, the confusion of wife and perch is equally at variance with what his own hero had recently differentiated from stagnation and from something strictly knowable:

> 'Tis true, that, like the bird of prey,
> With havoc I have mark'd my way—

> But this was taught to me by the dove—
> To die—and know no second love.
> This lesson yet hath man to learn,
> Taught by the thing he dares to spurn—
> The bird that sings within the brake,
> The swan that swims upon the lake,
> One mate, and one alone, will take.
> And let the fool still prone to range,
> And sneer on all who cannot change—
> Partake his jest with boasting boys,
> I envy not his varied joys—
> But deem such feeble, heartless man,
> Less than yon solitary swan—
> Far—far beneath the shallow maid
> He left believing and betray'd.
> Such shame at least was never mine—
> Leila—each thought was only thine!—
> My good, my guilt, my weal, my woe,
> My hope on high—my all below.
> Earth holds no other like to thee,
> Or if it doth, in vain for me—
> For worlds I dare not view the dame
> Resembling thee, yet not the same.
> The very crimes that mar my youth
> This bed of death—attest my truth—
> 'Tis all too late—thou wert—thou art
> The cherished madness of my heart! (1163–91)

The transformation of monogamy on the avian model into a grand passion is certainly an attention grabber. But in confirmation of what has emerged only in retrospect ("'Tis all too late") it is necessarily a mixed metaphor. Conferring value on an estate that both genre and custom frame differently, the amalgam speaks mostly to the way the ordinary, as distinct from the familiar, holds forth prospects that are unrepresentable save in these exaggerated terms.

The Corsair and *Lara* engage the issue differently, presenting marital life as a phenomenon closer to the epistolary exchange rather than the prospect/ retrospect that the Giaour all but calls paradise lost. Bracketed—but no longer bounded—by the life of sensation and by the stagnation that, in a virtual gloss, Byron had likened to an "insipid shore," *The Corsair* charts a third way over the pirates' "wild life" of "tumult" and "change" (1.7–8) and the equally codified, in this case moribund, world of domesticity that the corsair Conrad restlessly abandons. The poem's substance, then—the *durée* or time spent with the concubine Gulnare, who rescues Conrad after being saved by him earlier—is more than contingent and seemingly unscripted. It is sufficiently in process to be continued, which Byron doubled down on in allowing the anonymously published *Lara* to be advertised as a sequel even as the hero was significantly transformed. The sequel worked thanks to authorship, which readers instantly recognized, and to certain similarities between the "Byronic" protagonists. But what really made it fly was *The Corsair*'s initial replacement of the Penelope-like figure of Conrad's wife, Medora, with a new partner, who is fully present and removed from her sphere. Unlike the missed opportunity that *The Giaour* idealizes nostalgically and at a distance, the relational opportunity in *The Corsair* is missed by actual emergence now: as an unregulated formation from which the hero finally recoils in affirmation of his masculinity, and as a continuum into which the poem settles in defiance of both gender and genre.[17] Sequel or not, what *Lara* eventually provided was a perspective on this (im)possible history: both as an allegory of marriage/foredoomed, which all of the tales inscribe, and in honor of the Byron courtship, where marriage was primarily a signifier and the exchange with Milbanke, the abiding signified.

The Corsair hews to a now-typical triangulation, involving the Pacha Seyd and the non-Muslim Conrad, who invades the former's citadel and quickly gains the affections of his "Haram queen" (2.224), whose declarations echo Leila's in privileging desire and volition ("I saw thee—loved thee—owe thee all" [3.344]) over her previous, more primitive, coercion. In contrast to the previous tale, which remains an advertisement for Western modernity and its relational centerpiece, *The Corsair* imagines a different configuration in the way fidelity is tried, not just by Gulnare but by the separation of male and female domains generally, which is both a backdrop and increasingly a backstory. What counts as "marriage" in the poem is not Conrad's marriage. What counts, if only as an abstraction, is something more like "remarriage" or marriage "day after day" or even the "mutual acknowledgment of separateness," all figured in the shift to Gulnare and in the dynamic that this reset introduces, in which the hero's self-possession and the imperatives to both closure and homecoming are reciprocally undone.

A good deal of this is sublated in the tale's sensationalism, beginning with Conrad's raid and capture and culminating in his liberation by Gulnare, who eventually murders her master. But the referent becomes clearer when—in further defiance of all codes—Gulnare joins the corsair aboard ship. Here the opportunity of a relationship is suddenly at hand and just as suddenly a matter of history.

> And he was free!—and she for him had given
> Her all on earth, and more than all in heaven!
> And now he turned him to that dark-eyed slave
> Whose brow was bowed beneath the glance he gave,
> Who now seemed changed and humbled:—faint and meek,
> But varying oft the colour of her cheek
> To deeper shades of paleness—all its red
> That fearful spot which stained it from the dead!
> He took that hand—it trembled—now too late—
> So soft in love—so wildly nerved in hate;
> He clasped that hand—it trembled—and his own
> Had lost its firmness, and his voice its tone.
> 'Gulnare!'—but she replied not—'dear Gulnare!'
> She raised her eye—her only answer there—
> At once she sought and sunk in his embrace:
> If he had driven her from that resting place,
> His had been more or less than mortal heart,
> But—good or ill—it bade her not depart.
> Perchance, but for the bodings on his breast,
> His latest virtue then had joined the rest.
> Yet even Medora might forgive the kiss
> That asked from form so fair no more of this,
> The first, the last that Frailty stole from Faith—
> To lips where Love had lavished all his breath,
> To lips—whose broken sighs such fragrance fling,
> As he had fanned them freshly with his wing! (3.529–54)

In recognition of the peculiar infidelity, or acknowledgement of separateness, that the poem postulates, as an alternative mode of relation and an opening onto a different present, the lips that Conrad kisses are, in a slip signaled by the dash after "Faith," Gulnare's and no one else's. Spoken or heard, the lines clearly reference a "faith" to Medora that Conrad breaks in a moment of frailty. But in *reading*, and in the passage from one mode of relation to another, they are immured in a continuous present or series of "nows" following the principals themselves, for whom no two moments or subject-positions, or even a single, extended moment, are necessarily the same.

This is far from an easy place to be and its queerness (for there is no better term) is enhanced by the narrative apparatus, in which Gulnare shifts from an object of beauty (and an apogee by turns of femininity and passivity) to a "homicide" (3.463), and where the hero's action is increasingly consigned to being with her rather than doing. Thus in addition to beginning at the end, where from the moment of Conrad's departure Medora's death and the death of marriage are events waiting to happen, *The Corsair* "end[s]" in medias res—or "at the beginning," as Byron terms it in *Don Juan*—for what appear to be two related reasons. The first is that *The Corsair* is primarily about relation and, as the poem frames it, relation day after day rather than marriage on a codified model. The second is that, as a tale whose business is formally unfinished, *The Corsair* is manifestly about what might have been rather than what is foredoomed. There is pathos to Gulnare and to her valedictory kiss in contrast to Medora, whose consignment to the poem's "meanwhile" indexes a strictly probable world from which the narrative, no less than its protagonist, is in flight.[18] Thus it is the relationship, not the marriage, that proves to be the missed opportunity in nearly the same way that the exchange with Milbanke—what it modeled with marriage as an ostensibly "lost" cause—created a continuum, and a willingness for it, that marriage itself would relegate to abstraction.

The prospect of a sequel extended by ending *The Corsair* in a state of suspension was seized upon, not only to enhance sales, but also by a readership that had to wait until the very end of *Lara* for one to materialize. Here, in one of the great metamorphoses, Lara's page (Kaled) transforms from a male servant into a grieving spouse (presumably Gulnare) in something close to real time:

> He did not dash himself thereby, nor tear
> The glossy tendrils of his raven hair,
> But strove to stand and gaze, but reel'd and fell,
> Scarce breathing more than that he loved so well.
> Than that *he* lov'd! Oh! Never yet beneath
> The breast of man such trusty love may breathe!
> That trying moment hath at once reveal'd

> The secret long and yet but half-conceal'd;
>
> In baring to revive that lifeless breast,
>
> Its grief seem'd ended, but the sex confess'd;
>
> And life return'd, and Kaled felt no shame—
>
> What now to her was Womanhood or Fame? (2.508–19)

Reviewers detected signs of the page's true identity throughout the poem having read it, no doubt, more than once. The *Eclectic Review* (October 1814) took special note of the "unfeminine yet most womanly attachment of Kaled to her master,—unfeminine only in its origin and in the degree of the passion—most womanly in its disinterestedness, secrecy and truth" (397). Still, it is the opacity of the relationship, its impenetrability (in Byron's term), that remains key, especially in aftermath when the interaction of lord and page figures a world whose very possibility—day after day—is no longer in doubt "but half conceal'd" and perforce parallel.

There is also, of course, the matter of the narrative itself, recounting the hero's return to his Spanish domain, where, in defiance of his fellow lords, he finds common cause with his serfs, whom he eventually supports in what turns out to be his last great act. Thus in contrast to *The Corsair*, which for all its verve offers an alternative to the worlds of sensation and stagnation, *Lara* and Lara are mostly indices to something else from which the narrative is principally a distraction. Resorting to a "Byronic" vocabulary in describing the "chang[e]" (1.65) to Lara since he was last in residence, the speaker finds that attributes like the hero's "high demeanour" (1.71) or his secret "wound" (1.76) are limited in their explanatory power:

> All these seem'd his, and something more beneath
>
> Than glance can well reveal, or accent breathe.
>
> Ambition, glory, love, the common aim,
>
> That some can conquer, and that all would claim,
>
> Within his breast appear'd no more to strive,
>
> Yet seem'd as lately they had been alive;
>
> And some deep feeling it were vain to trace
>
> At moments lighten'd o'er his livid face. (1.77–84)

To the list of common traits that Lara no longer displays, there is also, not surprisingly, his rejection of a "destined bride" whom "[a]nother chief" currently "console[s]" (1.35).

While the poem's most enigmatic and therefore prominent feature—even before the reveal—remains the intimacy between Lara and Kaled, it is a relationship that is unwritable until the end, confirming *only then* the mismatch between narrative and the singularity of their situation. There is friction throughout, of course, beginning with the equivalency that Kaled shares with "his" ostensible superior:

> Still there was a haughtiness in all he did,
> A spirit deep that brook'd not to be chid;
> His zeal, though more than that of servile hands,
> In act alone obeys, his air commands;
> As if 'twas Lara's less than *his* desire
> That thus he served, but surely not for hire. (1.558–63)

If this sounds a bit like Captain Delano grappling with Babo in Melville's *Benito Cereno*, it is because, like Delano, for whom any disruption of the status quo is unthinkable, Lara's narrator is poised between a generic mindlessness, where he is in quest of what is not there, and a responsiveness, however inchoate, to what is ongoing and—in its otherness—impossible to conceive. Reflecting on the poem's hero, the speaker notes, that

> in youth all action and all life,
> Burning for pleasure, not averse from strife;
> Woman—the field—the ocean—all that gave
> Promise of gladness, peril of a grave,
> In turn he tried—he ransack'd all below,
> And found his recompense in joy or woe,
> No tame, trite medium; for his feelings sought
> In that intenseness an escape from thought. (1.115–22)

Unable to surmise what Lara calls thinking, the narrator does better in defining what "thought" opposes, beginning with certain romance conventions and continuing in the sensations and intensities where the *abyme* of thinking is variously foreshortened.

What Lara registers, as hero and focal point, is more than just an honorable, narratable, reluctance to fight duels or to support violent insurrection or to behave in ways that are strictly authoritarian. He registers, both in partnership with the poem and against it, a willingness for "something more," which is abstracted and "thought" in the impenetrable, unreadable world that he disappears into and in the "marriage" that finally figures it. Mortally wounded and speaking only to Kaled, Lara's "dying tones are in that other tongue"—what Byron would later call "the language of another world" (*Manfred* 3.4.7)—

> To which some strange remembrance wildly clung.
> They spake of other scenes, but what—is known
> To Kaled, whom their meaning reach'd alone;
> And he replied, though faintly, to their sound,
> While gaz'd the rest in dumb amazement round:
> They seem'd even then–that twain—unto the last
> To half forget the present in the past;
> To share between themselves some separate fate,
> Whose darkness none beside should penetrate. (2.444–53)

If the leap from this charged scene to the "conversation" with Milbanke seems too abrupt at this point, it is the case too that the separateness of *that* situation and the other world it figures, also involved a present in the past—and a past in the present—that was "half-forgotten": both as a "strange remembrance" of what might have been and as a series, more immediately, of "historical everydays" where what was missed, and foredoomed, was reenacted and briefly recovered. The concluding phase of *Lara*, featuring an outed, grieving Kaled attached to the site where Lara "lay his drooping head upon her knee" (2.613), may seem conventional and somewhat thoughtless in its representation of grief and loss. Yet the melancholy to which the poem reverts remains, in its filiation with the impenetrable and queer, a nostalgia for "what might have been." This is not only because the relationship has been foreclosed upon but also and, more important, because it is foreclosed at the very instant of disclosure: a longing for "what is," as Byron termed it, rather than for what was.[19]

V

Of the several poems and extracts associated with the Byrons' separation the most infamous is the poem "Fare Thee Well!" that Byron sent to Lady Byron immediately after their agreement was drafted. It is not "among Byron's most distinguished" works,[20] and its interest for my purposes lies in the parameters it assigns to the marriage controversy, which only Byron, in the end, was able to transgress. Beginning with an epigraph from Coleridge's *Christabel*, referring to a broken friendship between *men*, the speaker quickly settles into a more predictable posture, from his "undying" grief over the prospect that he and Lady Byron "no more may meet" (27–28) to his love for a daughter whom he may never see again:

> And when thou would solace gather—
>> When our child's first accents flow—
> Wilt thou teach her to say 'Father!'
>> Though his care she must forego?
> When her little hands shall press thee—
>> When her lip to thine is prest—
> Think of him whose prayer shall bless thee—
>> Think of him thy love has bless'd.
> Should her lineaments resemble
>> Those thou never more may'st see—
> Then my heart will softly tremble
>> With a pulse yet true to me,—
> All my faults—perchance thou knowest—
>> All my madness—none can know;
> All my hopes—where'er thou goest—
>> Wither—yet with *thee* they go. (33–48)

The turn to the speaker's faults and to a depth that none can possibly fathom is accompanied, not surprisingly, by a Byron who is steadfast in recognizing Lady Byron as his main chance. While this may bear on the opportunity to which marriage was always tantamount, it is insufficient in preventing Byron from making his solitary way:

> Fare thee well!—thus disunited—
>> Torn from every nearer tie—
> Seared in heart—and lone—and blighted,
>> More than this, I scarce can die. (57–60)

Leveraged by vocabularies like this one and by the antithetical, if related, discourse of domesticity, the controversy over the Byrons' separation worked primarily to probabilize what, at a different moment, was strikingly singular. Neither Thomas Moore's eventual description of the poet as a genius unsuited to "the calm affections and comforts . . . of domestic life"[21] nor Stowe's reiteration of the "very good, very bad" Byron managed to approximate what the Byrons—and

Byron in particular—were discovering or grappling with even as it clearly shows what they were pushing back against. For Byron this struggle was between the world of relation that courtship abstracted and the enticements of celebrity at a young age. It was easier to remain the unpredictable genius in trivial pursuit than to be Milbanke's friend, just as it proved easier for Lady Byron to become an icon of domesticity than to remain double-parked alongside the claims of morality and Christian virtue. There was much to be gained in this suspension and in the "situation" generally that the courtship incubated, just as there was something to domestic relations that was not only a challenge to Byron's inconsistency at the time but continuous as well with the version of "hope" or possibility to which he was committed, and for which quotidian life, along with poetry or poetical feeling, remained a site.

In a memo entitled "What is poetry?—The feeling of a Former world and Future," written during the composition of *Don Juan* in 1821, Byron returned once more to the life of sensation and to the "doubt or sorrow" that intrude "at the very height of desire and human pleasure." Although connected in some measure to "a fear of what is to come," what intrudes on such a life is more immediately a "doubt of what *is*" or, as Byron elaborates it, "a retrospect to the past, leading to a prognostication of the future." The "future," and the basis accordingly of what Byron proceeds to call "Hope," is not strictly hypothetical. It is linked to a "retrospect" and, by extension, to a "present," whose futurity *in relation* to the "past" maps a continuum, where the "present in the past" (to quote *Lara*) and the present that was once (and always) the future are the only "hope" or possibility there is. "It is useless," he continues, "to say where the Present is, for most of us know." However, in the temporal configuration he is working through, it is precisely this uncanny knowledge of "what is," no matter its obscurity, that remains key. For if "what predominates in memory" is ultimately "*Hope baffled,*" it is the case too that in "all human affairs" and at all times, "it is Hope—Hope—Hope" (*Letters*, 8: 37).[22] Performing as both subject ("it") and object in this clause, hope—that is, iterable hope—figures a world at once present and ongoing: a "former world and future" that, however unavailable to "memory," or riven by doubt, is always accessible to history, both as a "retrospect" of what was either missed or foreclosed on; and as the object, accordingly, of a still-secret knowledge where "what is," what was, and what is possible are subliminally allied. Thus if Byron's greatest poem—the one he was writing amid these reflections—eventually returns to England and to the gentrified, domestic world from which he had separated himself, it is because, as a work bound to the interlocutionary present and addressed to someone like Annabella Milbanke,[23] *Don Juan* is already there: a counterfactual, or enactment of what might have been had the Byrons not separated; and "a retrospect . . . leading to a . . . future" that the poem largely formalizes and whose "world," accordingly, is "all before [the poet] or behind" (14.9).

Nominally a riposte to Teresa Guiccioli's *My Recollections of Lord Byron*, where Lady Byron is depicted as the chilling scourge of the countess's late lover, Stowe's "The True Story of Lady Byron's Life" is best understood in conjunction with Moore's biography, which was first published in 1829, five years after the poet's death. An unabashed admirer of Byron as well as one of his confidants, Moore provided a perspective on the separation framed by the very codes that Stowe would embrace to different ends. Expatiating from the primary evidence of selected letters and journals and from conversations with Byron himself, Moore initially anticipates Stowe in identifying marriage as an event that Byron recognized as his "salvation" (Stowe 1970, 390). However where Stowe particularizes this salvation as residing in the impeccably virtuous Lady Byron, Moore is even more conventional in locating it in a paradigm of femininity usually found in conduct manuals. Speaking of another, characteristically unnamed, woman, whom Byron was apparently seeing "in the interval between Miss Milbanke's refusal and acceptance of him," Moore describes her in terms that are irreducibly trite:

Combining beauty of the highest order with a mind intelligent and ingenuous,—having just learning enough to give refinement to her taste, and far too much taste to make pretensions to learning,—with a patrician spirit proud as his own, but showing it only in a delicate generosity of spirit, a feminine high-mindedness, which have led her to tolerate his defects in consideration of his noble qualities and his glory, and even to sacrifice silently some of her own happiness rather than violate the responsibility in which she stood pledged to the world for his;—such was, from long experience, my impression of the character of this lady. (Moore 1830, 1: 390)

Invested, then, in a notion of femininity (and in a notion of genius by contrast) to which Lady Byron turns out to have been the heterodox (or for G. Wilson Knight "bisexual") counterexample, Moore's justification of the separation is essentially twofold: Byron was exceptional because he was a "genius," and Byron was an exceptional genius whose affections were the basis of extraordinary social feelings unsuited to marital fidelity. Noting that "men of the higher order of genius [have rarely, if ever,] shown themselves fitted for the calm affections and comforts that form the cement of domestic life," primarily because their "own mental stores are most abundant and self-sufficing" (1830, 1: 465), Moore argues that Byron was at the same time "a signal exception" to "that high class of human intelligences to which he belonged. . . . Born with strong affections and ardent passions, the world had, from first to last, too firm a hold on his sympathies to let imagination altogether usurp the place of reality, either in his feelings or the objects of them." Still,

[n]ot even that intense craving after affection, which nature had implanted in him, could keep his ardour still alive in a pursuit whose results fell so short of his "imaginings;" and though, from time to time, the combined warmth of his fancy and temperament was able to call up a feeling which to his eyes wore the semblance of love, it may be questioned whether his heart had ever much share in such passions, or whether, after his first launch into the boundless sea of imagination, he could ever have been brought back and fixed by any lasting attachment. . . . There needs no stronger proof of the predominance of imagination in these attachments than his own serious avowal . . . that often, when in the company of the woman he most loved, he found himself secretly wishing for the solitude of his own study. It was *there*, indeed—in the silence and abstraction of that study,—that the chief scene of his mistress's empire and glory lay. It was there that, unchecked by reality, and without any fear of the disenchantments of truth, he could view her through the medium of his own fervid fancy, enamour himself of an idol of his own creating, and out of brief delirium of a few days or weeks, send forth a dream of beauty and passion through all ages. (1830, 1: 467–69)

The "serious avowal" that Moore refers to comes from a journal entry (April 10, 1814) on the pleasures of solitude:

I do not know that I am happiest when alone; but this I am sure of, that I am never long in the society even of *her* I love, (God knows too well, and the Devil probably too,) without a yearning for the company of my lamp and my utterly confused and tumbled-over library. (Byron, *Letters*, 3: 257)

Given that Byron and Milbanke were scarcely in each other's presence prior to her acceptance of his proposal a few months later, the "love" who sends Byron running to his books and who, in Moore's interpretation, was always wanting by comparison to the "idol of his creat[ion]," is not Annabella but probably his sister Augusta, who, as it happened, gave to birth to Byron's daughter five days later. Thus in addition to conflating Byron's love and future wife as entities from which he was necessarily in flight, Moore projects a world that, in contrast to the one he describes, is no longer one of separate spheres, much less of incestuous proximity, but a distinctly possible world where the "library" could be a domestic sanctum and the home a scene of writing.

What Moore could never grasp about the Byrons, and about Byron in particular, was the always singular situation that marriage represented as an abstraction and in opposition to prevailing ideologies. In interpreting Byron's reported reflections on the separation late in life ("the causes . . . were too simple to be easily found out") to mean that the Byrons were "simply" incompatible and "that, at the time of their parting, there could have been no very deep sense of injury on either side" (1830, 1: 515), what continually eludes Moore (and Stowe) is the degree to which Byron, eventually by his own admission, was disabled by false consciousness. The marriage failed not because the "causes" were obscure but because given the ether that the Byrons breathed, that everyone around them breathed, and that Stowe and Moore continue to breathe, there was no way that the marriage could have succeeded.

Stowe tells an equally "simple" story of a "brilliant, seductive genius," who despite his current hold over the "youth of America" was, both during his marriage and in its aftermath, in "defiance" of "every principle of morality or decorum."[24] Indulging in the standard view of Byron as possessing "nobler feelings" suited to both marriage and possibly his salvation, "the transient rise of [those] feelings," she argues, "was choked and overgrown by the thorns of base, unworthy passions." Mincing neither words nor details, she continues: "From the height at which he might have been happy as the husband of a noble woman, he fell into the depths of a secret adulterous intrigue with a blood relation, so near in consanguinity, that discovery must have been utter ruin, and expulsion from civilized society" (Stowe 1970, 428). Concerned as much with telling "the true story" as with the competing—and, as far as she was concerned, mendacious—accounts of Moore, Guiccioli, and others, Stowe is committed to delivering not just a fallen Byron but a Byron whose ostensible superiority belongs now to someone else:

Young and gifted; with a peculiar air of refined and spiritual beauty; graceful in every movement; possessed of exquisite taste; a perfect companion to his mind in all the higher walks of literary culture; and with that infinite pliability to all his varying and capricious moods which true love alone can give; bearing in her hand a princely fortune, which,

with a woman's uncalculating generosity, was thrown at his feet,—there is no wonder
that she might feel for a while as if she could enter the lists with the very Devil himself,
and fight with a woman's weapons for the heart of her husband. (Stowe 1970, 431–32)

Crucial here, mostly because it stands in uneasy proximity to the discursive
parameters of the Byrons' relationship, is the recourse to a vocabulary that, for
the Byrons, was almost always a broader, subtler, language. When Byron speaks
of marriage as his salvation or when Milbanke urges him to good works in the
spirit of Christianity, these are not hard and fast notions but the constituents of
a developing friendship. By the time Stowe is writing this, however, that conversation and whatever willingness it registered are no longer missed opportunities,
much less history of them; they are circumscribed by the very discourses to
which the parties (and later their defenders) were fatally susceptible. "[R]eady to
relieve suffering in any form" (Stowe 1970, 443), Lady Byron is no longer Byron's
interlocutor or "parallel" so much as an "angelic woman . . . struggl[ing] with
fiends of darkness for the redemption of her husband's soul" (434) and, finally,
in Stowe's culminating stroke, a woman with "so much of Christ in her, that to
have seen her seemed to be to have drawn near to heaven. She was one of those
few whom absence cannot estrange from friends; whose mere presence in this
world seems always a help to every generous thought, a strength to every good
purpose, a comfort in every sorrow" (446).

And what of Byron? He goes "from shame to shame, and dishonor to dishonor" (Stowe 1970, 442) and, quoting Lady Byron directly, is finally an "egotis[t]"
whose heart "was hard and impenetrable" and "habitually destitute of that enthusiasm he so beautifully expresses" (456).

There is more in this vein in the *Atlantic Monthly* article and in the over
four hundred pages of *Lady Byron Vindicated*, which Stowe published almost
immediately in response to the nearly-universal criticism she received. It would
have been nice, then, if the general outcry had stemmed, however intuitively,
from a more nuanced appreciation of what Byron was working through, as a
writer and a potential mate. But, as Henry James's Mr. Bantling reminds us once
again, this was not the case. In addition to the repellent—and for many readers
unbelievable—disclosures made so long after the fact, the condemnation heaped
upon Stowe, especially in America, was motivated by a hagiographic, if always
titillating, view of the poet as a hero despite his weaknesses. Writing in the *Independent*, Justin McCarthy was representative in his two-pronged response.
Acknowledging Byron's moral flaws, endemic to his time and society, "when

morality was rare among men," McCarthy turns the other way and excoriates Stowe for her "sanctimonious imbecility" in "regard[ing] her sickening task as a moral and religious duty."[25] British commentators were generally more measured. The *Saturday Review* briefly acknowledged the truth of Stowe's allegations and was troubled mostly by her "bad taste in telling her story."[26] Even *Blackwood's*, which Stowe attacked endlessly in her second and more extensive defense, deferred to others in countering Stowe's "hideous tale": "All who glory in the fame of Byron—all who revere the memory of Mrs. Leigh—all, and they were not a few, who were attached by the ties of friendship to Lady Byron herself—all who guard the purity of home from pollution, and the sanctity of the grave from outrage—have joined in one unanimous chorus of condemnation."[27]

Just how this all bears on the American "glory in the fame of Byron," to return to Mr. Bantling once more—as distinct from, say, the British or Russian or French adulation—is a matter on which we can only speculate. But it would seem to involve the very dimension that Byron excoriated for its simplicity and that Stowe's own father enthusiastically displayed, when, upon learning of Byron's death, he was reported to have exclaimed, "Byron is dead—gone! . . . Oh, I'm sorry. I did hope he would live to do something for Christ. What a harp he might have swept!"[28] If for Lyman Beecher, Byron died before he could become something more than what he was, it can be argued that for the majority of Byron's American defenders the achievement of what to Beecher was only in a state of becoming took place conclusively at Missolonghi, where the poet, in the public imaginary, died tragically in the cause of freedom.

There is, however, at least one contemporaneous account of the Byrons and, by fortuitous coincidence, an account of them parting that captures the "present in the past" that remains the scene of the everyday's emergence generally. An American traveler with apparently more insight than those Mr. Bantling "supposes" had the privilege of actually witnessing the Byrons in what he assumed was domestic happiness. The scholar George Ticknor called on Byron when he was visiting London in 1815, and while they were conversing, Lady Byron made an appearance:

She is pretty, not beautiful,—for the prevalent expression of her countenance is that of ingenuousness. . . . She is a baroness in her own right, has a large fortune, is rich in intellectual endowments, is a mathematician, possesses common accomplishments in an uncommon degree, and adds to all this a sweet temper. She was dressed to go and drive, and, after stopping a few moments, went to her carriage. Lord Byron's manner to her was affectionate; he followed her to do the door, and shook hands with her, as if he were not to see her for a month.[29]

This affectionate parting may not have been charade. The Byrons were expectant parents and experiencing a respite from the primary source of Lady Byron's problems—the poet's sister—who had recently returned home (Eisler 1999, 468). But, more important, is how Ticknor captured—in the long goodbye to which the relationship was always tantamount—a retrospect leading to a future where a world previously lost to knowledge is suddenly present and, for the moment at least, the "Hope—Hope—Hope" that is.

5 DON JUAN AND THE ROMANTIC FRAGMENT

I

Two well-known poetical fragments by Coleridge, "Kubla Khan," whose composition was supposedly interrupted "by a person on business from Porlock," and the gothic ballad *Christabel*, break off in registers that are quite ordinary. The brief tableau of parental affect that concludes *Christabel*'s second part (originally from a father-to-father exchange with Robert Southey)[1] is no doubt interesting in tracking a domestic or pocket sublime where "pleasure" and "pain" are continually trading places. But compared to the Manichean allegory that precedes it, in which forces are at war, with a fair amount at stake, the poem's sudden modulation to a realistic (and contemporary) scenario takes it in a direction that is relatively aimless and, at the level of analysis, interminable.

So, too, the outsized struggle between authoritarian decree and "romantic" opposition in "Kubla Khan" segues to a wish-fulfilling fantasy of a banal—which is to say grandiose—sort, where in reviving the song sung by the Abyssinian maid, the speaker is besieged by admirers along with those who are simply awe-struck, even terrified:

> Could I revive within me
> Her symphony and song,
>   To such a deep delight 'twould win me,
> That with music loud and long,
> I would build that dome in air,
> That sunny dome! those caves of ice!
> And all who heard should see them there,
> And all should cry, Beware! Beware!
> His flashing eyes, his floating hair!
> Weave a circle round him thrice,
> And close your eyes with holy dread,
> For he on honey-dew hath fed,
> And drunk the milk of Paradise. (42–54)[2]

In an influential lecture delivered over a half century ago, Humphrey House was struck by a decidedly ordinary dimension to this concluding tableau, arguing that the "emphasis" in the lines "Could I revive within me / Her symphony and song" is actually quite "slight . . . like 'Could you make it Wednesday instead of Thursday, it would be easier for me.'" He hears the language as confidence, pointing—all fragmentation aside—to "the very possibility of creative achievement."[3]

My point is somewhat related. But it proceeds in a different direction, as I am concerned less here with ordinary language or tone (even in *Christabel*, where the ending departs from balladic hysteria) than with a turn to the everyday of which the fragment, in either instance, is seemingly both cause and effect. Discussions of the "Romantic fragment" typically run in other directions, from the radical, defamiliarizing aesthetics of the Schlegels writing in the aftermath of Kant, where "irresolution" (to quote Marjorie Levinson) "represent[s] . . . a generic deviation from some generic norm" of "perfection" (8), to Levinson's pragmatic assertion that the "Romantic fragment poem," particularly in British hands, demands "the substitution of a reading for a writing" that is nonexistent, creating a "mismatch between the text proper and an idea in [the reader's]—and perhaps the poet's—mind" (26–27) in which "a contradiction at once too seminal and too assimilated into individual historical consciousness" is gradually staged rather than resolved or transcended (13).[4]

Levinson has other issues apart from the everyday in mind. But her point about something new and sublimated on the model of either the uncanny or even the traumatic is relevant, since what the speaker's tone or positionality reflects in "Kubla Khan," in conjunction with the fragment it helps precipitate, is not bravado but a fantasy from the other side. Here—or better still "here and now"—creative achievement and fame are the products of what Keats under similar provocation calls a "waking dream" (of the kind explored in "Ode on Indolence") that as specimens of everyday phenomenology open onto other possibilities that the fragment, as part of a continuum, brings to view. It is not that "Kubla Khan" or *Christabel* or several of Keats's Odes end abruptly—and are thus fragments—due to some failure or impasse. They end the way they do because any ending, much less a teleology, is superfluous to the stratum to which—as fragments—they belong.[5]

"Kubla Khan" is particularly illustrative in the way its turn to ordinary fantasy at the end represents a third way in contrast to the poem's first two parts. The verse opens with a "decree" for something ordered, monumental and presumably enduring. The second stanza is insurrectionary, breaking with that "future," or that past, and with the decree intended to sustain it. Lingering at the edges of the "romantic" (12) and the oppositional, the third section stages something modest and different that—as emergence theory warrants—is more complex or, as the case may be, overdetermined. Rising at the point of fragmentation from the position of a daydreamer who can look only backward as a way forward ("could I revive"), is a history only partly continuous with the rupture that precedes it. For at the point of breakage or romantic revolt, creativity gives way to something anterior if unaccounted for, whose formal nod is no longer to a totality of which the poem is a microcosm but to a continuum of which the poem-as-fragment is a snapshot. There may be reason to dispute Coleridge's later assertion that the poem's composition was interrupted by a person on business from Porlock. But there is a sense, particularly on recollection or better still *as recollection*, that the poem as-is and the alleged circumstances of its stoppage are more intimately linked: that there is a continuity between a wish-fulfilling fantasy, which leaves the speaker situated in the comparatively ordinary place of longing, and the everyday life where people from Porlock come and go. Thus it is not just the fragmentary form that proves symptomatic but the prefatory materials that Coleridge added nearly two decades later, which—beginning with the disclosure that the poem was appearing at Byron's suggestion[6]—bear tribute to what "Kubla Khan" and its interruption (historically speaking) approach from different yet related angles.

II

"I never married," remarks *Don Juan*'s speaker early on as he is oscillating between the unhappy marriage of Juan's parents (replete with infidelities) and young Juan's stringent upbringing under his mother's panoptical supervision (1.53).[7] While this is clearly a lie—as it is impossible to imagine the speaker being anyone but Byron—it is also what, on the matter of lies in general, he later calls "[t]he truth in masquerade" (11.37). This would not only be with reference to the Byron marriage, which even in the period of courtship was already a doomed prospect secured by something close to contrived longing. It is with reference to the "marriage" that *Don Juan* instantiates where the qualifier "until now" is poised suddenly for addition. *Don Juan* is spectacularly rife with anti-conjugal sentiment, beginning with the marriage of Juan's parents and the description of his mother Donna Inez, whose morality and facility with mathematics are an unambiguous allusion to the very woman from whom Byron was recently separated. However this sociable poem is just as strikingly a conversation, where the consolations of form and the regressive patterns they follow give way, like "Kubla Khan," to something ongoing in which a relationship akin to what Eric Walker calls "remarriage, day after day" takes precedence over what Byron, when he was contemplating marriage, routinely disparaged as "love."[8]

The melding of marriage and the everyday in Walker's formulation originates with Stanley Cavell, whose anatomy of marriage, following the film genre he calls the "comedy of remarriage" and the "willingness for the everyday" it enshrines, has obvious bearing, since any marriage on Byron's part would have been a re-marriage. But its relevance is even more pressing, insofar as *Don Juan* is a do-over, among other things, whose implied reader—and there is no romantic poem more reader-directed—remains an intelligence to which Lady Byron can lay claim.[9]

Readers familiar with Byron's extensive correspondence, and the anecdotes about his famous sociability and equally infamous libertinage, will likely regard this elevation as counterintuitive, albeit of a piece with the counterfactual that marriage to the former Annabella Milbanke remained: beforehand, when it was already a missed opportunity and the more desirable for having been one; and subsequently, when anything resembling a marriage—good or bad—was (Ticknor's anecdote aside) barely manifest. But what this suggests is that *Don Juan* is a counterfactual as well: thematically, in the abiding preoccupation with marriage and its relation-ship to love and gender; and formally, where in "begin[ning] at the beginning" (1.7) with the matters aforementioned, the poem actually begins in medias res—albeit with the aim, we discover later, of "end[ing] ... with the beginning" (13.73) or what in the course of the poem will have amounted to a new start.[10] Well into the first canto, by which point we have witnessed Juan's upbringing, the dissolu-tion of his parents' marriage, and the burgeoning of the "hero's" sexuality at the instigation of Donna Julia, who is locked in an asymmetrical relationship with the much older Don Alphonso, the speaker expatiates on "sweetness" in a series of examples meant to highlight the disparity between life's various compensations and the unrivaled plenitude of first love. The passage is a long one and merits full citation, but its main point—as an exercise in narratology in tallying the toll of genre—is clear from just a few stanzas. " 'Tis sweet," Byron writes,

> to hear
> At midnight on the blue and moonlit deep
> The song and oar of Adria's gondolier,
> By distance mellow'd, o'er the waters sweep;

'Tis sweet to see the evening star appear;
   'Tis sweet to listen as the nightwinds creep
From leaf to leaf; 'tis sweet to view on high
The rainbow, based on ocean, span the sky.

'Tis sweet to hear the watchdog's honest bark
   Bay deep-mouthed welcome as we draw home;
'Tis sweet to know there is an eye will mark
   Our coming, and look brighter when we come;
'Tis sweet to be awaken'd by the lark,
   Or lull'd by falling waters; sweet the hum
Of bees, the voice of girls, the song of birds,
The lisp of children, and their earliest words.

   . . .

But sweeter still than this, than these, than all,
   Is first and passionate love—it stands alone,
Like Adam's recollection of his fall;
   The tree of knowledge has been pluck'd—all's known—
And life yields nothing further to recall
   Worthy of this ambrosial sin, so shown,
No doubt in fable, as the unforgiven
Fire which Prometheus filch'd for us from heaven. (1.122, 123, 127)

There are other instances of sweetness that I've omitted, some of which are more satirical and germane (in that register) to Lady Byron and her avatar Dona Inez. The ones I've chosen, though, proceed from the wisdom of the concluding stanza in finding strength in what remains behind and often overlooked, rather than in a telos toward which narrative (including biblical narrative) regresses in supposedly progressing. The "recollection" that matters most is not the Fall, whether as punishment or a prelude to paradise regained; what matters for Byron is a *paradise* that, as either a projected endgame or an experience that love as such can barely approximate (in the wake of "first . . . love"), actually suffers by comparison to what is ongoing and within reach: including the poem, the "conversation" it formalizes, and (as it happens) Adam's immediate future at the close of Milton's.[11]

   Given the speaker's—and the poem's—regressive tendencies, which are persistent and recurrent, from the celebration of Juan's sexuality, where the erotic object is typically a found mother, to the ridicule of married life in general, it might be a little early to call this procedure "marriage."[12] Still, even at his least conjugal and most misogynistic—beginning with the conflation of Juan's mother and Byron's wife—the speaker is no less mindful of the circumstances and structures that transform women into deformations. If there is one takeaway from the initial canto and the backhanded epithalamion it may be reckoned, it is that what's bad for women in "this sublime world" is equally bad for men. This is explicitly the point about the husbands here—Don José and Don Alphonso— for whom male prerogative, whether in womanizing or in marrying a younger woman, proves a passport to buffoonery. It has nearly equal bearing on the poem's speaker, for whom detachment, as one prerogative of authorship, proves a dead end as well. Dilating on the interchangeability of sin and pleasure and on the human dilemma they expose in conjoining the Byronic bookends of libertinage and Calvinism, the narrator comes to an impasse that is just as suddenly a vow:

> Man's a phenomenon, one knows not what,
>   And wonderful beyond all wondrous measure;
> 'Tis a pity though, in this sublime world, that
>   Pleasure's a sin and sometimes sin's a pleasure;
> Few mortals know what end they would be at,
>   But whether glory, power, or love, or treasure,
> The path is through perplexing ways, and when
> The goal is gain'd, we die, you know—and then—
>
> What then?—I do not know, no more do you—
>   And so good night. (1.133–34)

It may be a stretch to call this pillow talk. However in addition to sin and pleasure and their "perplexing ways," the juxtaposition of narrative on the regressive model with something ongoing, in which an interlocutor is clearly present, finds issue in an interrogative ("What then?") and, following that, a sign-off ("And so good night") that, far from peremptory or a way simply to "[r]eturn . . . to story" (1.134), recall the speaker to a continuum—and for the purposes of this analysis an opportunity—where conversation and the primary discursive mode here that Byron calls "digression" take precedence over anything goal-oriented or, for that matter, monologic.[13]

Digression is so much a feature of *Don Juan*—or a "fault" (3.96), as the speaker disingenuously describes it—that to emphasize it even slightly seems hardly a production of knowledge. What does bear emphasis is the way the constellation of form, subject matter and other-directedness is further specified by a woman (Inez, Julia, Haidée, Gulbayez, Lady Adeline, Aurora Raby, even Fitz-Fulke) who, in focalizing what the speaker memorably terms "their she condition" (14.24), figures an interlocutor—and by extension a conversation—where digression is frequently a form of listening or paying attention. A good example would be the narrator's transcription of Julia's letter to Juan at the end of the first canto which she writes after her adultery has been discovered and she has been dispatched to a convent where she will be immured indefinitely:

> 'I loved, I love you, for that love have lost
>   State, station, heaven, mankind's, my own esteem,
> And yet can not regret what it hath cost,
>   So dear is still the memory of that dream.
> Yet, if I name my guilt, 'tis not to boast,
>   None can deem harshlier of me than I deem:
> I trace this scrawl because I cannot rest—
> I've nothing to reproach or to request.
>
> 'Man's love is of his life a thing apart,
>   'Tis woman's whole existence; man may range
> The court, camp, church, the vessel, and the mart,
>   Sword, gown, gain, glory, offer in exchange
> Pride, fame, ambition, to fill up his heart,
>   And few there are whom these can not estrange;
> Man has all these resources, we but one,
> To love again, and be again undone. . . .
>
> 'You will proceed in beauty, and in pride,
>   Beloved and loving many; all is o'er
> For me on earth, except some years to hide
>   My shame and sorrow deep in my heart's core;
> These I could bear, but cannot cast aside
>   The passion which still rends it as before,
> And so farewell—forgive me, love me—No,
> The word is idle now—but let it go.
>
> 'I have no more to say, but linger still,
>   And dare not set my seal upon this sheet,

And yet I may as well the task fulfil,

    My misery can scarce be more complete:

I had not lived till now, could sorrow kill;

    Death flies the wretch who fain the blow would meet,

And I must even survive this last adieu,

And bear with life, to love and pray for you!'

This note was written upon gilt-edged paper

    With a neat crow-quill, rather hard, but new;

Her small white fingers scarce could reach the taper,

    But trembled as magnetic needles do,

And yet she did not let one tear escape her;

    The seal a sunflower; '*Elle vous suit partout*,'

The motto, cut upon a white cornelian;

The wax was superfine, its hue vermilion. (1.193–94, 196–98)

It has been noted more than once that this passage strongly resembles the exchange between Anne Elliot and Captain Harville at the end of Austen's *Persuasion*, where the former delineates the differences between the sexes in matters of love and the differences, more generally, that they underscore. Insisting that women "do not forget [men] as soon as you forget us," which squares with Julia's prediction, Austen's heroine goes on to enumerate other differences that Julia reiterates, suggesting (among other things) that Byron had access to Austen's novel in advance of its posthumous publication by John Murray, who was his publisher too.[14] Observing, in the same self-recriminatory vein, that women "cannot help themselves," that "[w]e live at home, quiet, confined," where "our feelings prey upon us," Anne is also quick to note that men "are forced on exertion. You always have a profession, pursuits, business of some sort or other, to take you back into the world immediately, and continual occupation and change soon weaken impressions" (183). When pressed on the matter of constancy, which, Harville insists, is a virtue shared by men and women both, Anne not only disagrees but observes as well that the differences here, like those aforementioned, are quite detrimental:

I believe you equal to every important exertion, and to every domestic forbearance, so long as—if I may be allowed the expression—so long as you have an object. I mean while the woman you love lives, and lives for you. All the privilege I claim for my own sex (it is not a very enviable one; you need not covet it), is that of loving longest, when existence or hope is gone. (186)

If Byron were somehow miming a writer his wife clearly admired, it is not because he is a resourceful plagiarist; it is because he was *listening*: in taking the measure of Julia's plight (and of Anne's, Austen's, and Annabella's by extension) and in allowing a text committed to the rigors of ottava rima to lapse, auditorily, into what reads and sounds like prose. And not just any prose but writing of the kind that Walter Scott, in reading Austen, described as "prosing" and that Maria Edgeworth saw similarly as having "no story." In addition to hearing Julia in every sense possible, Byron (like Austen) is focused on the details, from her writing implements to her cursive style, to the material circumstances marking the slippage (here as in Austen) between privilege by class and subordination by gender. Slippage of this sort was a matter of interest at the time and women readers, as Susan Wolfson reminds us, were taken with this moment in the poem.[15] But the passage is directed just as specifically to someone whose favored author is being channeled, stylistically and thematically, in demonstrating an attentiveness that is conjugal (for want of a better term) or prosaic rather than strictly poetical.

This attentiveness can appear short-lived—especially when Juan, who is also sent away, is observed reading Julia's letter aboard ship and, beset apparently by seasickness, visibly and hilariously nauseated. Even here, however, the nausea is far from localized, proceeding from physical circumstances at sea, to juvenile disgust at the prospect of remaining faithful at so early a moment, to revulsion at the "phenomenon" that the letter delineates, which is dialogic at this point and directed, in Byron's equally public letter, to an equally specific "you." Thus in the shipwreck episode that immediately ensues when, after drawing lots from the shredded remnants of the letter, the famished passengers and crew (save for Juan) set about eating one of their company (Juan's tutor), the speaker digresses to reflecting on the most immediate structural imperative—that "man" is "a carnivorous production" (2.67) and, by that mandate, a cannibal-in-waiting—before rounding back to where Julia and Austen (and I would further venture Lady Byron) have directed him: a "condition" where "he" and "she" are, like the productions of carnivorousness, arbitrary and limiting.

Describing the behavior of two fathers, charged with tending to sons who are about to die, the speaker lets the events speak for themselves and, like Julia's letter, to similar effect.

> There were two fathers in this ghastly crew,
>   And with them their two sons, of whom the one
> Was more robust and hardy to the view,

But he died early; and when he was gone,
His nearest messmate told his sire, who threw
    One glance on him, and said, 'Heaven's will be done!
I can do nothing,' and saw him thrown
Into the deep without a tear or groan.

The other father had a weaklier child,
    Of a soft cheek, and aspect delicate;
But the boy bore up long, and with a mild
    And patient spirit held aloof his fate;
Little he said, and now and then he smiled,
    As if to win a part from off the weight
He saw increasing on his father's heart,
With the deep deadly thought, that they must part.

And o'er him bent his sire, and never raised
    His eyes from off his face, but wiped the foam
From his pale lips, and ever on him gazed,
    And when the wish'd-for shower at length was come,
And the boy's eyes, which the dull film half glazed,
    Brighten'd and for a moment seem'd to roam,
He squeezed from out a rag some drops of rain
Into his dying child's mouth—but in vain.

The boy expired—the father held the clay,
    And look'd upon it long, and when at last
Death left no doubt, and the dead burthen lay
    Stiff on his heart, and pulse and hope were past,
He watched it wistfully, until away
    'Twas borne by the rude wave wherein 'twas cast;
Then he himself sunk down all dumb and shivering,
And gave no sign of life, save his limbs quivering. (2.87–90)

Beyond the anatomy of gender that the appropriately designated "other father"
performs in showing that life and love are no longer things apart, the equally
important aspect of the passage involves the time of description, which is a varia-
tion in many ways on the sweetness elaboration earlier. In the very way that the
time and texture of life are typically overlooked and subordinated to a goal that

holds the promise (however illusory) of some imperishable bliss, the momentum toward closure in this instance, however inevitable, obscures and mitigates the critical difference that being in the present can make and, more important, be shown to make regardless of where things are headed. The aperture onto gender troubles, and the opening to which it leads in extending and feminizing the masculine, is of a piece with the larger conversation it is incorporated into in going nowhere, or to any resolution, apart from what is immediately possible.

Joined to a sense of the poem as interlocution, the "immediately possible" displaces possibility on a grand or deferred scale, of which the ensuing idyll involving the island princess Haidée, into whose love and nurturance Juan literally washes up, is a defining instance.[16] Bound, like Adam's recollection, to a regressive and totalizing paradigm where, in a telling moment, language acquisition and carnal knowledge are administered to Juan in what amounts to a single stroke, the episode of the young lovers is riven by opposing viewpoints: Juan's, which is akin to Adam's before his fall, and an "end" accordingly that the poem resists in form and in function; and Haidée's, which gradually morphs from the gratification of having a man or child she can partake of and control to something more obscure, where the "other minds" problem, so central to Cavell's sense of marriage as a reading or unreading performed daily, gradually takes hold. Thus in addition to the cocoon-like business of "love" and being "beloved" (2.191), which proves a cul-de-sac for both parties, the episode migrates to a series of digressions, where—here as before—a conversation is in progress.

The most important of these involves the recurrent theme of marriage versus love in which, as the opposite of sex, marriage names a desire or willingness that is distinctly hermeneutical rather than hormonal:

> 'Tis a melancholy, and a fearful sign
>   Of human frailty, folly, also crime,
> That love and marriage rarely can combine,
>   Although they are born in the same clime;
> Marriage from love, like vinegar from wine—
>   A sad, sour, sober beverage—by time
> Is sharpen'd from its high celestial flavour
> Down to a very homely household savour.
>
> There's something of antipathy, as 'twere,
>   Between their present and future state;

A kind of flattery that's hardly fair
  Is used until the truth arrives too late—
Yet what can people do, except despair?
  The same things change their names at such a rate;
For instance—passion in a lover's glorious,
But in a husband is pronounced uxurious. . . .

There's doubtless something in domestic doings,
  Which forms, in fact, true love's antithesis;
Romances paint at full length people's wooings,
  But only give a bust of marriages;
For no one cares for matrimonial cooings,
  There's nothing wrong in a connubial kiss:
Think you, if Laura had been Petrarch's wife,
He would have written sonnets all his life?

All tragedies are finish'd by a death,
  All comedies are ended by a marriage;
The future states of both are left to faith,
  For authors fear description might disparage
The worlds to come of both, or fall beneath,
  And then both worlds would punish their miscarriage;
So leaving each their priest and prayer-book ready,
They say no more of Death or of the Lady. (3.5–6, 8–9)

If the speaker is insistent on exploring the link between marriage and a literary
genre with which it is dispositionally at odds, be it comedy or Petrarchanism, it
is not because marriage is constitutionally unrepresentable, which is the usual
argument. It is because marriage is representable by other means: by commitment to a "future" and a "lady" that is both a "serious matter" (as Byron famously
described it in a deleted stanza)[17] and a recurrent possibility that only a text
bent on "doing something," with no end or closure that "might disparage," can
fulfill. There is plenty that moves in the opposite direction as well, notably the
"vinegar" into which marriage declines. Still, in the very way that the unequaled
sweetness of first and passionate love (which the Haidée episode restages) was
already overwhelmed by the contingent if unappreciated sweetness of everyday
life, the unsustainability of love—and love, it bears repeating, on the regressive
model—quickly tilts in the direction of the conjugal, whether in the interroga-

tory cry for an alternative to despair, or in the scenes of domestic love, however unappealing, or in the concluding reflections on genre and representation, where the focus is not on tragedy but on comedy the day after or, as the speaker puts it, "the world to come." As in the two fathers episode, the threshold to which the passage leads thematically is negotiated discursively in a practice that, line by line, moment to moment, is about what's "to come" in the recognition that this *is* the representable event, the marital event, the everyday, for which no genre apart from what's going on and ongoing can effectively answer.

All of which leads shortly—and not surprisingly—to a defense of poetry as an instigation to thought, along with an interpolated poem, "The Isles of Greece," to which the larger poem is turned in demonstrating, even theorizing, a poetical thinking that, like the marriage genre, is hard-working, a lifelong commitment (like and unlike Petrarch's) and increasingly a vitiation of form. Recited amid a revelry by a chameleon poet who, as the speaker describes him, knows "the way to wheedle" (3.80), "The Isles" takes the hard way by commitment to engagement rather than to nostalgic or regressive lament. The poem's seemingly rhetorical question in response the degradation of modern Greece—"Must *we* but weep o'er days more blest"? (stanza 7)—is not a call to restorative action or to some new "despot" (stanza 12) to lead the country back to its former or lost glory (as the "wheedler" piquantly notes). It is a call to reflection or response, where following *Pride and Prejudice*'s first sentence and its pivotal "must," the imperatives of narrative are met by exasperation over how the present and, by extension, the future are typically subordinated to a plot where lives, bodies, and nations (in this instance) are visible only as accompaniments to the usual story.[18]

Byron has something else in mind, both in identifying poetry as thinking, in which the "Isles of Greece" is surprisingly exemplary, and in the way the Haidée episode overall is in flight from felicity as well as facility: both in the paradise it misrecognizes as bliss and in its Homeric intertext where the domesticity that Odysseus's homecoming consolidates turns out to be a pathological patriarchy in which there are no winners even and especially on the winning side of history. The metamorphosis of Homer's hero into Haidée's "piratical papa" (3.13) Lambro (and of Haidée into Penelope) is one of many complex allusions in a text marked—lest we forget—by a heightened literacy and intertextuality consistent with its sociability.[19] But like so many of these knowing asides, this particular citation moves from parody and something relatively stable into what, with the specter of incest, is decidedly unstable—much like Haidée's dream, in fact, where readability, with its horizon of cognition, gives way to opacity in the recognition that projective identification or mind reading, however constituted, only goes so far. For all its incentives to psychoanalytic understanding in, for example, a love object that, as Haidée dreams it, effectively morphs from son to lover to father, Haidée and her dream are about difficulty and a "mutual separateness" that the episode flatly acknowledges.

The dream actually incorporates two orders of difficulty: one thematic or allegorical in scenarios of entrapment or limitation that Haidée invokes (being chained to rock like Andromeda, walking on "sharp shingles," and standing in a cave hung with icicles with a "wet . . . and lifeless [Juan] at her feet" [4.32–34] who fades gradually into the waking and terrifying specter of her father); and another that, for want of a better term, is simply arresting in the way the dream-work and allegoresis are inconclusive and, like all fragments, ongoing and inter-ruptible. Dreams rarely end with anything resembling formal elegance. What's interesting here is the continuity between the dream, which ultimately conjures up Lambro, and the succeeding material where he is already present at the mo-ment of Haidée's waking. In addition to a return to story, and to a now-typical triangulation involving Juan, a woman, and a proprietary and potentially danger-ous older man, this transition, like the segues to and from the "Isles of Greece," is incorporated into a process that is consistently outward bound: in the other mind that it has opened onto; in the *other* other mind it is perpetually engaging through inducements of various kinds; and finally, in the formal parameters it rejects in the way story and digression morph into each other. There is a prac-tical as well as symbolic necessity in getting Juan from place to place and from woman to woman, even if it costs Haidée her life and Julia, for all practical pur-poses, hers. Still, just as Juan's womanizing, in which he is altogether passive, quickly wanes as a parodic inversion of the Don Juan / Don Giovanni topos, so the force of narrative on the grand or regressive models chronically dissipates in detours like this one, where thought—and thought, it must be stressed, with another thinker somehow present—takes precedence over the usual incentives to absorption or interest.

When Byron's speaker imagines therefore—apropos of poetry's overarch-ing purpose—that "words" and, more materially, a "small drop of ink" have the potential to make "thousands, perhaps millions think" (3.88), he appears to be transforming what I've been arguing is an everyday affair into a virtuoso perfor-mance, in which he is the very hero of whom he is initially and paradoxically in quest ("I want a hero"). But what this larger claim points to more is the degree to which thinking, with the speaker/hero as provocateur, is a broadly speculative process where other minds are theoretically present and a means, accordingly, by which the poem may be internally judged, found wanting, and is always a work in progress.[20] The well-known harem episode that follows, for example, where the reader is asked to consider what it means (or not) for gender roles to be reversed, is a thought experiment that actually founders: not because it provides what Wolfson aptly calls a "critical perspective on the ordering schemes of gender" (a perpetual theme here [187]) but because the experiment's principal device— Juan's gender reassignment and relocation to a harem at the behest of Gulbeyaz (the sultan's wife) where he must (as "Juanna") persuade the other odalisques that he is one of them when he is destined ironically to become one—is largely a bedroom farce where, as the Sultana shows similarly, authority and resistance, or power and subservience, are positions in a familiar, never-ending loop. When Juan pushes back, then, by sanction of either manly or liberal prerogative in refusing to "serve [the] sultana's sensual phantasy" (5.126) as her sexual toy, and provokes in the process a characteristically female outburst of rage, shame and finally humiliation replete with tears, the experiment collapses: in reverting to type and in the difference this reversion marks between "thinking as it has been traditionally" (as Heidegger put it) and "what is to be thought" (Heidegger 1977, 352) in something like the two fathers episode.

Don Juan is a sprawling poem and much of its dilation is instrumental in its capture of the everyday as a continuum where conversation "rules" over either "Cash" or "Love" (12.14). But not every digression or detour is linked to the poem's conjugal demands and to the possibilities they provide. There are plenty of moments beside the one immediately at hand where the speaker holds forth to didactic or oracular effect—in, for example, the siege of Ismail (cantos 6–8)— where the interlocution and the conjugal present, if still in play, are secondary to more general, or public, interest. Nevertheless, by the time the poem relocates to England's manorial culture, where it continues on indefinitely, and to the scene specifically of a marriage that has been reconstituted in thought (or thinking) more than really thought about, the internal or critical mechanisms at the heart of the poem's willingness for the everyday, in which another mind is always present, take on greater prominence. There is a great deal still that the poem pronounces upon, from geopolitical wealth and influence, in which the speaker stumbles into anti-Semitic fantasy, to questions of skepticism where, in repudiating the narcissism of "English" idealism, he throws in with physical, even metaphysical, certainty.

But overall there is a fallibility, for want of a better term, that takes over—in the admission, preeminently, that Lady Byron made a monstrous choice in marrying the poet—that no amount of irony or attentiveness or bravado can suppress. In returning to the scene of a courtship that has in many ways been extended here and of a separation that has been functionally forgotten (the allusions to it notwithstanding), *Don Juan* has no choice now but to remember: in honor of the facts, including possibilities foreclosed on, and as a retrospect that only a present steeped in separation, and a separation or reflexivity inflected by another mind, can recall and possibly recuperate. What characterizes the English cantos, above all, is a mobility or improvement conditional upon error: whether in the lapses already mentioned, or in the claim that the miser is "your only poet" (12.8), or in the postulate that "Love may exist *with* marriage, and *should* ever" (12.15) that, in contradicting the shape and substance of the poem thus far (where love and marriage are generically opposed), traces a learning curve—"ever" and everyday—of which *Don Juan* is the genre par excellence.[21]

Nowhere is the capacity resulting from error more of an issue—and more materially and socially connected to the Byrons as a missed and suddenly recoverable opportunity—than in the example of Lady Adeline and Lord Henry Amundeville, who, although grist for what looks to be Byronic thinking at its most "traditional," are in fact much closer to "what is to be thought" in light of limitations that are simultaneously in view. Habituées of the "Great World" (XI. 45) that Byron traveled in his moments of both fame and dalliance and at the moment as well of separation from wife and country, the Amundevilles are clearly a condensation of persons and environments (the marriage market, the London season, the country house) with which the poet (for whom Juan is now a stand-in) was both familiar and notoriously unhappy.

Yet beyond figuring a world populated by the *"Bores* and the *Bored"* (13.95), the Amundevilles, and it is important to stress the Amundevilles as a unit, are clearly an enigma that the speaker contrives, with considerable ingenuity but little success, to penetrate. This is mostly in regard to Lady Adeline, whom he takes considerable relish in analyzing even as analysis proves interminable. While her husband poses less of a problem, thanks to a superiority matched by a pride that renders all judgments final, the commentary on the Amundeville marriage is, with no particular irony, a pretty good imitation of Lord Henry's view. In a display of free indirect discourse that, for all its cleverness, makes Austen's the more remarkable by comparison, the poem's speaker offers an assessment of the marriage that is limited—quite purposely—by its own authority:

> She loved her lord, or thought so; but *that* love
> > Cost her an effort, which is a sad toil,
> The stone of Sisyphus, if once we move
> > Our feelings 'gainst the nature of the soil.
> She had nothing to complain of, or reprove,
> > No bickerings, no connubial turmoil:
> Their union was a model to behold,
> Serene, and noble,—conjugal, but cold. (14.86)

The speaker goes on to speculate on Adeline's investment in Juan and *his* marital prospects where the effort to criticize and in that way to comprehend, with particular focus on Adeline's potential or unrealized infidelity, is met by a marriage (and by a fidelity as it happens) to which there is only an outside. If the Amundeville union is as cold as the speaker suggests, it is not because he is especially discerning. It is because there is a necessary link between the speaker's surmise of icy impenetrability and *his* lack of penetration, which is flagged by a greater intelligence that the poem has gradually introjected in thinking that is reflexively superficial and in a work that is increasingly all *inside* in which— questions of Byron's performance apart—the possibility of revision and the possibility of (re)marriage are effectively one and the same.[22]

This dynamic gains particular traction in two final examples, Aurora Raby and the Duchess of Fitz-Fulke. They enter the poem as surprises or possibilities rather than challenges. The model already in place is Adeline, who, in being "strongly acted on by what is" always "nearest," is the apogee suddenly of both "sincer[ity]" and the "mobility" at its center. Such pliancy or receptivity might have earlier been called dissembling insofar as Adeline is remarkable in her ability to "ac[t] . . . all and every part" (16.97). But her transformation, like so much else here is the result, it would appear, of hard-earned, cooperative wisdom in which the "mobility" to act and to reform (literally and figuratively) is linked similarly to an intelligence that, as I've been arguing, is necessarily close by. As a result, the mystery that surrounds the "marriageable" Aurora Raby comes from two sides or rather two sides in one: from the other mind she figures in appearing more like an "aura" and from the proximity of someone "nearest" who neutralizes and mitigates any effort to comprehend her beyond following her example. Although a suitable mate for the nominally Spanish Juan, Aurora is not only a Catholic. She is, the speaker enthuses, "a Catholic too" (15.46), whose religiosity, far from definitive, is supplementary and, like Milbanke's in the period of courtship, consistent with a worldview where things are "scarcely [knowable]" (15.47) and where the trappings of piety—specifically a "heavenly ignorance / Of what is called the world, and the world's ways" (16.108)—are decidedly of this world and, in the present case, self-referential.[23]

By this point Juan has already encountered the spectral "Black Friar" and is moved, in thinking about Aurora, to thoughts of marriage that are alternately metaphysical and specific to the poem in the way his heart has been "entrance[d] from "an existence of its own" into "another's bosom" (16.108). The ghostly friar, as readers familiar with *Don Juan* will remember, is only partly a fiction. An embodiment, who emerges as the last, and possibly most illustrative, of the poem's other minds, the "friar" manages to unite an oppositional past, involving a monk's refusal to leave Norman Abbey following the Act of Supremacy (as Adeline details in a ballad about the history of her current residence), and an ongoing present where "opposition" comes from within the poem and its world of relation rather than the position of exteriority (or, in Byron's case, exile) that the speaker claims that he was "born for" (15.22). It is not that either Byron or his poem retreat from such opposition. It is that, following Michel de Certeau, both of them know better than to construe oppositionality in just one way, which is precisely the point of both the history and the masquerade, where the original monk first and eventually the stalking Fitz-Fulke are internal to their environments and, in the case of the duchess, a force literally from within that, however visceral, is doing and signifying more in the climactic moment of encounter:

> Juan put forth one arm—Eternal powers!
>   It touched no soul nor body, but the wall. . . .
> He shuddered, as no doubt the bravest cowers
>   When he can't tell what 'tis that doth appal.
> How odd, a single hobgoblin's non-entity
> Should cause more fear than a whole host's identity! (16.120)

The question of nonentity vs. identity is a fairly complicated one by this point, since the identity or intelligence on which the poem has come to rest is clearly distributed and, like "friar" herself, who turns out to be a cowled Fitz-Fulke,

close by yet daunting and difficult to locate. However, when we turn to the succeeding canto 17 (left uncompleted by Byron and omitted in some editions), in
which the poem fragments, joining the continuum it has been formalizing all
along, there is something close to a moment of clarity or reckoning regarding
the missed opportunity that has been the impetus throughout. Appearing at
breakfast the next morning with the duchess, who has just preceded him, Juan
and "her frolic Grace" (16.123) are bound together in a state of confusion that,
if not the most felicitous figure for a poem-as-remarriage, leaves it fittingly not
far from where Milton leaves his great work: in an everyday "world" of relation
that is "all before [the speaker], or behind" (14.9).

III

The move from *Don Juan* to Shelley's *The Triumph of Life* is in one sense very
direct given the circumstances of their fragmentation (the death of the author)
and that each is seemingly a work of epic ambition. But to proceed in this way
reduces the fragment to an accident and the poet, paradoxically, to a writer seeking greatness. Epic in *Don Juan* is not aspirational so much as proportional and,
apart from the persistent intertext (e.g., *The Odyssey* or *Paradise Lost*), a matter of
extended duration in which the end is incorporated into what eventually stops.[24]
Shelley's poem is an ostensibly different matter, with its serious nod to Dante and
the arc of Western Civilization from antiquity on, that, however stymied at the
moment of closure (with the famous question "Then, what is Life?"),[25] is neither
finished with what it has been engaging (the ravages of "life") nor inured, like
Byron's poem, to the absence of a generic compass apart from the "world to come."

And yet, if the conjugal world inscribed in *Don Juan* is an exemplary instance
of a willingness for the everyday that the fragment registers in highlighting a
"world" or continuum without end, *The Triumph of Life* is, even more than
"Kubla Khan," the litmus test for the fragment's responsiveness to the "missable" or to an order of experience that narrative partializes by framing. While
there has probably been no poem more central to the debates swirling around
canonical romanticism in the past half century, it is the case too that the fragmentary status of Shelley's poem—for all its grist for theoretical mills of one
kind or another—is in many ways a foregone conclusion, beginning with the title
itself, which, although grimly ironic on most interpretations, remains by force
of some internal logic a powerful and abiding intuition. There are readings of
the poem that show or can be enlisted to show that, in inevitably allowing "life"

to drive it, *The Triumph of Life* doubles back on itself and its infernal vision.[26] However, one in particular, Tilottama Rajan's 1990 interpretation, stands out in the way it extends, and sophisticates, the skeptical position, adopted foremost by Paul de Man, in carefully demonstrating how "negative statements" in Shelley's poem "are in their turn negated, so as to produce the trace of something positive . . . as a shadow that futurity casts upon the present."[27] Such a dialectic, needless to say, is more sophisticated than Harold Bloom's (the standard reading for many years), where the apparent failure of imagination in the face of mutability and the overwhelming materiality that the poem calls "life" remains personal, local and, by the humanistic ideology central to both Shelley's mythmaking and British romanticism generally, the equivalent of a bad day's work.[28] In recruiting the poem to the endless work of reading and living, Rajan takes a crucial step forward in removing *The Triumph of Life*, and the peculiar idealism of which it is still a repository, from a final solution, good or bad.

At the same time, by substituting direction for an ending or teleology, if only to argue that the poem is not unidirectional in a purely deconstructive sense (de Man's argument), Rajan provisionally sets aside what for me is the most extraordinary aspect of Shelley's achievement, underscored by its fragmentary status: the "futurity" toward which the poem supposedly inclines is already with us and in plain (hind)sight. Rajan very nearly acknowledges this reversal when she equates the experience of (reading) the poem with the experience or condition effectively prophesied by the poem's actual process. Yet the commitment of this interpretation to a process of which futurity is the goal (however deferred), as opposed to what Byron calls a "serious matter," misses the materiality, the plenitude (to get back to Byron's litany of sweetness) or the anteriority for that matter that displaces futurity as both a vanishing point and a horizon of possibility.

The Triumph of Life is less about the vitiation of romantic narrative—about the paradise that, having been lost, can never be regained except in a process destined to repeat itself—than a work whose title must be interpreted at face value. That's because the narrative to which *The Triumph of Life* is ostensibly most responsive and most vulnerable in consequence—the romantic narrative of wholesale change in and over time as registered in among other places the second stanza of "Kubla Khan"—is one that, along with the *Triumph*'s two key figures, is literally beside the point.

Against the dismay and disengagement of both the poet and his Dantean guide, Rousseau, who maintain a prophetic and critical distance from the seemingly infernal world, *The Triumph of Life* produces an engagement by textual means in permitting a reading from the *inside* and from the perspective of those caught in life's "jubilee" (111) for whom disenchantment, much less distance, is seemingly nonexistent. It is a reading, or, better, an experience (to follow Rajan) to which a tradition-bound interpretation guided by the poem's seeming allegiance to a visionary legacy, beginning with Dante, cannot possibly gain access:

> The crowd gave way, and I arose aghast,
>   Or seemed to rise, so mighty was the trance,
> And saw like clouds upon the thunder blast
>
>   The million with fierce song and maniac dance
> Raging around; such seemed the jubilee
>   As when to greet some conqueror's advance
>
> Imperial Rome poured forth her living sea
>   From senatehouse and prison and theatre
> When Freedom left those who upon the free
>
>   Had bound a yoke which soon they stooped to bear.
> Nor wanted here the just similitude
>   Of a triumphal pageant, for where'er
>
> The chariot rolled a captive multitude
>   Was driven; all those who had grown old in power
> Or misery,—all who have their age subdued,
>
>   By action or by suffering, and whose hour
> Was drained to its last sand in weal or woe,
>   So that the trunk survived both fruit and flower;
>
> All those whose fame or infamy must grow
>   Till the great winter lay the form and name
> Of their own earth with them forever low—
>
>   All but the sacred few who could not tame
> Their spirits to the Conqueror, but as soon
>   As they had touched the world with living flame
>
> Fled back like eagles to their native noon (107–31)

To read this poem from the position of the "captive multitude" (119) does not require an especially disciplined or even a perverse refusal to follow the incentives to recrimination at life's spectacle that the poem presents and to which, like those caught in life's procession, it has largely succumbed. Such a reading requires only a responsiveness to what is of the surface—life itself—whose dynamism overwhelms the discourse of blame in the same way that it takes hold of the poetic discourse, where meaning and judgment are compromised by the chronic enjambment into which the poem is thrown by its subject.

This is not to suggest that Shelley's poem does not also invite a reading in depth. It is that such a reading, beyond enlarging the discursive field in accordance with *The Triumph*'s mythological resonance, is ultimately parasitic on the everyday world it resists, specifically the "untamable" procession of those caught in life's jubilee. The position of exteriority occupied by the narrator, Rousseau (and by almost every commentator on this poem), is, for all its aspirations, instrumental in resisting the possibility and—pursuant to the poem's very last statement— the "happ[iness]" it presumably cherishes. Regardless of how we read the poem, whether from the inside out or the outside in, *The Triumph of Life* situates the visionary against a prospect so close at hand that to represent it in vision is also to displace it from view.[29] Modeling himself on those personages who have resisted or rejected life, Shelley's speaker is surely among the visionaries he dubs the "sacred few" (128). But the poem he narrates or the one he makes readable abolishes that designation in deference to a multitude (including the "Happy those" [547] of the penultimate line), who in retrieving romanticism from its teleological straitjacket have—in life or happiness—retrieved romanticism from its discontents.

Finally, and by way of conclusion, I want to take these claims regarding the fragment and the everyday in a somewhat different direction, which on the face of it is counterintuitive, since the poems that are fragmentary on this claim—Keats's Odes—are, in contrast to his Hyperion poems, which *are* fragments, universally regarded as among the most formally elegant not only in the romantic canon but also in the English canon tout court. Nevertheless, in the greatest of these poems, "Ode to a Nightingale," "Ode on a Grecian Urn," and "To Autumn," the imperatives of form, especially closure, are sharply tried by an open-endedness where, as enactments of quotidian thinking, the everyday is a site, a phenomenology, in which an otherwise consolidated and isolated subjectivity is, as Heidegger notes in reference to it, suspended. While there are certainly ways in which the endings of these three poems can be forged into resounding closures of one kind or another—from the existential resolve to remain engaged regardless of cost, to the definition of beauty as truth as opposed to a version of perfection or the divine—it is just as much the case that these conclusions, as aspects of ordinary rumination, or engagement on the fly, are throwaways, where thinking modulates (as it always does) to the more mundane business of getting on or, to borrow from Heidegger directly, being-in-the-world.

What is especially important about that these texts, particularly the Nightingale and Grecian Urn poems, is that they are set, however artificially, in real time, tracking the mind's gyrations, random or foolish or mawkish or self-ironic. The speaker hears a nightingale and, in weighing the options of either dying in a state of ecstatic audition (which is already a little silly) or continuing to benefit from what sensory experience the world continues to offer, comes to the unsurprising, and not particularly brilliant, decision to hang in there, making the poem's famous conclusion—which may be paraphrased on one reading as "what have I been up to?"—continuous with what precedes and follows rather than formally discontinuous and decisive. Similarly, the Grecian Urn poem nicely captures what it's like to look at an object in, say, a museum while moving in and "out of thought" in ways that are alternately clever, mysterious, mocking, and even juvenile. There is art here certainly: Keats is never not brilliant, regardless of his subject. But it is in their service to the moment, an internal moment that typically goes unmarked in contrast to the real-time sublime of Shelley's "Mont Blanc" or the real-time reflection of Wordsworth's "Tintern Abbey," that these poems maintain a unique place among romantic-era revelations. Moments of comparatively short, even instantaneous, duration, are formalized and extended—and here, I think, Keats's notion of "slow time" is altogether symptomatic—so as not to be missed or overlooked or, most important of all, forgotten. Honoring the larger continuum or temporal dimension of which they are therefore fragments, these poems parse the time of being-in-the-world and the interior time of everyday phenomenology, which meets Heidegger half way in its necessary disarticulation from a narrowly mnemonic or personal function. There's history in these poems, to be sure, but it is one that is strangely generic and depersonalized into which the speaker and the reader are, in yet another Heideggerean figure, *thrown*. And it is a history to which these poems cleave by way of honoring what can only be fathomed in aftermath as a history of missed opportunities.

Nowhere is this cleaving more evident than in the concluding phase of "To Autumn," where the speaker strains to register and to preserve a moment—an altogether ordinary or anonymous moment[30]—that is being lost (as we read it) in the procession of time as the landscape turns to dark and sensation, here as in "Ode to Nightingale," is gradually limited to audition:

> Where are the songs of Spring? Ay, where are they?
>   Think not of them, thou hast thy music too,—
> While barrèd clouds bloom the soft-dying day,
>   And touch the stubble-plains with rosy hue;
> Then in a wailful choir, the small gnats mourn
>   Among the river sallows, born aloft
>   Or sinking as the light wind lives or dies;
> And full-grown lambs loud bleat from hilly bourn;
>   Hedge-crickets sing; and now with treble soft
>   The red-breast whistles from a garden-croft;
>   And gathering swallows twitter in the skies. (23–33)[31]

If the death of the author was the ostensible or material cause for the truncations of *The Triumph of Life* and *Don Juan*, its elevation to figural status in "To Autumn," where poetic and somatic closure meet in a lights-out moment (and figures and premonitions of "dying" are *everywhere* in this stanza), suggests that the fragmentary disposition of the two works that were literally left unfinished was, once again, a foregone conclusion. In all the fragments I've been discussing, cessation discloses a continuum or ongoing-ness that poetry, certainly subjective poetry of the sort we associate with British romanticism, typically leaves behind. What the fragment performs in all of these instances is a romantic chiasmus of sorts, in which personal history or memory is essentially forgotten in deference to a history of either being in the world, or of just regarding it, that is typically overlooked and the more valuable upon recovery, since it is a history that we live and in living make, despite ourselves.

NOTES

PRELUDE

1. Richard Altick, *Shows of London* (Cambridge, MA: Harvard University Press, 1978), 128–220. See also Ralph Hyde, *Gilded Scenes and Shining Prospects: Panoramic Views of British Towns, 1575–1900* (New Haven, CT: Yale Center for British Art, 1985), and Hubert Pragnell, *The London Panoramas of Robert Barker and Thomas Girtin Circa 1800* (London: London Topographical Society, 1968). I discuss the panorama at length in *The Return of the Visible in British Romanticism* (Baltimore: Johns Hopkins University Press, 1993), 34–71.

2. "The Panorama," *Art Journal* (1857): 46.

3. Maurice Blanchot, "Everyday Speech," *Yale French Studies* 73 (1987): 14–17.

4. One visitor to the London panorama took special note of the "baker knocking at the door, in Albion place," especially when he "did not move!" (B. G., "First Panorama," *Notes and Queries* [July 12, 1851]: 21 [cited in Markman Ellis, "'Spectacles within doors': Panoramas of London in the 1790s," *Romanticism*, 14 (2008): 133–48]). In this case, and many others presumably, nothing seen or seeable in the panorama just once, giving rise to various possibilities.

5. William Wordsworth, *The Major Works*, ed. Stephen Gill (Oxford: Oxford University Press, 1984). References to Wordsworth's poems are to the texts in this edition.

6. Paul de Man, "Intentional Structure of the Romantic Image," in *The Rhetoric of Romanticism* (New York: Columbia University Press, 1984), 13.

7. Peter Galassi, *Before Photography: Painting and the Invention of Photography* (New York: Museum of Modern Art, 1981). Galassi includes the London panorama in his survey and while observing that the "popularity of panoramas is often cited as a symptom of the thirst for realism that is thought to have prompted the invention of photography," he notes too that "the particular character of this realism rarely has been carefully considered" (119). I identify that "character" in terms that are identical to the ones Galassi uses elsewhere in his account but is apparently too distracted by the panoramic sweep (as it were) to apply in this instance. For further discussion of the Panorama and of the "photographic" during the romantic moment, see my *Return of the Visible in British Romanticism*, 34–71, 207–43.

8. Camilo José Vergera, *Harlem: The Unmaking of a Ghetto* (Chicago: University of Chicago Press, 2013), 17. Cartier-Bresson takes a somewhat different view of this "whole." A "joint operation of the brain, the eye and the heart," the decisive moment is one in which "the elements in motion are in balance" and sufficiently "inside movement" that the moment itself is only partly in "unison with movement" and with the continuum from which, as a "fugitive moment," it has escaped and is then "capture[d]." Henri Cartier-Bresson, *The Decisive Moment* (New York: Simon & Schuster, 1952), 3–8.

INTRODUCTION

1. David Hume, "Of Miracles," in *An Inquiry Concerning Human Understanding* (New York: Bobbs-Merrill, 1955), 124. See also Lorraine Daston, *Classical Probability in the Enlightenment* (Princeton, NJ: Princeton University Press, 1988). A version of this Introduction originally appeared in *Constellations of a Contemporary Romanticism*, ed. Jacques Khalip and Forrest Pyle (New York: Fordham University Press, 2016), 17–36.

2. Malcolm Elwin, *Lord Byron's Wife* (New York: Harcourt Brace, 1962), 159. For a full discussion of the early response to Austen, see my essay "Austen's Earliest Readers and the Rise of the Janeites," in *Janeites: Austen's Disciples and Devotees*, ed. Deidre Lynch (Princeton, NJ: Princeton University Press, 2000), 87–114.

3. "It is a truth universally acknowledged, that single man in possession of a good fortune, must be in want of a wife." Jane Austen, *Pride and Prejudice*, ed. Claudia L. Johnson and Susan J. Wolfson (New York: Longman, 2003), 5.

4. Marilyn Butler, *Maria Edgeworth: A Literary Biography* (Oxford: Clarendon Press, 1971), 46.

5. Roland Barthes, "L'Effet de réel," *Communications* 11, no. 1 (1968): 84–89.

6. *The Journal of Mary Frampton, from the Year 1779, until the Year 1846*, ed. Harriot Mundy (London, 1885), 226.

7. *Romilly–Edgeworth Letters, 1813–1818*, ed. Samuel Henry Romilly (London: John Murray, 1936), 92.

8. *Jane Austen: The Critical Heritage*, ed. B. C. Southam, 2 vols. (London: Routledge, 1968), 1: 65–68.

9. For a fuller discussion of the implications of Austen's revisions, particularly in the movement from epistolarity to free indirect discourse, see my *The Historical Austen* (Philadelphia: University of Pennsylvania Press, 2003), 109–37. See also B. C. Southam, "*Lady Susan* and the Lost Originals, 1795–1800," in *Jane Austen's Literary Manuscripts: A Study of the Novelist's Development through the Surviving Papers* (London: Oxford University Press, 1964), 45–62.

10. D. A. Miller, *Jane Austen, or The Secret of Style* (Princeton, NJ: Princeton University Press, 2003), 2

11. Jane Austen, *Mansfield Park*, ed. R. W. Chapman, rev. Mary Lascelles (Oxford: Oxford University Press, 1965–66), 455.

12. *Literary Gazette*, March 30, 1833, 199.

13. Edmund Husserl, *On the Phenomenology of the Consciousness of Internal Time*, trans. John Barnett Bough, ed. Rudolf Bernet (Dordrecht: Kluwer, 1991), 37.

14. Martin Heidegger, "Letter on Humanism," in *Basic Writings*, ed. David Farrell Krell (San Francisco: Harper Collins, 1977), 196.

15. I have used Kevis Goodman's phrase from *Georgic Modernity and British Romanticism: Poetry and the Mediation of History* (Cambridge: Cambridge University Press, 2004), 65. Goodman is interested in the role of Georgic in mostly preromantic texts as a mode of accounting and recovery particular to poetry in an age of new media. However our interests broadly intersect in the "history" simultaneously manifest as a result.

16. Cathy Caruth, *Unclaimed Experience: Trauma, Narrative, and History* (Baltimore: Johns Hopkins University Press, 1998), 5.

17. Harry Harootunian, *History's Disquiet: Modernity, Cultural Practice, and the Ques-*

tion of Everyday Life (New York: Columbia University Press, 2000). Focusing primarily on Japan, Harootunian is concerned (like Heidegger) with the residual disposition of everyday practice in a culture seemingly in the throes of modernization.

18. Ernst Bloch, *The Principle of Hope*, trans. Neville Plaice, Stephen Plaice, and Paul Knight, vol. 1 (Cambridge, MA: MIT Press, 1985), 194–222.

19. Jane Austen, *Emma*, ed. James Kinsley (Oxford: Oxford University Press, 2003), 138.

20. Samuel Taylor Coleridge, *Biographia Literaria*, ed. James Engell and W. Jackson Bate, vol. 2 (Princeton, NJ: Princeton University Press, 1983), 7.

21. Eric C. Walker, *Marriage, Writing and Romanticism: Wordsworth and Austen after War* (Stanford: Stanford University Press, 2009), 10, 69. Stanley Cavell, *In Quest of the Ordinary: Lines of Skepticism and Romanticism* (Chicago: University of Chicago Press, 1988), 153–78.

22. *Byron's Letters and Journals*, ed. Leslie Marchand, vol. 8 (Cambridge, MA: Belknap Press of Harvard University Press, 1978), 37. "It is useless to say where the Present is, for most of us know." Svetlana Boym, *The Future of Nostalgia* (New York: Basic Books, 2001), xvi.

23. For the relationship between historiographic practice and narrative practice, particularly along a realistic axis, see Hayden White, *The Content of Form: Narrative Discourse and Historical Representation* (Baltimore: Johns Hopkins University Press, 1987), and Paul Ricœur, *Time and Narrative*, trans. Kathleen McLaughlin and David Pellauer, 2 vols. (Chicago: University of Chicago Press, 1984–85). See also Everett Zimmerman, *The Boundaries of Fiction: History and the Eighteenth-Century British Novel* (Ithaca, NY: Cornell University Press, 1981).

24. Norman Bryson, *Looking at the Overlooked: Four Essays on Still Life Painting* (London: Reaktion Books, 1990); Henri Lefebvre, *Critique of Everyday Life*, trans. John Moore, vol. 2 (London: Verso, 2008), 64. In alluding to the form of historical content I'm purposely inverting the title of Hayden White's investigation of historical practice (cited in the preceding note) in which the possibilities for historical recovery remain linked to form, notably narrative form, as "the mode of discourse in which a successful understanding of matters historical is represented" (60).

25. Walter Benjamin, "On the Concept of History," in *Selected Writings*, trans. Edmund Jephcott, ed. Howard Eiland and Michael W. Jennings, vol. 4 (Cambridge, MA: Harvard University Press, 2003), 390. My interest bears obvious affinities with Anne-Lise François's exploration of the "literature of uncounted experience" in her *Open Secrets: The Literature of Uncounted Experience* (Stanford: Stanford University Press, 2008), which treats romantic-period texts, including those by Austen and Wordsworth. Apart from the transhistorical sweep of François's interests, which takes her beyond and before romanticism, what differentiates our positions on the way literature accounts for what is typically missed boils down to a distinction between what François calls "recessive experience"—a finely grained reckoning, onto which a passive or meditative disposition effectively and mimetically opens—and what for my part is an experience or event that, thrown suddenly into historical relief, focalizes a possible world that, far from recessive, is forever close at hand and hiding in plain sight.

26. For Stanley Cavell the "ordinary" is always "missable," but as a prelude to the particular "existence" of which it is on recovery an "ecstatic attestation." Cavell, *Philosophy the Day after Tomorrow* (Cambridge, MA: Harvard University Press, 2005), 26.

27. Raymond Williams, *Politics and Letters* (London: New Left Books, 1979), 164–65. Lefebvre, for example, speaks of how the "true critique of everyday life" by which the modern everyday gives way to an antecedent or agrarian paradigm "will have as its primary objective the separation between the human (real and possible) and bourgeois decadence, and will imply a *rehabilitation of everyday life*" (*Critique of Everyday Life*, trans. John Moore, vol. 1 [London: Verso, 1991], 127). And Heidegger, in discussing "everyday modes of being," speaks of the "possibility of distraction" and the "possibilities of abandoning [one]self to the world" (*Being and Time*, trans. John Macquarrie and Edward Robinson [New York: Harper & Row, 1962], 216–17).

28. The preeminent figures here are Heidegger (*Being and Time*) and Lefebvre who variously mobilize the everyday or what Heidegger calls the world against an alienated or consolidated subjectivity. For the self-critical aspects of romantic writing more generally, see Phillipe Lacoue-Labarthe and Jean-Luc Nancy, *The Literary Absolute: The Theory of Literature in German Romanticism*, trans. Philip Barnard and Cheryl Lester (Albany: State University of New York Press, 1988), and Paul Hamilton, *Metaromanticism: Aesthetics, Literature, Theory* (Chicago: University of Chicago Press, 2003). See also Simon Jarvis, *Wordsworth's Philosophic Song* (Cambridge: Cambridge University Press, 2007). Jarvis invokes what he calls "poetical thinking," both to reexamine the "truth" onto which Wordsworth's poems open in surprising and fundamental ways and, like Hamilton, to give the poet a hand in understanding and in superseding the materialisms by which he is often either explained or found wanting. In "metaromantic" fashion, Wordsworth's writing "provides resources for truer apprehensions of some of the problems" that historicist critique has routinely turned up, which, far from period-specific or a question of context, are matters ("need, desire and pleasure") that "extend back through centuries . . . rather than decades" (5–6). For Heidegger's conception of everydayness, see chiefly *Being and Time*.

29. Benjamin, "On the Concept of History," 397, 391. For a more recent treatment of this messianism under the general rubric of "nostalgia," where the past, and specifically the history of modernity, harbors "unrealized possibilities" in which the "retrospective" is "also prospective," see Boym, *The Future of Nostalgia*, xvi.

30. See especially M. H. Abrams, *The Mirror and the Lamp: Romantic Theory and the Critical Tradition* (New York: Oxford University Press, 1953), which follows on Coleridge's effort in the *Biographia* both within and as establishing its own critical/theoretical tradition.

31. Walter Benjamin, *The Arcades Project*, trans. Howard Eiland and Kevin McLaughlin (Cambridge, MA: Harvard University Press, 1999), 462–63.

32. James Chandler, *England in 1819: The Politics of Literary Culture and the Case of Romantic Historicism* (Chicago: University of Chicago Press, 1998), 5–6.

33. Mary Favret, *War at A Distance: Romanticism and the Making of Modern Wartime* (Princeton, NJ: Princeton University Press, 2010), 9.

CHAPTER 1: THE EVERYDAY, HISTORY, AND POSSIBILITY

1. Jean-François Lyotard, "Answering the Question: What Is Postmodernism?" in *The Postmodern Condition: A Report on Knowledge*, trans. Geoff Bennnington and Brian Massumi (Minneapolis: University of Minnesota Press, 1984), 71–82.

2. See Jane Bennett, *The Enchantment of Modern Life* (Princeton, NJ: Princeton University Press, 2001) and "The Force of Things: Steps Toward and Ecology of Matter,"

Political Theory 32, no. 3 (2004): 347–72. See also Thomas Dumm, *A Politics of the Ordinary* (New York: New York University Press, 1999).

3. Michel de Certeau, *The Practice of Everyday Life*, trans. Steven Rendall (Berkeley: University of California Press, 1984).

4. The most comprehensive reiteration of this position remains Henri Lefebvre's *Critique of Everyday Life*, trans. John Moore and Gregory Elliott, 3 vols. (London: Verso, 1991–2008).

5. Michel de Certeau, *The Writing of History*, trans. Tom Conley (New York: Columbia University Press, 1988), 4.

6. See especially Michel Foucault, *Discipline and Punish: The Birth of the Prison*, trans. Alan Sheridan (New York: Vintage Books, 1979), 194–228. De Certeau is preeminently concerned with Foucault.

7. For a more moderated account of agency amid routine, see Anthony Giddens, *The Constitution of Society* (Berkeley: University of California Press, 1984), whose theory of "structuration" is based on a "duality of structure" "grounded in the knowledgeable," indeed agential, "activities of situated actors" in which "social systems" become "both the medium and outcome of the practices" that these agents or actors "recursively organize" (25).

8. See, in particular, Wlad Godzich's "Foreword" in Michel de Certeau, *Heterologies*, trans. Brian Massumi (Minneapolis: University of Minnesota Press, 1986). See also the special issue of *diacritics* 22, no. 2 (Summer 1992), on de Certeau, edited by Tom Conley and Richard Terdiman.

9. Harootunian, *History's Disquiet*, 155.

10. Something similar obtains for Benjamin for whom, as Harootunian notes, "it was the everyday of the present that housed this labyrinth of time and provided the place to enact the synchronic drama in which past, present, and future are interwoven in an endless tapestry of temporality . . . [in] such strategies as 'dialectics at a standstill,' 'messianic cessation,' and 'dialectical image' as a way of getting out of conventional theories of progress" (ibid., 104).

11. Reinhart Koselleck, *Futures Past: On the Semantics of Historical Time*, trans. Keith Tribe (New York: Columbia University Press, 2004).

12. Heidegger, *Being and Time*, 38.

13. Hubert Dreyfus. *Being-in-the-World: A Commentary on Heidegger's Being and Time, Division 1* (Cambridge, MA: MIT Press, 1991), 90.

14. See especially David Lewis, *On the Plurality of Worlds* (Oxford: Blackwell, 1986).

15. Henri Bergson, *Matter and Memory*, trans. N. M. Paul and W. S. Palmer (New York: Zone Books, 1988), 73, 66.

16. Cavell, *In Quest of the Ordinary*, 52.

17. Harold Bloom, *The Ringers in the Tower: Studies in the Romantic Tradition* (Chicago: University of Chicago Press, 1971), 3–35.

18. For a related, but ultimately different take, on romanticism's proto-ecological openness to the "incommensurate materiality of nature" and to the "particularity of the moment captured and/or represented by poetry" (13–14), see Onno Oerlemans, *Romanticism and the Materiality of Nature* (Toronto: University of Toronto Press, 2002). Romanticism's "material sublime" amounts, on Oerlemans's formulation, to a block-

age where ideation and consciousness are fundamentally powerless in the face an "impenetrable reality" (35), whereas the things and events that I consider in romantic texts (especially in Wordsworth), though at odds with a certain intentionality or consciousness, are indices to a possible or parallel world that emerges on reflection and as a "matter" specifically of history.

19. Stanley Cavell, "The Ordinary as the Uneventful," in *Themes Out of School: Effects and Causes* (Chicago: University of Chicago Press, 1984), 190.

20. Fernand Braudel, *Civilization and Capitalism: 15ᵗʰ–18ᵗʰ Century*, vol. 1: *The Structures of Everyday Life: The Limits of the Possible* (New York: Harper & Row, 1981), 27.

21. Kevis Goodman has recently backdated this claim—or one cognate—in showing how the eighteenth-century Georgic registered "poetry's concern for its specificity as a rival to contemporary visual, auditory and print channels of perception and communication . . . and . . . its corollary attentiveness to the receptive consciousness *as* a medium, a 'sensible path' for a circumambient, historical presentness" (*Georgic Modernity*, 108). While circumambience is clearly the province of the Georgic—certainly in a writer like James Thomson—rather than of what I'm exploring, where history is missed and subsequently restored in its immediacy and locality, there is no question that "historical presentness" nicely describes the phenomenon I'm trying to get at.

22. Paul de Man, *Blindness and Insight: Essays in the Rhetoric of Contemporary Criticism*, 2nd ed. (Minneapolis: University of Minnesota Press, 1983), 200, 203.

23. Orrin Wang, *Romantic Sobriety: Sensation, Revolution, Commodification, History* (Baltimore: Johns Hopkins University Press, 200), 135.

24. Marjorie Levinson, "A Motion and a Spirit: Romancing Spinoza," *Studies in Romanticism* 46, no. 4 (2007): 391. See also Mary Jacobus, *Romantic Things: A Tree, a Rock, a Cloud* (Chicago: University of Chicago Press, 2012). Although the everyday figures in Jacobus's engagement with romantic thing-ness, chiefly by allusion to Heidegger, her interests are primarily with the lyric, both as a "thing" in itself (pace Derrida) and as a discourse directed toward the inanimate or to "things," as she puts it, that "look back at us" (5). Such engagements invariably intersect with the everyday and with "states," more broadly "that are often overlooked" (3), but there is an assumption throughout that the everyday is there to be registered rather than a dimension to which writing of the period (and not just poetry) is recovering for the first time.

25. Jacques Derrida, "Typewriter Ribbon: Limited Ink 2," in *Material Events: Paul de Man and the Afterlife of Theory*, ed. Tom Cohen, Barbara Cohen, J. Hillis Miller, and Andrej Warminski (Minneapolis: University of Minnesota Press, 2001), 281.

26. Working with both Derrida's and Benjamin's heterodox notions of materiality, particularly in dialogue with de Man's late work on aesthetic ideology, a number of critics, including Warminksi (" 'As the Poets Do It': On the Material Sublime," in *Material Events*, 3–31) have followed what they take to be de Man's lead in tracking a potentiality in Kant's formal materialism, notably his statements about the sublimity of the ocean as something "we must regard as the poets do." The possibility embedded in this sublime apparently involves something prior and concrete that eludes or transcends "the rhetoric of temporality," in which the sign, again, is all the past we know or can access. Concerned instead with an anterior referent, Warminski and others have settled variously on the "material event" as something that, by definition, avoids any tropological

and interpretive system, in which the past would be indistinguishable from ideology and from the kind of history that Benjamin and de Certeau roundly reject. See also Cohen, Miller, and Cohen, "A 'Materiality without Matter'?" ibid., vii–xxv, and Michael Sprinker, "Art and Ideology: Althusser and de Man," ibid., 32–48.

27. Alain Badiou, *Being and Event*, trans. Oliver Ferguson (London: Continuum, 2005), 197.

28. For discussion of the bearing of "possible worlds" theory on literature, with particular focus on fiction, see Ruth Ronen, *Possible Worlds in Literary Theory* (Cambridge: Cambridge University Press, 1994). See also Marie-Laure Ryan, *Possible Worlds, Artificial Intelligence, and Narrative Theory* (Bloomington: Indiana University Press, 1991). Still, with respect to the everyday as such a world—as a condition again of its emergence—my interests are more directly philosophical rather than applicatory.

29. Lewis, *On the Plurality of Worlds*, 193

CHAPTER 2: WORDSWORTH'S DOUBLE TAKE

1. Tilottama Rajan, "Imagining History," *PMLA* 118, no. 3 (2003): 428, 433. Sections of this chapter originally appeared in *The Wordsworth Circle* 41, no. 3 (2010): 123–27, and in *Romanticism and the City*, ed. Larry Peer (New York: Palgrave, 2011), 25–41.

2. Cavell, *In Quest of the Ordinary*, 52–53.

3. Walter Benjamin, "Short History of Photography," trans. Phil Patton, *Artforum* (February 1977): 47.

4. On the romantic proclivity to internalization and to repressing or erasing historical and material reality, see Jerome J. McGann, *The Romantic Ideology: A Critical Investigation* (Chicago: University of Chicago Press, 1983).

5. This commentary begins as early as the poem's initial epigraph taken from Vergil— *paulò majora canamus* usually translated as "let us sing a loftier strain" but which, as Anahid Nersessian reminds us, is better translated as "let us sing of slightly greater things" (*Utopia Limited: Romanticism and Adjustment* [Cambridge, MA: Harvard University Press, 2015], 61). As something emergent, the ordinary world that the poem discovers and effectively postulates as a third way against either the probable or the marvelous is indeed "slightly greater" or, better, something at once slight and great.

6. Harry Harootunian, "Remembering the Historical Present," *Critical Inquiry* 33, no. 3 (2007): 477.

7. I read "heart of hearts" (192) as metonymic with intimations of both mortality and solidarity and of a piece, then, with what in this same and final stanza Wordsworth calls "the human heart by which *we* live" (203; emphasis added). Early readers, not surprisingly, read the poem as an epochal elegy rather than a personal statement.

8. Wordsworth, *Major Works*, ed. Gill, 595. The "more than common" would also bear on the peculiar affect that "war at a distance," as Favret shows, effectively transmits to everyday life and routine. And in many ways that is where this poem leaves us but only after the "more than common" irrupts in the wake of being overlooked, missed.

9. Galperin, *Return of the Visible in British Romanticism*, 99–128.

10. For discussion of the romantic sublime, see Thomas Weiskel, *The Romantic Sublime: Studies in the Psychology of Transcendence* (Baltimore: Johns Hopkins University Press, 1976); Frances Ferguson, *Solitude and the Sublime: Romanticism and the Aesthetics*

of Individuation (New York: Routledge, 1992); and, with particular relevance to this passage in book 7, Neil Hertz, *The End of the Line: Essays on Psychoanalysis and the Sublime* (Baltimore: Johns Hopkins University Press, 1985), 40–60.

11. Heidegger, *Being and Time*, 91–148.

12. For a reading of Wordsworth that picks up on these same tendencies toward the material, see Oerlemans, *Romanticism and the Materiality of Nature*, 30–64.

13. There have been numerous readings of this passage, suffice it say, but the one from which most commentary proceeds is of course Geoffrey Hartman's in *Wordsworth's Poetry, 1787–1814* (New Haven, CT: Yale University Press, 1964), 33–69, which lays stress on the autonomy of imagination over and against nature or natural materiality.

14. Jacques Derrida, "Of Spirit," *Critical Inquiry* 15, no. 2 (1989): 463.

15. References to are to the text of Dorothy Wordsworth's *The Grasmere Journals*, ed. Pamela Woof (Oxford: Oxford University Press, 1991).

16. Anne K. Mellor, *Romanticism and Gender* (London: Routledge, 1993), 160; Margaret Homans, *Women Writers and Poetic Identity: Dorothy Wordsworth, Emily Brontë, and Emily Dickinson* (Princeton, NJ: Princeton University Press, 1980), 96.

17. Kurt Heinzelman, "The Cult of Domesticity: Dorothy and William Wordsworth at Grasmere," in *Romanticism and Feminism*, ed. Anne K. Mellor (Bloomington: Indiana University Press, 1988), 52–78.

18. Susan Wolfson, *Romantic Interactions: Social Being and the Turns of Literary Action* (Baltimore: Johns Hopkins University Press, 2010), 178.

19. Martin Heidegger, "What Calls for Thinking," in *Basic Writings*, ed. Krell, 350.

CHAPTER 3: HISTORIES OF THE PRESENT

1. *The Journal of Mary Frampton*, 226. Sections of this chapter originally appeared in *ELH* 73, no. 2 (2006): 355–82; in *A Companion to Jane Austen*, ed. Claudia L. Johnson and Clara Tuite (Malden, MA: Wiley-Blackwell, 2009), 123–32; and *Re-Drawing Austen: Picturesque Travels in Austenland*, ed. Beatrice Battaglia and Diego Saglia (Naples: Liguori Editore, 2004), 45–56.

2. Elwin, *Lord Byron's Wife*, 159.

3. William S. Ward, "Three Hitherto Unnoted Contemporary Reviews of Jane Austen," *Nineteenth-Century Fiction* 26, no. 4 (1972): 473.

4. *Jane Austen's Letters*, ed. Deirdre Le Faye (Oxford: Oxford University Press, 1995), 311.

5. Thomas Gisborne, *An Enquiry into the Duties of the Female Sex* (London, 1797), 11–12.

6. See especially Leonore Davidoff and Catherine Hall, *Family Fortunes: Men and Women of the English Middle Class, 1780–1850* (Chicago: University of Chicago Press, 1987).

7. Austen, *Mansfield Park*, ed. Chapman, 415.

8. "Opinions of *Mansfield Park*: Collected and Transcribed by Jane Austen," in *Jane Austen: The Critical Heritage*, ed. Southam, 1: 48.

9. "Everything is natural, & the situations & incidents are told in a manner which clearly evinces the Writer to *belong* to the Society whose Manners she so ably delineates" (ibid., 1: 51).

10. Jane Austen, *Northanger Abbey, Lady Susan, The Watsons, and Sanditon*, ed. John Davie (Oxford: Oxford University Press, 1980), xliii.

11. Galperin, *The Historical Austen*, 138–53.

12. For an anatomy of the regulatory realism that Austen apparently helped inaugurate, see especially George Levine, *The Realistic Imagination* (Chicago: University of Chicago Press, 1981). See also D. A. Miller, *The Novel and the Police* (Berkeley: University of California Press, 1989).

13. See Ruth Bernard Yeazell, "The Boundaries of Mansfield Park," *Representations 7* (Summer 1984): 133–52, and Julia Prewitt Brown, *Jane Austen's Novels: Social Change and Literary Form* (Cambridge, MA: Harvard University Press, 1975), 80–100.

14. I am indebted to Margaret Kirkham (*Jane Austen: Feminism and Fiction* [Totowa, NJ: Barnes & Noble, 1983]) for this connection.

15. Austen, *Northanger Abbey*, 112

16. For *Clarissa*'s influence on the phase of the novel, see also Alistair Duckworth, *The Improvement of the Estate* (Baltimore: Johns Hopkins University Press, 1971), 76, and Joseph Wiesenfarth, *The Errand of Form* (New York: Fordham University Press, 1967), 103.

17. See White, *The Content of Form*. See also Mark Saber Philips, *Society and Sentiment: Genres of Historical Writing in Britain, 1740–1820* (Princeton, NJ: Princeton University Press, 2000), and Everett Zimmerman, *The Boundaries of Fiction: History and the Eighteenth-Century British Novel* (Ithaca, NY: Cornell University Press, 1996).

18. Butler, *Maria Edgeworth*, 445.

19. In referring to Austen's style, I am appropriating D. A. Miller's idea in *Jane Austen, or The Secret of Style*. Where Miller locates this style (and its secret) in a positionality of absolute exteriority to which the heroines aspire in imitation of the narrator or "stylothete," I am concerned with how *Emma*'s style (rather than Emma's style) is, as Edgeworth complained, immersive, inclusive, particularly on multiple encounters.

20. *Jane Austen: The Critical Heritage*, ed. Southam, 2: 265–66.

21. Mary Favret, *Romantic Correspondence: Women, Politics, and the Fiction of Letters* (Cambridge: Cambridge University Press, 1993), 134.

22. This adds a complication to Benedict Anderson's oft-cited thesis on the "novel and the newspaper" in "the eighteenth century" as serving similar functions in "'re-presenting' the kind of imagined community that is the nation" (*Imagined Communities: Reflections on the Origin and Spread of Nationalism* [London: Verso, 1983], 25). For if the "letter, in Austen hands, took the tone of a village newspaper" (Favret 1993, 136), the novel in Austen's hands, its ur example on many accounts, is actually doing something quite different.

CHAPTER 4: LORD BYRON AND LADY BYRON

1. An early version of this chapter appeared in *The Traffic in Poems: Nineteenth-Century Poetry and Transatlantic Exchange*, ed. Meredith L. McGill (New Brunswick, NJ: Rutgers University Press, 2008), 125–38.

2. *The Portrait of a Lady*, ed. Robert D. Bamberg (New York: Norton, 1995), 127.

3. Leon Edel, *Henry James: The Middle Years, 1882–1895* (London: Hart-Davis, 1963), 157.

4. See Jerome Christensen, *Lord Byron's Strength* (Baltimore: Johns Hopkins University Press, 1993), 80–87. See also Benita Eisler, *Byron: Child of Passion, Fool of Fame* (New York: Knopf, 1999), 499–500, and G. Wilson Knight, *Lord Byron's Marriage: The Evidence of Asterisks* (London: Routledge & Kegan Paul, 1957). Although Knight does not focus on the courtship, which is a parenthesis bracketed in his account by Byron's love life (involving members of both sexes) prior to his meeting Annabella Milbanke,

and by the Byron marriage as viewed through the lens of the separation controversy, he makes the interesting point that "in marrying a woman of bisexual temperament, [Byron] probably knew what he was doing, and it might have succeeded, as it succeeded with the Brownings" (251). Bisexuality may well be a shorthand for immasculation here, conflating sex and gender, rather than a statement about sexuality per se.

5. Peter J. Manning, *Byron and His Fictions* (Detroit: Wayne State University Press, 1978).

6. "Byron was read and admired in the Stowe household" and "was the single greatest literary and imaginative influence" on Harriet's writings, according to Alice Crozier ("Harriet Beecher Stowe and Byron," in *Critical Essays on Harriet Beecher Stowe*, ed. Elizabeth Ammons [Boston: G. K. Hall, 1980], 195–96).

7. Elizabeth Cady Stanton, "The Moral of the Byron Case," in *Critical Essays on Harriet Beecher Stowe*, 174.

8. Elwin, *Lord Byron's Wife*, 443.

9. Milbanke remarked with no great enthusiasm on Byron's "*theoretical* idea of my perfection." But her stance, it turns out, was no less theoretical or, on her part, exploratory. Concerned, though she was, about Byron's irreligious nature, which together with his theoretical bent, she thought, "would suffice to make [her] decline a connection," she observes in this same letter that "matrimonial unhappiness is often the consequence of one or both the parties having believed that they should be too easily contented" (Elwin, *Lord Byron's Wife*, 152–53).

10. The act itself may have been regressive, but Byron and his half-sister were consenting (if adulterous) adults who effectively met as adults, having been separated in their youth.

11. Harriet Beecher Stowe, *Lady Byron Vindicated: A History of the Byron Controversy, from Its Beginning in 1816 to the Present Time* (Boston: Osgood, Fields, 1870; repr. New York: Haskell House, 1970), 397.

12. Wolfson notes the parallel between the character of Darcy in *Pride and Prejudice*, with whom Milbanke was quite taken, and Byron, and speculates that Byron and Darcy became something of a condensation for her. The first encounter, however, came about a year before Milbanke had read the novel, originally titled "First Impressions," where Elizabeth Bennet finds herself responding to Darcy in ways that echo Milbanke's initial response (Wolfson, *Romantic Interactions*, 244–45).

13. References to Byron's letters are to the texts in Byron's *Letters and Journals*, ed. Leslie Marchand, 12 vols. (Cambridge, MA: Belknap Press of Harvard University Press, 1973–82).

14. Bharat Tandon, *Jane Austen and the Morality of Conversation* (London: Anthem, 2003).

15. References to Byron's poems in this chapter are to the texts in *Lord Byron: The Complete Poetical Works*, ed. Jerome J. McGann, vol. 3 (Oxford: Clarendon Press, 1981).

16. Caroline Franklin sees very little difference between Hassan's patriarchal Turkish view of woman and the Christian view espoused by the Giaour, since in both instances the woman/Leila remains a construct. However, the Giaour's "fervent belie[f] in monogamous love" is more than simply continuous either with his Western view or with Hassan's, which treat women as "possession[s]" (Franklin, *Byron's Heroines* [Oxford: Clarendon Press, 1992], 43–47). It speaks more immediately to Byron's grapplings with marriage as a matter of fact, for which the Giaour's vocabulary is at once indexical but ultimately insufficient.

17. Franklin (ibid., 65–68, 78–86) is right in noting the rejection of domesticity represented by Medora and the possibility of "woman as companion" that Gulnare presents to Conrad. Where Franklin pulls up short (in my view) is in the conclusion that such companionship is masculine and desexualizing rather than a prospect of marital and domestic relations in an alternative—and for much of the poem—fully present formation.

18. This was a difficult point for reviewers given the poem's "infidelity," diegetically and formally. The *Eclectic Review* (October 1814) noted that the "love which [Conrad] may be supposed to have felt for [Gulnare], is never made to appear of the same nature as his love for Medora, and consequently it does not offend us as a violation of the consistency of the character" (397). But it was a dimension to the poem that was both evident and clearly problematic.

19. This reading obviously sidesteps the homoerotic implications of the Lara/Kaled coupling, which, beginning at least with Louis Crompton's reading in *Byron and Greek Love: Homophobia in Nineteenth-Century England* (Berkeley: University of California Press, 1985), 206–10, have inflected the interpretation of the poem. These readings would also include Robert Gleckner, who argued earlier that Lara has no knowledge of Kaled's sexual identity (*Byron and the Ruins of Paradise* (Baltimore: Johns Hopkins University Press, 1967), 163, as well as Franklin (*Byron's Heroines*, 86–89). From my perspective, however, everyday domesticity as Byron explores it, here and elsewhere, is a good deal queerer and less normative than "love" on either the "Greek" or heterosexual models.

20. Eisler, *Byron*, 501. Conceding that the poem is susceptible to being read as "stupid and sentimental," Jerome McGann argues that "[i]ts minute particulars tell a set of contradictory stories, and finally make up one story whose central subject is contradiction itself—a contradiction we know as the torments of love and jealousy which were realized and played out though the break-up of the Byron marriage" (*Byron and Romanticism*, ed. James Soderholm [Cambridge: Cambridge University Press, 2002], 229). One such contradiction, then, would be marriage itself: that is, marriage in theory (and before the fact) vs. marriage in practice (and after the fact), both of which are in play in the poem. See also Wolfson, *Romantic Interactions*, 224–31, who focuses on the poem's reception, where it effectively went viral, putting the reading public, including many notables, in the addressee's position and creating, in the process, a "differentiating sympathy" for Lord Byron "at [Lady Byron's] expense" (225). Lady Byron, as Wolfson details, recognized this all too well (and was naturally not pleased) even as there is a strain to the poem—and to the marriage before and after—of an opportunity that had been missed.

21. Thomas Moore, *Letters and Journals of Lord Byron: With Notices of His Life* (New York, 1830), 1: 465.

22. This memo is not without apparent skepticism, but ultimately it turns on the "Ergo" that precedes the reference to "Hope." Far from a deduction based on memory, where hope is routinely "baffled," "ergo" redirects the memo to an intuition based on history, where possibility naturally resides.

23. There is no evidence that Lady Byron read more than two cantos of *Don Juan*, but that is not the point.

24. Harriet Beecher Stowe, "The True Story of Lady Byron's Life (as originally published in the *Atlantic Monthly*)," in *Lady Byron Vindicated* (1970), 415, 417.

25. Justin McCarthy, "Mrs. Stowe's Last Romance," in *Critical Essays on Harriet Beecher Stowe*, 171.

26. "The Byron Mystery," *Saturday Review*, October 23, 1869, repr. in *Critical Essays on Harriet Beecher Stowe*, 173.

27. "Lord Byron and His Calumniators," *Blackwood's Edinburgh Magazine*, February 1870, repr. in *Critical Essays on Harriet Beecher Stowe*, 183.

28. Crozier, "Harriet Beecher Stowe and Byron," 195.

29. George Ticknor, *Life, Letters, and Journals* (Boston, 1876), 1: 60.

CHAPTER 5: *DON JUAN* AND THE ROMANTIC FRAGMENT

1. In a letter to Southey dated May 6, 1801, Coleridge prefaces what became *Christabel*'s conclusion with a reference to the poet's son Hartley: "we are times alarmed by the state of his Health—but at present he is well—if I were to lose him, I am afraid, it would exceedingly deaden my affection for any other children I may have" (*Collected Letters of Samuel Taylor Coleridge*, ed. Earl Leslie Griggs, vol 2. [Oxford: Clarendon Press, 1956], 397–98).

2. Citations of Coleridge are from the versions of his poems in *Samuel Taylor Coleridge: A Critical Edition of His Works*, ed. H. J. Jackson (Oxford: Oxford University Press, 1985).

3. Humphrey House, *Coleridge: The Clark Lectures, 1951–52* (London: Rupert Hart-Davis, 1967), 115.

4. Marjorie Levinson, *The Romantic Fragment Poem* (Chapel Hill: University of North Carolina Press, 1986), 8, 26–27, 13. Levinson regards *Christabel*'s close, focusing on the "psychic vicissitudes of a father," as directing attention to Christabel's father, Sir Leoline, whose "strong paternal love promotes a conflict relieved by an act of aggression" (90–91). Such a connection undoubtedly exists, but the deflection of the poem's ending, stylistically and phenomenologically, moves it beyond the poem's narrative or representational field, and the gothic and supernatural apparatus that both defines and circumscribes it, into a world where paternity is suddenly a matter (however overdetermined) of everyday domesticity, following the letter in which it originally appeared. All discussion of the romantic fragment begins, of course, with the Schlegels, and Friedrich Schlegel in particular, whose aphoristic fragments, specifically the *Critical Fragments*, the *Athenaeum Fragments*, and *Ideas* along with the essay "On Incomprehensibility," are responses in various registers to Kant's Critiques, particularly that of Pure Reason, whose limits in turn the Schlegels actively embrace. See especially, then, *Friedrich Schlegel's Lucinde and the Fragments*, trans. Peter Firchow (Minneapolis: University of Minnesota Press, 1971). The most far-reaching recent theoretical engagement with the Schlegels and their bearing on the function of literature rather than just philosophy (although these are closely aligned) is Lacoue-Labarthe and Nancy, *The Literary Absolute*. Cristopher A. Strathman, *Romantic Poetry and the Fragmentary Imperative* (Albany: State University of New York Press, 2006), builds upon *The Literary Absolute* (and Schlegel before it) in seeing the romantic fragment as a site and symptom of the incomprehensible or, as he puts it in reference to Byron, of a truth-telling (in effect) where there is ultimately no "correspondence between word and thing" (104). See also Alexander Regier, *Fracture and Fragmentation in British Romanticism* (Cambridge: Cambridge University Press, 2010), which enlists romantic fragmentation and its resistance to "totalisation" or to

an "original totality" in arguing that, at the level of theory and auto-critique, "we are still part of Romanticism" (5–25). Finally, in a more general register, Hans-Jost Frey, *Interruptions*, trans. Georgia Albert (Albany: State University of New York Press, 1996), sees the fragment as something, paradoxically, that *defines* a panopoly of discourses, emotions and affects.

5. Although his interests are (as I've suggested) more aligned with the poetry-as-theory (and vice versa) and aspects of the romantic fragment construed through the Schlegels and their successors, Strathman's *Romantic Poetry and the Fragmentary Imperative* gets at something cognate in observing that the "linguistic density" of romantic "fragmentary writing"—rather than a "retreat into some kind of transhistorical linguistic idealism"—"is better understood to offer a kind of passage . . . outside the dualism of self and other and into an unsettled or unsettling region" that "Blanchot by turns calls the outside or the neutral" (20), and which for my part may be linked in turn to Blanchot's sense of the "everyday" as that which "escapes" and is only "seen again." Thus for all the differences in focus there remains a fair amount of overlap—not the least involving a theoretical archive including Blanchot, Benjamin, Heidegger, de Man, and others—between Strathman's sense of a fragmentary imperative and the imperative lurking in the fragment as I adduce it. Like Strathman, Regier also takes his lead in *Fracture and Fragmentation* from Benjamin and Blanchot, but in a strange way the fragment's anti-totalizing bent (on his argument) runs athwart the continuum onto which the romantic fragment, as I see it, necessarily opens. There is a difference obviously between what Regier means by "totalisation" and the emergent notion of the everyday as the history that repeats—in this case as a source of wonder rather than farce. However, the possibility—the sense of something ever more about to be—unleashed by this emergence, and marked by the fragment, is a very clearly a "plenitude" that, for Regier's part, is both the target and the opposite of critique as administered through "fragmentation" (9).

6. "The following fragment is here published at the request of a poet of great and deserved celebrity and, as far as the Author's own opinions are concerned, rather as a psychological curiosity, than on the ground of any supposed poetic merits."

7. Citations of *Don Juan* are from the text of the poem in *The Complete Works of Lord Byron*, ed. Jerome J. McGann, vol. 5 (Oxford: Clarendon Press, 1986).

8. Walker, *Marriage, Writing and Romanticism*, 10, 69. Writing to his publisher Murray in 1821, Byron makes clear that canto 5 is "so far from being the last of D. J. that it is hardly the beginning. I meant to take him on a tour of Europe—with a proper mixture of siege—battle—and adventure—and to make him finish *Anarchis Cloots*—in the French revolution.—To how many cantos this may extend—I know not—nor whether (even if I live) I shall complete it" (*Letters*, 8, 77–78). On this aspect of the poem, see especially Jerome J. McGann, *"Don Juan" in Context* (Chicago: University of Chicago Press, 1976), 1–10. Elsewhere McGann takes more seriously the plan that Byron related to Thomas Medwin (and to Murray his publisher) in which Juan ends up "guillotined in the French Revolution" as a basis for reading the poem in a more historical, post-revolutionary context (McGann, "The Book of Byron and the Book of a World," in *The Beauty of Inflections: Literary Investigations in Historical Method and Theory* [Oxford: Clarendon Press, 1988], 255–93). But his earlier sense of a plan that has been abandoned,

if there was one, seems the more germane. McGann also notes that the poem is "down-to-earth" in the Ciceronian tradition of focusing on "everyday matters" or "on ordinary rather than heroic subjects," and whose style, accordingly, is "chatty and conversational" (*"Don Juan" in Context*, 74, 79). But where McGann regards this inclination as a critique of high romanticism on Byron's part, it is of a piece with writing of the period in any number of registers, including the fragment. Bernard Beatty likens the "conversational flow of the narrator" to a kind of "love-making," which he analogizes in turn to "writing poetry" as Byron construes it. This may well be the case given the poem's addressee on my claim, but the erotics in play are those of the everyday (as detailed in the sweetnesss digression) rather than what Beatty has in mind (B. G. Beatty, *Byron's "Don Juan"* [London: Croom Helm, 1985], 122). Noting the "raffish" letters that Byron was writing from Italy during the poem's composition, Beatty observes that "*Don Juan*, in comparison with such letters and Byron's own proclamation of his outspokennesss in the poem, is noticeably discreet" (112).

9. Cavell, *In Quest of the Ordinary*, 153–78. Chief among the "other things" *Don Juan* seeks to do, particularly as a kind of satire, is "to correct the degenerate literary practices of the day; and second, to expose the social corruption which supports such practices" (McGann, *"Don Juan" in Context*, 65). But these aims are subsumed by the conversation that is the primary function here, save when the speaker is plainly holding forth. That conversation, as McGann observes subsequently, is an ongoing discourse—and a deeply conjugal one, as I see it—regarding what for Byron was the "world: men and women, facts, things, the events that involve them all in the matter of existence, past, present, and future" (134) or, to boil it down still further, the common things alluded to in the phrase from Horace that is the poem's epigraph. In *Pursuits of Happiness: The Hollywood Comedy of Remarriage* (Cambridge, MA: Harvard University Press, 1981), Stanley Cavell gets at many of the key elements of a poem that is a "remarriage" in the way "the achievement of human happiness" in *Don Juan* anticipates the wisdom of the film genre in "requir[ing] not the perennial and fuller satisfaction of our needs," which the poem continually frames as regressive, "but the examination and transformation of those needs" (4–5) through what Cavell terms "conversation." Cavell regards "the conversation of . . . the genre of remarriage" (19) as documenting the "struggle . . . for the reciprocity or equality of consciousness between a woman and a man" (17) leading to what he calls "acknowledgment" or the "reconciliation of genuine forgiveness . . . the achievement of a new perspective on existence" (19). All of this is apposite to Byron's achievement, especially the generic parameters that Cavell outlines where marriage and conversation are conjoined.

10. Needless to say, this view runs against the position of most critics, including, for example, Franklin (*Byron's Heroines*) who regards the poem as flatly "anti-feminist" and against marriage as an institution that destroys the "freedom of the individual" (115–21). It also runs athwart the facts of the Byron marriage: the crushing debt that drove Byron to marry Milbanke in the first place and the financial plight in which Lady Byron was left following the separation. But this is just another way of observing that, while based (like all counterfactuals) on certain irrefutable facts, *Don Juan* is (like all counterfactuals) a refutation in which the flight from individuality to the more complicated separation-amid-relation that counts as marriage or remarriage is predicated (with grounding in the courtship) on the prospect/retrospect of woman as another mind.

11. McGann rightly describes this regressive paradise as "prepubescent" (*"Don Juan"* *in Context*, 144). Thus if it is the case that Eros in the poem, as Beatty argues, is "associated" with "Nature," it is nature of a distinctly primitive kind. It may well be part of the poem's "forward movement" (Beatty, Byron's *"Don Juan,"* 110–11), but that movement is at odds with what is vitally present, line-by-line, and opposed to any momentum toward closure, which is to say, erotic closure. On Byron's preoccupation with the present both as a site of possibility and, with bearing on this discussion, as "history," see Emily Rohrbach, "'Must the event decide?'" Byron and Austen in Search of the Present," *Keats-Shelley Journal* 61 (2012): 122–32.

12. For the persistence of "a dominating motherhood" in Juan's sexual encounters, see Manning, *Byron and His Fictions*, 177–99.

13. Although his primary interest involves *Don Juan*'s "carnivalesque irreducibility . . . [m]ost obviously revealed in its polymorphous attitudes to the act of writing," which in turn forces "consistent readjustments in the reader's positions," Philip W. Martin notes too that the "activity of reading is itself participatory, dialogic, as page by page the reader is consistently moving into new relations with the discourse." It is this "disturbance[e]" of what Martin calls the "social contract of reader and writer," or what Bakhtin calls "monoglossia," that is at the heart as well of what, for my part, is the poem's marriage contract. Martin, "Reading *Don Juan* with Bakhtin," in *Don Juan*, ed. Nigel Wood (Philadelphia: Open University Press, 1993), 104–5.

14. See, e.g., Caroline Franklin, *The Female Romantics: Nineteenth-Century Women Novelists and Byronism* (New York: Routledge, 2013), 100. References to *Persuasion* are to the text of the novel in my edition (New York: Longman, 2008).

15. *Borderlines: The Shapings of Gender in British Romanticism* (Stanford: Stanford University Press, 2004), 180–83. Wolfson's chapter on "Gender as Cross-Dressing in *Don Juan*" is the most comprehensive treatment of gender in the poem, to which all subsequent discussions of the topic, including this one, are indebted.

16. Discussing Catherine the Great's role as yet another apotheosis of "love" later in the poem, Cecil Y. Lang calls her a "fucking machine" ("Narcissus Jilted: Byron, *Don Juan*, and the Biographical Imperative," in *Historical Studies and Literary Criticism*, ed. Jerome J. McGann [Madison: University of Wisconsin Press, 1985], 153). The episode, in other words, is simply a more debased version of the Haidée episode.

17. "I wish to heaven that I were so much clay, / As I am blood, bone, marrow, passion, feeling— / Because at least the past were passed away— / And for the future—(but I write this reeling, / Having got drunk exceedingly today, / So that I seem to stand upon the ceiling) / I say—the future is a serious matter— / And so for God's sake—hock and soda water!"

18. Although his interests are more historically and politically contextual, McGann recognizes an "integrity" in "The Isles of Greece" "through its aspiration toward the whole truth, toward complete freedom from cant" ("The Book of Byron," 284).

19. On intertextuality in *Don Juan*—both literary and historical—see, most recently, Jane Stabler, *Byron, Poetics and History* (Cambridge: Cambridge University Press, 2002), 106–71.

20. Although he detects some skepticism on Byron's part regarding language in the "words are things" passage (*Byron and His Fictions*, 237–43), Manning later observes that

Don Juan "is remarkably unprescriptive of its reader," functioning "not so much centrip-etally, directing attention to its uniqueness . . . as centrifugally, returning each reader to the complex of private and public experiences that make up his particular life" ("*Don Juan* and Byron's Imperceptiveness to the English Word," in *Reading Romantics: Texts and Contexts* [New York: Oxford University Press, 1990], 139–40). With marriage, however, as the dialogic model for cooperative thought, it may be safer to say that the poem functions both centripetally and centrifugally.

21. Here Beatty's point that "*Don Juan* engages us because we do not only find out what Byron knows but what he is learning" (120) is especially relevant, particularly if we consider who the poem is actually or potentially engaging and, in its "learning," engaged by.

22. McGann gets at this point in a more general sense in noting that "*Don Juan* is poem that is, in fact, always in transition" (*Don Juan*, 95), or "a poem of openness and possibility" (99) or, paraphrasing Wordsworth, that "[s]omething is indeed evermore about to be for Byron, but equally"—and here the notion of missed opportunities is quite apposite—that "something is evermore about *not* to be" (102).

23. Stowe was among the first to make the Milbanke connection, citing the poem directly in describing Lady Byron (*Lady Byron Vindicated* [1970], 206). Lang, by varia-tion, notes that the figure of Aurora "coincides in every particular with what we know of Annabella Milbanke" and takes issue, as a result, with readings such as Stowe's that see her as an ideal. "Byron would have married Juan to Aurora and . . . they would have lived unhappily ever after—in the hell of an unhappy marriage" ("Narcissus Jilted," 169–76). Obviously this view differs from mine in all respects but particularly on the question Au-rora's/Annabella's alterity and the separation-amid-union that it figures. Beatty is much closer to my position in noting that "Byron is at pains to enlarge, in a way to secularise, his clearly religious conception of Aurora" as a figure "manifestly in the world but not of it, yet is so in substance not in the narrator's vocabulary" (155).

24. Christensen makes a similar point in noting that the "English Cantos are the perfect *un*ending for a poem whose textual drift demands that any ending be contin-gent" (*Lord Byron's Strength*, 311), although his focus is on the hell to which Juan/Byron is consigned in returning to England, fulfilling in that way the Don Juan / Giovanni myth.

25. References to Shelley's poem are to the version in *Shelley's Poetry and Prose*, ed. Donald H. Reiman and Sharon B. Powers (New York: Norton, 1977), 453–70.

26. See especially Jerrold E. Hogle, who argues (in the wake of de Man and with a similar attention to the poem's "radical" or, as elaborates them, "transferential" dynam-ics) that "*The Triumph of Life* highlights a moment of choice, hints at a better choice, and laments the effects of the wrong choice so often made throughout Western history, even as the poem's organization allows the reader either to see or to ignore the fact that there is a choice" (Hogle, *Shelley's Process: Radical Transference and the Development of his Major Works* [New York: Oxford University Press, 1988], 335). Hogle's reading is in particular dialogue with de Man's deconstructive analysis "Shelley Disfigured," which proved to be the most enduring and influential of a series of deconstructive readings of the poem in *Deconstruction and Criticism* (New York: Continuum, 1979) by Harold Bloom, Jacques Derrida, Geoffrey Hartman, and J. Hillis Miller, in addition to de Man.

27. Tilottama Rajan, "The Broken Mirror: The Identity of the Text in Shelley's *The*

Triumph of Life," in *The Supplement of Reading: Figures of Understanding in Romantic Theory and Practice* (Ithaca, NY: Cornell University Press, 1990), 331.

28. Harold Bloom, *Shelley's Mythmaking* (Ithaca, NY: Cornell University Press, 1969), 220–75.

29. On the "delusions of imagination" in the poem that "enlis[t] poets in [the] same defeat" that they envision, see William A. Ulmer, *Shelleyean Eros: The Rhetoric of Romantic Love* (Princeton, NJ: Princeton University Press, 1990), 156–82.

30. For anonymity in romanticism and in Keats especially, see Jacques Khalip, *Anonymous Life: Romanticism and Dispossession* (Stanford: Stanford University Press, 2009), 40–65. There has been a great deal written on Keats's cognate notions of "negative capability" and the "characterless" or "chameleon" poet. But with respect, again, to the everyday and to ordinary phenomenology, as it were, anonymity seems more apposite and a fundamentally different idea.

31. Citations are from *Selected Poems and Letters by John Keats*, ed. Douglas Bush (Boston: Houghton Mifflin, 1959), 247–48.

INDEX

Page numbers in italics refer to figures.

CPSIA information can be obtained
at www.ICGtesting.com
Printed in the USA
LVOW10*1550140517

534490LV00020B/640/P